The Canada Fire
Radical Evangelicalism in British North America, 1775–1812

The Canada Fire is an examination of the remarkable growth and evolution of "radical evangelicalism" in what is now English-speaking Canada from the American Revolution to the War of 1812.

Both rank-and-file evangelists and prominent preachers such as Henry Alline, William Black, David George, Freeborn Garrettson, and Harris Harding figure in *The Canada Fire*. Through letters, diaries, and autobiographies the actors and actresses in this unfolding religious drama speak for themselves, and their voices are permeated with a disconcerting vulnerability and honesty.

Rawlyk argues that radical evangelicalism was the leading edge of Protestantism in what is now English-speaking Canada, and was more democratic and populist than contemporary evangelicalism in the United States. Relative to evangelicalism elsewhere in the English-speaking world, radical evangelicalism in Canada was defined centrally (often almost exclusively) by the New Birth experience or by similar experiences, such as sanctification. Over time, however, there has been a significant change regarding the centre of Canadian evangelicalism. This change, sometimes gradual and sometimes sudden, is of crucial importance in understanding all aspects of evolving Canadian Protestantism in the nineteenth and twentieth centuries.

The Canada Fire is not only a book about the distant past; it also throws light on the changing face of Canadian Protestantism in general, and Canadian evangelicalism in particular.

G.A. RAWLYK is professor of history, Queen's University.

The Canada Fire

Radical Evangelicalism in British North America, 1775–1812

G.A. RAWLYK

McGill-Queen's University Press
Kingston & Montreal • London • Buffalo

© McGill-Queen's University Press 1994
ISBN 0-7735-1221-7 (cloth)
ISBN 0-7735-1277-2 (paper)
Legal deposit fourth quarter 1994
Bibliothèque nationale du Québec

Printed in Canada on acid-free paper

This book has been published with the help of grants
from the Evangelical Fellowship of Canada, Queen's
University, and the Alex Zander Foundation.

Canadian Cataloguing in Publication Data

Rawlyk, George A., 1935–
    The Canada fire: radical Evangelicalism in British
North America: 1775–1812
    Includes bibliographical references and index.
    ISBN 0-7735-1221-7 (bnd)
    ISBN 0-7735-1277-2 (pbk)
    1. Evangelical Revival – Canada. 2. Great Awakening.
3. Canada – Church history – 1763–1887. I. Title.
BR1642.C3R39 1994   277.1'09'033   C94-900342-5

Typeset in Baskerville 10/12 by
Caractéra production graphique inc., Quebec City.

For
Anna and Miriam
and
Miriam and Anna
who for decades have attempted to persuade me of the powerful
message, especially directed at me, in Ecclesiastes 12:12

Contents

Maps and Tables

Illustrations

Acknowledgments

Without the generous financial support of the Pew Charitable Trusts I would not have been able to write this book. I also appreciate, of course, the financial assistance provided by Queen's University and especially the encouragement given me by Professor Bob Malcolmson, the chairman of the Department of History. Much of the book was written while I was at the University of Notre Dame as a visiting scholar in the Cushwa Center for the Study of American Catholicism during the fall term of 1993. The center's director, Professor Jay Dolan, did everything possible to make my sojourn there both enjoyable and profitable. I also owe a great deal to the Reverend Thomas Zurcher, the superior/rector of Moreau Seminary, and to the wonderful men of that religious community who provided me with food, fellowship, friendship, and lodging while I was at Notre Dame. I shall never forget my time with them.

Five very good friends and two anonymous assessors read the book in manuscript form and offered many suggestions for improvement. They have helped immeasurably in making this a better book; I, however, remain responsible for its remaining sins of commission and omission. Professor George Marsden of the History Department, University of Notre Dame, ensured that I would not be too enamoured with Canadian exceptionalism, and he also graciously provided me with the title for the book; Professor Grant Wacker of the Duke Divinity School compelled me to make connections I had not previously seen, and Professor Carman Miller of the Department of History, McGill University, gave me the courage to make significant changes to my original introduction and conclusion. Professor Mark Noll of Wheaton College urged me not to forget the exceptions to the rule, and Professor Susan Juster of the History Department, University of Michigan, perceptively pointed out to me the importance of gender in the growth of radical evangelicalism – whether in New England or what is now Canada.

I have recycled some previously published material, sometimes significantly revised, especially in part 1. Some sections of chapters 1, 4, and 5 were originally published in my introduction to *The New Light Letters and Spiritual Songs, 1778–1793* (Hantsport: Lancelot Press, 1983), 4–56. This material is published with the permission of the Editorial Committee of the Baptist Heritage in Atlantic Canada Series. Some of chapter 2 was originally published in *The Contribution of Methodism to Atlantic Canada*, edited by C.H.H. Scobie and J.W. Grant (McGill-Queen's University Press, Montreal and Kingston, 1992), 79–91, and is used with the permission of McGill-Queen's University Press. Chapter 8 is revised from *Evangelicalism in Comparative Studies of Popular Protestantism in North America, the British Isles, and Beyond, 1700–1990*, edited by Mark A. Noll, David W. Bebbington, and George A. Rawlyk. Copyright © 1994 by Oxford University Press, Inc. Reprinted by permission.

I am very indebted to Ms Cindy Butts for her considerable skill and good humour in translating my hieroglyphics into recognizable printed form. She has been a marvellous editor and critic as well. For this I am, I hope she realizes, very grateful. Ms Patricia Townsend, the archivist of the Acadia University Archives, and two of my graduate students and colleagues, Lorraine Coops and David Plaxton, have been joyfully assiduous in finding some suitable illustrations for this book; and Ms Carlotta Lemieux has been a superb copyeditor. I also appreciate the work done by Ms Kathy Sutherland-Huard in preparing the index and Mr Victor Dohar for his splendid maps.

The Canada Fire is dedicated to my two daughters, Anna and Miriam, whose love, friendship, and understanding have supported and encouraged me for decades. My deep love and affection for them has not been expressed often enough.

Introduction

During the first half of the eighteenth century, English-speaking Protestantism was profoundly affected by a series of revivals or religious awakenings that helped to define the emerging new evangelical impulse. The most visible Anglo-American human agents involved in these early pulsating religious and revitalizing movements were larger-than-life figures – men such as George Whitefield, the remarkable transatlantic itinerant; John Wesley, the saintly founder of Methodism; and Jonathan Edwards, the extraordinarily gifted New England theologian and preacher. But for every Whitefield in the eighteenth century, there were hundreds of lesser known evangelists, both men and women, who felt themselves to be the special conduits of the Holy Spirit in bringing about the defining evangelical moment – the New Birth – which was often a sudden and transforming experience involving all sensory perceptions and permanently branding Christ's salvation upon the "redeemed of the Lord." Perhaps the popular evangelical hymn, "Amazing Grace," published in 1779 by John Newton, a slave trader turned Anglican parson, captures best the crucial importance of the New Birth experience for evangelicals, whether in the eighteenth century or the twentieth:

Amazing Grace! how sweet the sound
That saved a wretch like me!
I once was lost, but now am found,
Was blind, but now I see.

John Wesley, in his published journal, described what took place on Wednesday, 24 May 1738, at a religious gathering on Aldersgate Street, London, when "one was reading Luther's preface to the *Epistle to the Romans*. After a quarter before nine, while he was describing the change which God works in the heart, through faith in Christ, I felt my heart strangely warmed. I felt I did trust in Christ, Christ alone for salvation; and an assurance was given one that he had taken away *my* sins, even *more*, and saved *me* from the law of sin and death."[1] In the spring of 1779, William Black, a nineteen-year-old emigrant from Yorkshire, who was to become a well-known Methodist itinerant, experienced his New Birth in Nova Scotia. In his journal, Black observed:

We tarried . . . singing and praying for about two hours when it pleased the Lord to reveal his free grace; his fulness and his suitableness, as a Saviour: his ability and willingness to save *me*. So that I was enabled to venture on the sure mercies of *David*, and claim my interest in his blood, with "I am thine and thou art mine": while our friends were singing

"My pardon I claim,

For a sinner I am,

A sinner believing in Jesus's name"

Now I could lay hold of him, as the hope set before me: *The Lord my righteousness*, My burden dropped off: my guilt was removed: condemnation gave place to mercy: and a sweet peace and gladness were diffused through my soul. My mourning was turned into joy, and my countenance, like *Hannah's* was no more heavy. After tarrying some time, and returning public thanks, I went home with my heart full of love, and my mouth full of praise.[2]

Other eighteenth-century North American evangelicals would describe their conversion as an experience of being "ravished with a divine ecstasy . . . as if I were wrapped up in God,"[3] or being overwhelmed by "a lively sense of the excellency of Christ,"[4] or being ecstatically redeemed "by God's mercy – that my sins had crucified Christ; and now the Lord took away my distress."[5]

There are a number of ways to try to come to grips in a book such as this with the slippery concept of what I refer to as Canadian radical evangelicalism; one can see it as a powerful religious ideology that provides what has been called "conceptual" and "theological unity – not only for the élite but also for the rank and file." During its late-eighteenth-century and early-nineteenth-century period of development, conversionism and revivalism largely defined this conceptual and theological core, which also included biblicism (a reliance on the Bible as the ultimate religious authority), activism (a concern with spreading the faith), and crucicentrism (a focus on Christ's redeeming work on the cross).[6] Of course, radical evangelicalism may also be seen as a kind of loose religious "denomination" – "a dynamic movement with common heritages, common tendencies, an identity, and an organic character."[7] In its formative stage, the period covered by this volume, radical evangelicalism was largely a powerful, populist religious ideology permeated by what Ronald Knox once called "enthusiasm" and by a particular hermeneutic. Not all evangelicals, however, were radical evangelicals. Some, mostly Anglicans and Presbyterians, accepted the quadrilateral of evangelical ideology, but they tended to marginalize activism and play down the trauma of the New Birth, replacing it with a largely intellectual acceptance of Christ as Saviour. Evangelicalism has always, as far as I am concerned, been a complex kaleidoscope. During the 1775–1812 period, in North America and Great Britain, dominating the centre of the evangelical kaleidoscope was the ecstatic New Birth. In other words, radical evangelicalism was the heart of Canadian evangelicalism. As the nineteenth century unfolded, other pieces challenged the New Birth for dominance; and by the twentieth century, some have convincingly argued, the authoritative and divinely inspired Bible had taken central place in the evangelical kaleidoscope, having pushed to the periphery conversionism, crucicentrism, and activism.

At the popular religious level, during the period linking the American Revolution and the War of 1812, the language of evangelicalism – whether in sermons, prayers, hymns and spiritual songs, or testimonies – provided the sacred canopy for the dynamic religious movement. Any religious observer knew whether she or he was attending a radical evangelical or a non-radical evangelical service. The experiential language of the New Birth, emphasizing a personal relationship of the convert with the Almighty through Jesus Christ, characterized evangelical worship and daily life – whether within a Congregational, Methodist, Baptist, New Light, Anglican, or Presbyterian context. Similar evangelical code words and phrases were used and reused, and it should not be surprising that radical evangelicals from different denominations, classes, and ethnic backgrounds could ardently agree where "the true gospel of Jesus Christ was being preached." There was, it seems clear, an evangelical litmus test for evangelical orthodoxy – a test that any believer could conduct and often did; for spiritual boundary making was also an essential characteristic of evangelicals, who were determined not only to wall themselves from the unsaved but also to foster their own unique brand of intense Christian fellowship.

In its eighteenth- and early-nineteenth-century formative stage, conversionism and revivalism largely defined the central core of what

I refer to throughout this study as radical or populist evangelicalism. This central organizing principle needs to be emphasized. The New Birth, often what would be called a New Light version of conversion – instantaneous, ecstatic, and thrilling – crystallized the essence of evangelicalism in general and radical evangelicalism in particular.

As far as the late-eighteenth-century British North American variant of radical evangelicalism was concerned, Biblicism and crucicentricism were fundamentals that were shared with other orthodox Christian denominations, such as the Presbyterians, Anglicans, and Congregationalists. What many members of these Protestant denominations did not have in common with most radical evangelicals was, of course, the latter's heavy stress on the New Birth experience and on an activistic witnessing, or sharing of the faith. These two tenets created considerable theological space between the radical evangelicals and non-evangelicals as well as between radical evangelicals and many other so-called moderate evangelicals, as did an openness to the emotions and to "enthusiasm" together with a dynamic accommodating spirit.

It has become increasingly clear to me in recent years that in order to understand Canadian evangelicalism, whether in the late eighteenth, nineteenth, or twentieth centuries, it is essential first to try to understand and to explain the importance of the New Birth paradigm in and immediately following the American Revolution. This is the underlying rationale for this book. It is my contention that despite the fact that what is now Canada rejected the American Revolution and all it represented, Canadian evangelicalism, during its early years, from the revolution to the outbreak of the War of 1812, whether in Upper Canada (today's Ontario) or in New Brunswick or Nova Scotia, was more radical, more anarchistic, more democratic, and more populist than its American counterpart. In my view, radical evangelicalism was the energizing faith for most Protestant believers and adherents during these years. Unlike the new American evangelicalism, described so persuasively by Nathan Hatch in his *Democratization of American Christianity*,[8] Canadian radical evangelicalism did not have to carry the baggage of civic humanism, republicanism, and the covenant ideal and possessive individualism.[9] Without these heavy secular encumbrances and fortuitously avoiding what Mark Noll has recently referred to as "the interaction of conceptual 'languages,'"[10] Canadian radical evangelicalism – a broad spectrum of belief connecting Antinomian anarchists on one extreme and Calvinist Baptists and British-oriented Methodists on the other – was able to cut itself free from largely secular concerns and preoccupations. For many British North Americans, religious concerns, concentrating on the "state of the soul," were of primary importance. For most Canadian evangelicals in the 1775–1812 period, regeneration was the pivotal and quintessential Christian experience – the only experience – the Christ-inspired means whereby finite time and space were smashed by "the Eternity you once were and knew."[11]

The religious trajectories of five influential radical evangelicals in revolutionary and post-revolutionary British North America reveal something about the way in which the radical evangelical New Birth paradigm was first etched and then impressed upon the pliable religious landscape, especially in Maritime Canada. These five important exponents of radical evangelicalism were Henry Alline (1748–1784), a New Light Congregationalist; William Black (1760–1834), a British-born Methodist; David George (1743–1810), a Loyalist black Baptist; Freeborn Garrettson (1752–1827), a Maryland-born Methodist; and Harris Harding, (1761–1854) a New Light Baptist and a native of Nova Scotia.

Of course, by examining the beginnings of radical evangelicalism, especially its New Birth emphasis, through the lens of the careers of five men, and in particular through their ecstatic conversion experiences, a rather impressionistic picture emerges. There are hundreds of faceless people they helped to convert, but we know virtually nothing about the spiritual journeys of these converts. These men and women are largely frozen in time; they seem almost lifeless figures – some of the ten or twenty converted in this revival or that, in this year or that – at least, according to the reports of the evangelists. However, some biographical material about rank-and-file British North Americans is available, and this material makes it abundantly clear that the popular radical evangelicalism was virtually identical with that being projected by Alline, Black, Garrettson, George, and Harding.[12] This is the central argument of chapter 6, "The Nova Scotia New Lights: From the Bottom Up, 1785–1793."

Chapter 7, "The Canada Fire," attempts to deal with the amazing growth of Methodism in Upper Canada between 1784 and 1812, and chapter 8 tries to argue the case for a "special" Canadian brand of radical evangelicalism. The last three chapters of the book are concerned with three important Protestant rituals, the Methodist camp meeting, the Baptists and believer's baptism, and the Presbyterian long communion. In this concluding section, I have tried to understand, from the vantage point of both the emerging ministerial élite and the ordinary believer, something of the appeal of ritual to both radical evangelicals and evangelicals.

I have also endeavoured, through my examination of the long communion, to draw attention to the gap that existed between Presbyterian evangelicalism and the radical evangelicalism of most

Canadian Baptist New Light Congregationalists and Methodists. I
have also tried to show, in a variety of ways, what some of the
important similarities were.

This book is a history written, it is hoped, from the bottom up. It
is a history that takes religious belief seriously within the context of
the late eighteenth and early nineteenth centuries and also within
the framework of recent Anglo-American historiography. I have not
been afraid to permit the principal actors and actresses in this
unfolding religious drama to speak for themselves. Their authentic
voices are permeated with a disconcerting vulnerability and honesty.

Four interrelated and sometimes overlapping themes implicitly and
explicitly undergird this book. First, what I call radical evangelicalism
was, as far as I am concerned, the leading edge of Protestantism in
what is now English-speaking Canada before 1812. Second, this
radical evangelicalism was more democratic and more populist than
contemporary evangelicalism is in the United States. Third, relative
to evangelicalism elsewhere in the English-speaking world, this Canadian radical evangelicalism was defined centrally (often almost exclusively) by the New Birth experience or by the experiences functionally
similar to the New Birth, such as sanctification. Fourth, there is a
significant change over time with regard to the actual centre of
gravity of Canadian evangelicalism; and this change, sometimes
gradual and sometimes sudden, is of crucial importance in understanding all aspects of evolving Canadian Protestantism, whether in
the nineteenth century or the twentieth.

This book, of course, has not been written in splendid scholarly
isolation. It owes a great deal to the pioneering work of S.D. Clark,
Church and Sect in Canada (Toronto: University of Toronto Press,
1948), and Goldwin French, *Parsons and Politics* (Toronto: Ryerson
Press, 1962). Clark and French both took evangelical Christianity
seriously in central Canada and the Maritimes, and both authored
landmark studies that still reverberate within the field of Canadian
religious history. I have also been greatly influenced by three very
different kinds of book, each of which has been published during
the past decade. David Bell's superbly edited *Newlight Baptist Journals
of James Manning and James Innis* (Hantsport: Lancelot Press, 1984)
is, without question, the best available study dealing with any aspect
of New Brunswick's religious history during the colony's first twenty-
five years of existence. While I have learned a great deal from Bell
about the evolving radical evangelical movement in his much-beloved
native province, I have been taught a great deal about Protestant
religious rituals in general by Leigh E. Schmidt's *Holy Fairs: Scottish
Communions and American Revivals in the Early Modern Period*

(Princeton: Princeton University Press, 1989). Schmidt has helped me come to grips with Canadian variations of the evangelical rituals of believer's baptism, the long communion, and the camp meeting. But if any single volume has shaped virtually every chapter of *The Canada Fire*, it is Nathan Hatch's prize-winning *Democratization of American Christianity*. Hatch, in a direct and indirect manner, has compelled me to look at Canadian radical evangelicalism in a totally different manner. Even though I may spar with him in the text and in the footnotes, his conclusions weigh heavily on the pages of this volume. I owe more than he probably realizes to his many brilliant insights and suggestions.

The Canada Fire

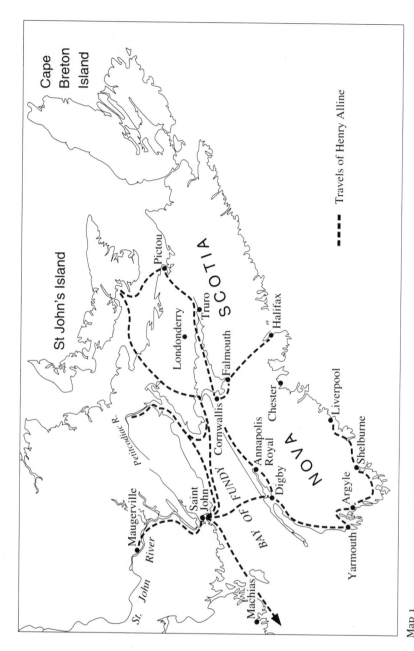

Map 1
Nova Scotia at the Time of the American Revolution

PART ONE

The Radical Evangelical
Paradigm Established:
The Maritime Experience

INTRODUCTION

Nathan Hatch has perceptively observed that "modern church historians ... have had difficulty identifying with dimensions of their own ecclesiastical heritage that are diametrically opposed to the modern embrace of intellectual, liturgical, and ecumenical respectability."[1] In the 1780s and early 1790s, Henry Alline, William Black, David George, Freeborn Garrettson, and Harris Harding were anything but "respectable." Their aggressive proselytizing, together with their obsession with religious ecstasy and dramatic conversionism, helped them communicate with their Nova Scotia and New Brunswick contemporaries – who, like them, were determined to "storm heaven by the back door."[2] These five men were truly charismatic leaders because their evangelistic power came directly from the ordinary folk, like themselves, to whom they preached their different versions of radical evangelicalism and with whom they so obviously resonated, at every level of existence.

The "radical evangelical paradigm" which these men helped stamp on the religious culture of Maritime Canada was permeated by an exaggerated emphasis both on the emotions and on all sensory perceptions. Even though their New Birth conversionist gospel had a certain Puritan/Pietist formulaic quality – sin, salvation, service[3] – it was, in a great many respects, fundamentally different.

It was the older Protestant piety but a piety infused by a remarkable degree of anarchistic ecstasy and intense spirituality.[4]

It would be wrong to suggest that the Maritime radical evangelical paradigm of such men as Alline, Black, George, Garrettson, and Harding significantly influenced the religious culture of central Canada. Another version of radical evangelicalism emerged in what is now Ontario and in parts of Quebec – an evangelicalism that owed far more to American Methodism than it did to New Light enthusiasm. This central Canadian variant clicked into fragile place a decade after the Maritime version did. The former, in the British North American context – at least, in the decades spanning the American Revolution and the War of 1812 – was, without question, just as important as the latter. It will therefore be examined later in the book.

What follows are five loosely connected biographical sketches, each of which attempts to deal with the ways in which radical evangelicalism evolved and developed, during and immediately following the revolution, in the religious experience and expression of five influential evangelists: William Black, David George, Freeborn Garrettson, Harris Harding, and especially Henry Alline.

1 Henry Alline (1748–1784): The Shaping of the Conversion Paradigm

Henry Alline was born in Newport, Rhode Island, in 1748 and moved in 1760 with his parents, as part of the large Yankee emigration movement, to Falmouth in the Minas Basin region of Nova Scotia. He died in New Hampshire in early February 1784. Like most of his contemporaries in the so-called Yankee heartland of the British colony, Alline was raised in a pious, Calvinist, and Congregational Church atmosphere. There was little in his isolated and rural upbringing that was even to suggest that Alline, the well-known fun-loving "tanner and farmer," would be transformed by his traumatic conversion experience in 1775 into what one Canadian scholar has recently described as "the greatest 'Canadian' of the eighteenth century, the greatest Maritimer of any age and the most significant religious figure this country has yet produced."[1] Even though Professor David Bell's glowing assessment of Alline's importance may be somewhat exaggerated – helping to create what one caustic critic has referred to as a mythical New Light superman[2] – the young Falmouth preacher nevertheless succeeded in casting a huge shadow over the religious development of Nova Scotia, New Brunswick, and New England from the 1770s until the present-day.[3]

Many of Alline's contemporaries regarded him as Nova Scotia's own George Whitefield, a powerful vehicle of the Almighty, truly charismatic and uniquely spiritual, who had, virtually single-hand-edly, coaxed into existence, as the conduit of the Holy Spirit, a series of intense religious revivals, which swept the region during the American Revolution. Not only was Alline an unusually gifted charismatic revivalist, he was also the author of over five hundred hymns, some of which are still being sung, as well as two long and convoluted books of theology – *Two Mites*, published in 1781, and *The Anti-Traditionist*, in 1783 – neither of which is read today. In addition, three of his sermons were published while he was still alive; but his journal, though it was circulating in manuscript form a few years after his death in 1784, was not published until 1806.[4]

Alline's *Journal* was laboriously copied soon after his death by his many disciples as it was passed from New Light family to New Light family and from isolated community to isolated community. In the process, it became not only the inspiration for his followers and other Christians in the area but also the manual describing the morphology of a revival inspired by the New Light–New Birth triggered by the Holy Ghost. Although the *Journal* followed a well-worn stylistic format, this did not invalidate Alline's experiences; it merely permitted them to roll along predictable tracks. Alline's remarkable spiritual trajectory was considered by his contemporaries to be far more significant than the often confused, opaque, disjointed, and difficult theology contained in his two big books and three published sermons. Nova Scotians and, later, New Brunswickers, as well as a surprising number of New Englanders, could relate to Alline as a person very much like themselves. He was indeed one of them; each line of his *Journal* and each sentence of his sermons emphatically underscored this obvious point. If the Falmouth farmer-tanner could experience the intense spiritual ecstacy and also the certainty of the New Light–New Birth, then they could do so too. If Alline could be "ravished" by the Holy Spirit, they could as well. If he could miraculously recover from his black introspection and find peace of mind and a mystical oneness with the divine – what he called the "One Eternal Now" – so could they. And if the uneducated Yankee Nova Scotian, in his late twenties and early thirties, could help bring about a widespread religious awakening, then they could as well. They all possessed the spiritual potential, they confidently believed, that God could so easily actualize. Alline, in a very real sense, became a model and an inspiration; his life was convincing proof that with God all things were indeed possible. But these "things" could not happen until Alline's New Birth became their own New Light "experience." His description would be their reality; his words would shape their conversion experience and their Christian lives and, in the process, the radical evangelical tradition of an entire region of North America.

In the early months of 1775, the twenty-seven-year-old Alline experienced what to him was an unforgettable spiritual and psychological crisis. It was a crisis that when resolved would provide the turning point in his all-too-brief life. It seems clear that Alline's conversion – his New Light–New Birth – was significantly affected by his finely developed morbid introspection, his tuberculosis, his fear of imminent death and the possible end of the world, and by the mounting pressure he felt to commit himself one way or another during the early months of the American Revolution. Alline's conversion, without question, was the central event of his life, and he felt compelled to make his ecstatic experience the universal norm. One perceptive nineteenth-century observer shrewdly noted that Alline was "converted in a rapture; and ever after he sought to live in a rapture; and judged of his religious condition by his enjoyments and raptures."[5] He could have added that this also was the case for Alline's many followers, not only in the late eighteenth century but throughout much of the early nineteenth.

It is of some interest that Alline's memorable and detailed description of his conversion experience captured the attention of William James who, in his *Varieties of Religious Experience*, first published in 1902, used it as a "classic example" of the "curing of the 'sicksoul.'"[6] According to Martin Marty, James had far "more respect for mystics, mossbacks, and misfits than for adaptive Protestant modernists."[7] Alline may have been a Nova Scotian version of a Protestant mystic, but he certainly was neither a mossback nor a misfit. It is noteworthy that his first explicit reference in his *Journal* to an actual day, month, and year occurred on 13 February 1775:

When about midnight I waked out of sleep, I was surprised by a most alarming call as with a small still voice, as it were through my whole soul; as if it spoke these words, How many days and weeks, and months and years has God been striving with you, and you have not yet accepted, but remain as far from redemption as at first; and as God has declared, that his spirit shall not always strive with man, what if he would call you no more, and this might be the last call, as it might be; *what* (where, where) would your unhappy doom be? O how it pierced my whole soul, and caused me to tremble in my bed, and cry out for a longer time. O Lord God do not take away thy spirit! O leave me not, leave me not; give me not over to hardness of heart, and blindness of mind.[8]

For some three years before February 1775, Alline had been, in his own evocative words, "plunged into inexpressible horrors and racking views of despair; yea I thought never a poor soul could be in more horror on this side of hell; so that I was many times constrained to cry out with an audible voice and horrid groans."[9] He was tempted to commit suicide, but just at the moment of darkest despair "God kept me from laying violent hands on myself." Because of his "keen despair," Alline tried to find solace in "young company" and "carnal mirth." "O what a wonder that ever I was snatched from that alluring snare," he observed. He continued:

The Lord still followed me, and would not give me up; I began to be more and more afraid of the condemning power of sin, and my lost and undone condition. I then engaged more closely into morality and followed my duties; but all did not take away the fear of death and hell: yea, I was so burdened at times, that I could not rest in my bed; when I had been to any frolick or into carnal company I was often afraid to close my eyes for fear that I should awake in hell before morning. I was one of the most unhappy creatures that was on earth. When I felt the least disorder in my body, I would be in such distress that I could hardly contain myself, expecting that God was about to call me away, and I unprepared.[10]

Expecting, in good Calvinist fashion, that the Almighty, without any human initiative, would "call me by and by,"[11] Alline still felt a deep inner compulsion to take the first step, thus breaking his "chain to the covenant of works."[12] But at this stage he was unable, as he put it, "to be saved by free grace." Instead, he became even more morbid in his introspection, "begging for mercy and fighting against it at the same time." Seeing visions and being "surrounded with an uncommon light," Alline expected the imminent return of Jesus Christ and the final judgment. His "distress was so great" that he felt his soul was separated from his body: "For my very flesh seemed to consume off of my bones with the weight; everything conspiring to load me with unspeakable distress."[13]

Alline immediately turned round to see "how far the burning flood and sweeping deluge, which I imagined to be coming after me, was from me, that I might know how long I should be out of hell, or how long it would be, before my doom should be finally settled." But to his "unspeakable satisfaction," he saw that it was not as he expected: "The day [of judgment] was not really come, therefore I had an opportunity of repentance, and a possibility of escaping from that awful and eternal gulf. O how my heart seemed to leap for joy, and at the same time began to groan for mercy. I found the day of judgment was not come, nor the world in flames as I expected."[14] There appeared instead, Alline was absolutely certain,

a large blaze of light in the shape of a circle, with that side next to me open as though it yawned after me, and as it drew very nigh me, it closed up in a small compass, then broke out in small sparkles, and vanished away ...

When the light seemed to vanish, and the scene to withdraw, my whole soul seemed to be engaged to implore mercy and grace. O mercy, mercy, mercy, was every groan of my soul, and I began to make many promises, that I would never ... sin as I had done, nor rest another day, *unless* I had found a Saviour for my poor soul. I thought very much of the goodness of God to me in giving me one moment more for repentance, and that there appeared yet a possibility of my being saved.[15]

Soon after Alline returned home, following these unforgettable experiences, he rushed to his bedroom "crying for mercy like a person in agony." But instead of finding any relief, Alline was confronted in his imagination by the devil in the shape of "a beautiful woman" – "the most beautiful object that I ever beheld."[16] His "passions were so inflamed" by his explicitly sexual dream that he was afraid he "might grieve the holy spirit." All of a sudden, Alline's sexuality seemed to be getting in the way of his search for salvation. Seeing Satan setting the ultimate snare for him, a disturbed Alline promised God, "Neither will I think of marrying or enjoying anything in this world, until (if God gives me grace) I find a Saviour for my soul."[17]

What took place in Alline's bedroom that night in late 1774 or early 1775? Was a battle going on for his love and affection between Jesus Christ and an attractive young woman? Alline had to admit that the "most beautiful object" he had "ever beheld" was in reality a disconcerting image of a female acquaintance. The dream had made her even more beautiful. Obviously, there was a complex sexual dimension to Alline's religious quest, a dimension that he was not afraid to share with his contemporaries, who could both empathize and resonate with his "creature ... enjoyments" and his guilt. According to Alline, using sexual imagery, he was tempted to "plunge" himself in and, in the process, find himself "snare[d] ... on the devil's ground."[18] Would he "ravish" his woman friend or would he be "ravished by the Spirit"?

Unable to answer this question, Alline remained in acute distress "still night and day." As he stressed over and over again in his *Journal*, he was waiting for the Almighty to "bring me in by an arbitrary power when he pleased, but [He] would not."[19] Then came the remarkable and "alarming call" heard on 13 February 1775. For more than a month after 13 February, Alline struggled even more fiercely to find salvation – or, as he would often put it, "to be stripped of self-righteousness." But the harder he tried, the "further from conversion" he actually felt. Then something very unusual happened: Alline, for "the first time," was able to read the Bible in such a way that he actually "saw the word of God."[20] "Without premeditation" he cast his eyes on the 38th Psalm:

1 O Lord, rebuke me not in thy wrath; neither chasten me in thy hot displeasure.

2 For thine arrows stick fast in me, and thy hand presseth me sore.

3 There is no soundness in my flesh because of thine anger; neither is there any rest in my bones because of my sin.

4 For mine iniquities are gone over mine head: as a heavy burden they are too heavy for me.

5 My wounds stink and are corrupt because of my foolishness.

6 I am troubled; I am bowed down greatly; I go mourning all the day long.

7 For my loins are filled with a loathsome disease: and there is no soundness in my flesh.

8 I am feeble and sore broken: I have roared by reason of the disquietness of my heart.

9 Lord, all my desire is before thee; and my groaning is not hid from thee.

10 My heart panteth, my strength faileth me: as for the light of mine eyes, it also is gone from me.

11 My lovers and my friends stand aloof from my sore; and my kinsmen stand afar off.

12 They also that seek after my life lay snares for me; and they that seek my hurt speak mischievous things, and imagine deceits all the day long.

13 But I, as a deaf man, heard not; and I was as a dumb man that openeth not his mouth.

14 Thus I was as a man that heareth not, and in whose mouth are no reproofs.

15 For in thee, O Lord, do I hope: thou wilt hear, O Lord my God.

16 For I said, Hear me, lest otherwise they should rejoice over me: when my foot slippeth, they magnify themselves against me.

17 For I am ready to halt, and my sorrow is continually before me.

18 For I will declare mine iniquity; I will be sorry for my sin.

19 But mine enemies are lively, and they are strong: and they that hate me wrongfully are multiplied.

20 They also that render evil for good are mine adversaries; because I follow the thing that good is.

21 Forsake me not, O Lord: O my God, be not far from me.

22 Make haste to help me, O Lord my salvation.

Believing that the psalmist was speaking both explicitly for him and directly to him, Alline cried as he read and reread the 38th Psalm. He then tested God again by opening the Bible "without design"[21] and placed his finger on the 40th Psalm, verses 1 to 3:

1 I waited patiently for the Lord; and he inclined unto me, and heard my cry.

2 He brought me up also out of a horrible pit, out of the miry day, and set my feet upon a rock, and established my goings.

3 And he hath put a new song in my mouth, even praise unto our God: many shall see it, and fear, and shall trust in the Lord.[22]

Alline's new way of seeing the word of God took hold of him, he stated, "with such power, that it seemed to go through my whole soul, and read therein every thought of my heart, and raised my whole soul with groans and earnest cries to God, so that it seemed as if God was praying in, with, and for me ... Things appeared new, and I could not tell what to make of it."[23]

Just when it seemed that he had reached the mental breaking point, Alline experienced, in his bedroom, what seemed to him to be the exhilarating and transforming power of spiritual regeneration. He described the beginning of his life-changing conversion in the following manner:

O help me, help me, cried I, thou Redeemer of souls, and save me or I am gone for ever; and the last word I ever mentioned in my distress (for the change was instantaneous) was O Lord Jesus Christ, thou canst this night, if thou pleasest, with one drop of thy blood atone for my sins, and appease the wrath of an angry God ... At that instant of time when I gave up all to him, to do with me, as he pleased, and was willing that God should reign in me and rule over me at his pleasure: redeeming love broke into my soul with repeated scriptures with such power, that my whole soul seemed to be melted down with love; the burden of guilt and condemnation was gone, darkness was expelled, my heart humbled and filled with gratitude, and my will turned of choice after the infinite God ... Attracted by the love and beauty I saw in his divine perfections, my whole soul was inexpressibly ravished with the blessed Redeemer ... my whole soul seemed filled with the divine being.[24]

As far as the ecstatic Alline was concerned, the black gloomy despair of his acute and prolonged depression had been miraculously and suddenly lifted. "My whole soul," he proudly proclaimed,

that was a few minutes ago groaning under mountains of death, wading through storms of sorrow, racked with distressing fears, and crying to an unknown God for help, was now filled with immortal love, soaring on the wings of faith, freed from the chains of death and darkness, and crying out my Lord and my God; thou art my rock and my fortress, my shield and my high tower, my life, my joy, my present and my everlasting portion.[25]

The sudden, transforming power of the New Light–New Birth experience compelled Alline to declare: "O the infinite condescension of God to a worm of the dust! For though my whole soul was filled with love, and ravished with a divine ecstasy beyond any doubts or fears, or thoughts of being then deceived, for I enjoyed a heaven on earth, and it seemed as if I were wrapped up in God."26

These emotionally and sexually charged words were to energize and encapsulate Alline's Christian message until his death in 1784. Over and over again in his *Journal* and published sermons and books, as well as in his very popular "hymns and spiritual songs," Alline referred to his having been "ravished" by "divine ecstasy" and "married" to the "heavenly charmer." Divine love had overwhelmed him to such an extent in 1775 that he viewed his own "instantaneous" emotion-charged religious experience as being the divinely shaped pattern for all others who wished to experience true regeneration. Alline therefore expected his followers and all true Christians to share his unique version of the New Light–New Birth, which he regarded as the only satisfactory means of regeneration. It was not difficult for Alline to generalize from his own particular conversion experience and to force it upon all who came to hear him or all who read his works or sang his hymns. His audacity – some might call it spiritual hubris – had a tremendous appeal during and after the American War of Independence for those North Americans who were particularly confused and disoriented by the powerful divisive forces unleashed by the revolution.

After his conversion, Alline relentlessly attacked what he regarded as the evil underpinnings of Calvinist predestination, stressing instead the crucial importance of the New Light–New Birth and "free grace" in enabling each believer to choose freely to return to his or her "paradisiacal state." An emotionally charged conversion, shaped by all sensory perceptions, bridged the huge chasm existing between the sinner and the Almighty. Because of the New Birth, Alline maintained, "for that love they now enjoy, that beauty they behold, and that glory they admire is one glimmering Ray of the perfections of God; for that Moment the Will and Choice was turned after God, they acted with God, and therefore partake of God; and thus again brought to enjoy the Tree of Life, which they had lost; and are reinstated in that Paradise that they fell out of."27 Alline felt strongly that his conversion had returned him, in a very real sense, to the pristinely pure paradise that Adam and Eve had once inhabited.

Since God inhabited what Alline liked to refer to as the "One Eternal Now," surely, the Falmouth preacher contended, the redeemed of the Lord "must inhabit the same." For the truly converted, there was no sense of "Time, and Space, and successive Periods." According to Alline:

Salvation and Damnation originates here at your own Door; for with God there never was any such Thing, as before or after, Millions of Ages, before time began, and as many more, after Time is at a Period, being the very same instant; consider neither Time past nor Time to come, but one ETERNAL NOW; consider that with God there is neither Succession nor Progress; but that with Him the Moment He said let us make Man, and the Sound of the last Trumpet, is the very same instant, and your Death as much first as your Birth ... with God all things are NOW ... as the Centre of a Ring, which is as near the one side as the other.[28]

As far as Alline's very unsystematic theology was concerned (a theology, it should be noted, that seemed to be obsessed with locating the New Birth within a cosmic reality), conversion was not only the readily available means whereby those who had freely chosen the "electing love of God" were able in a spiritual sense to return to Paradise, but it was also the God-given means for telescoping all time within the "Eternal Now." Thus, for Alline, regeneration was the process that demolished artificial and finite time and space, and astonishingly transformed for each person the mundane (what was described as the world of "turnips, cabbages and potatoes")[29] into the cosmic and heavenly – the "Eternity you once [were], and knew."[30]

Since Alline held that each person was emphatically "capable of consenting to Redeeming Love" and that "the great Work of the Spirit of God"[31] was essential in transforming the individual, he felt it necessary to add to his *Journal* account, in his sermons and elsewhere, a detailed description of what actually occurred in regeneration. Conviction, "bringing the Sinner to a Sense of its fallen, helpless and deplorable condition," was, he had to admit, as had been case with others, sometimes perceived to be a gradual process, "altho' the work of conversion" was always "instantaneous."[32] The conviction of what he called "actual and original sin" operated with such power that the converted sinner was not only made aware intellectually of his or her being a sinner, but, of greater consequence, the real convert actually felt this reality in his or her own soul:

He is convinced of his lost and undone Condition in his own Conscience, without having any claim to God's Mercy or the last Favor from his Hand. He is so convinced of his helpless Condition that he finds his utter inability, either to obtain Relief for his perishing and immortal soul, or to extricate himself out of that deplorable state of Sin and Misery which he is now convinced that he has plunged himself into. He has long been trying perhaps to recommend himself to Christ by Repentance and Humility; he has been labouring with Prayers and Tears to love God & Holiness, to hate his evil Ways, and be sorry for his Sins: But the Spirit of God has now wrought so powerfully on his Heart, that he appears worse than ever. He finds his heart is hard, and his will stubborn; His Nature is at Enmity against God, and all that is good, and perhaps filled with blasphemous thoughts against God and his Way.[33]

Generalizing yet again from the particulars of his own conversion, Alline stressed that the truly converted person feels both drawn to and repelled by the Almighty. The emphasis was again placed on the feelings involved – the so-called frames of emotional experience. Such a person, as had certainly been the case with Alline, "tried every possible way to flee from the Wrath to come and to recommend himself to Christ, or to prepare to be converted, but now all appears in vain, and he finds no way to step another step and all his Supporters are now gone."[34] The depressed and disoriented seeker sees

that to fly from his Guilt and misery is impracticable: and to reform or make Satisfaction, as much impossible; and therefore like the four Lepers at the Gates of Samaria (2 Kings 7:3,4) he is determined to try the last Remedy; for to stay where he is, is certain Death, and to return back unto his former State of Security, will be Death, and therefore, altho' he cannot see, that Christ has any Love for him, or Pity towards him, neither doth he see, whether He intends to have Mercy on him or not; yet, he is determined to cast himself at his Feet, and trust wholly to his Mercy, and Free Grace for Salvation; and cries out with the trembling Leper. *Lord if thou wilt* (Mark 1:40)[35]

At this precise moment, when the convicted person is finally "willing to be redeemed out of his fallen state on the Gospel-Terms," the "Redeeming Love enters into his soul," as Christ "the Hope of Glory takes possession of the inner Man."[36] George Whitefield, the remarkable eighteenth-century Anglo-American revivalist, had contended that it was "as easy for any adult to tell the dealings of God with their soul as to tell when they were married";[37] the born-again felt "the Burden of their Sin gone, with their Affections taken off of this World, and set on things above."[38] Moreover, their "hearts," their inner feelings, were "drawn out after Christ, under a feeling sense of the Worth of his Redeeming Love; at the same Time with a sense of their own Vileness, and the Verity of all things here below, together with the worth and Sweetness of Heavenly Things, and the

Amiableness of the Divine Being." Then came "an increasing Thirst after more Liberty from Sin and Darkness, and a continued panting after the Enjoyment of God, and the Likeness to the meek and the lowly Saviour for their Hearts which before were set on Things below, are now set on Things above."[39]

Because of the almost mystical union with Christ, fused by "free grace," "every new born Soul is daily hungering and thirsting after its Original Source, viz, spiritual and Divine Food; panting after Light and Love, from which it has been so long a miserable Deserter, and to which it is now returning."[40] Each of "these newborn souls, being united inseparably to the Lord Jesus Christ, became Members of his Body."[41] There was, therefore, a "final Perseverance of the Saints" (this is what regeneration both promised and delivered) and a redemptive assurance that resulted not in antinomian excesses but in a somewhat vaguely defined form of "sanctified" behaviour, which always involved "witnessing to the true faith."

It should always be remembered that Alline contended that his own extraordinary conversion experience had convincingly persuaded him that Calvinism was an especially pernicious heresy. "The lesson, why those, that are lost, are not redeemed," he maintained, "is not because that God delighted in their Misery, or by any Neglect in God, God forbid." Rather, it resulted "by the will of the Creature: which, instead of consenting to Redeeming love, rejects it, and therefore cannot possibly be redeemed." "Men and Devils that are miserable," Alline stressed, "are not only the Author of their own Misery, but that against the Will of God, the Nature of God, and the most endearing Expression of his Love."[42]

It should be emphasized, however, that despite his anti-Calvinism, and possibly because of it, Alline believed in the "final Perseverance of the Saints." What else could be expected of the New Birth moment when "the Will and Choice was turned after God" and the regenerate "acted with God, and therefore partake of God; and thus again are brought to enjoy the Tree of Life, which they had lost; and are reinstated in that Paradise that they fell out of?"[43] Of course, as long as one lived on this earth, there would be an often-bitter struggle between the sanctified "inmost Soul" and the "fallen immortal Body," as Alline knew from personal experience. But because of this dualism and the tremendous emphasis that he placed on the centrality of the "ravishing of the soul by Christ" (conversion having blurred into sanctification), Alline found himself asserting, "That which is born of God cannot sin."[44]

Realizing the real threat posed to his unique brand of evangelicalism by antinomianism, Alline carefully tried to balance his stress on "perseverance" with what has accurately been referred to as a powerful "asceticism and bodily mortification worthy of the most austere monasticism."[45] Carefully blended, Alline's "perseverance of the spiritually ravished saints" and his tough-minded asceticism produced what he once called "true zeal."[46] Perseverance without asceticism, he knew all too well, would lead directly to the evils of Calvinist antinomianism, which he both denounced and detested. He also knew that New Light perseverance without New Light asceticism was mere hypocrisy. Alline therefore carefully wove these two themes in his evangelistic preaching and in his writing, producing in the process the clear impression not only that he was a special spokesman for the Almighty – the region's John the Baptist preparing the way for the Lord – but also that he was the Nova Scotia articulation of the evangelicalism of George Whitefield and Jonathan Edwards. There was in Alline's New Light message, despite his many unorthodox theological views, what has been called an orthodox "Whitefieldian sound."[47] In other words, Alline in the late 1770s and early 1780s sounded very much like a New England New Light from the 1730s and 1740s. His dynamic and charismatic preaching produced many of the same results. Moreover – and this point needs to be highlighted – the Falmouth evangelist intuitively realized that his New Light movement could fragment quickly into warring antinomian and anti-antinomian factions, just as Whitefield's had done. Despite his attempts to keep antinomianism in check, Alline could do little to put a brake on the fragmentation process once it manifested itself, and his legacy could do even less after his death in 1784.[48]

How does one account for Alline's amazing success as an itinerant evangelist and for the continuing influence of the Allinite New Light gospel throughout the region of New Brunswick, Nova Scotia, and New England for at least a century after his death? Obviously, for thousands of Maritimers and New Englanders during and after the American Revolution, Alline's New Light evangelical message gave compelling answers to those who were disoriented and confused and were desperately looking for meaning at a particularly difficult time in their lives. New England was at war with the mother country; Patriots were battling Loyalists; and families were splitting along political and religious lines. In particular, the New Light–New Birth emphasis provided a new and powerful spiritual relationship between Christ and the enlightened and redeemed believer in a world in which all traditional relationships seemed to be falling apart. As is evidenced in everything Alline wrote and preached, he was concerned especially with the emotional and spiritual relationship of Christ and the regenerate individual, and because of this he was able to use his charismatic powers to drill this reality into the minds and hearts of his followers. He was obviously a person who was very sensitive to disintegrating relationships and one who could, directly and indirectly, relate to those who were similarly preoccupied with disintegrating relationships. For Alline and for his followers, a New Light relationship to Christ was the means of resolving all the difficulties arising from a myriad of disintegrating human relationships. Conversion was thus both perceived and experienced as the short-circuiting of a complex process – a short-circuiting that produced instant and immediate sacred and secular satisfaction as well as solace and intense relief in a revolutionary and post-revolutionary situation.

It should be remembered that in his *Journal* and his preaching Alline always stressed, in good gnostic fashion, that he was in direct communication with the Almighty, who inspired his every word and action. Here was another reason for his success. Not only had Alline experienced God directly through "the scriptures," and not only had he heard "the still small voice" of God, but he had also, for what seemed to be an eternal moment, actually seen the Almighty face to face. At all levels of sensory experience, Alline had been overwhelmed by the divine presence, which had penetrated the deepest recesses of his being. His intimate association with the Almighty was so close that he could, without embarrassment, inform his followers, "The Lord is come with a stammering tongue, to seek you."[49]

Because of his "stammering tongue," Alline, like his contemporary John Wesley, was regarded by his many followers as "unique, irreplaceable, mysterious." He was seen less like a regular minister of the gospel and more "like the God figure in the Scriptures of the Hebrews, the God whose attributes are all paradoxical."[50] Alline was the godlike personage that any of his followers could become. Those North Americans who were converted through his preaching or that of his many disciples wished to replicate all aspects of Alline's own transforming religious experience. They, too, wished to have an immediate experience of Paradise; they, too, were eager to "taste but one glimmering ray" of the "Eternal Now"; and they yearned – how many of them deeply yearned! – for Alline's Christ to ravish them and make them at one with the divine, just as the Falmouth preacher himself had been sanctified by Christ. Many of those who had actually heard Alline preach tumbled to the depths of despair soon after his death. But most soon recovered, inspiring those who had never seen or heard the Nova Scotian to remember that magic New Light moment when they, like Henry Alline, had connected with Christ and become a human extension of His pristine spirituality and perfectibility. They had reached out and Christ had touched them. They were certain that it could happen again – and it did, only a few months after Alline's death, as periodic revivals, significantly shaped by the Allinite New Light–New Birth emphasis, became a noteworthy and distinguishing feature of the entire region's religious culture.

The last line of the inscription chiselled into Henry Alline's New Hampshire tombstone reads: "He was a burning and shining light and was justly esteemed the Apostle of Nova Scotia."[51] Most of his Nova Scotian contemporaries, and even many who in the nineteenth century had never heard him, would have endorsed this cogent statement. Despite the fact that Alline did not always preach what one Yankee Nova Scotian described in July 1784 as "right sound doctrine,"[52] he was widely perceived in his lifetime and afterwards as a man "sent of God" who had promoted a remarkable "Work of God."[53] Amos Hilton, one of Alline's most influential Nova Scotia converts, expressed in 1782 what he must have realized was a widespread view regarding Alline's so-called heretical views. When pressed by the Reverend Jonathan Scott, Alline's most vociferous ministerial critic, on why he could accept a gospel in which "all the Revelation of God's Word is overthrown," Hilton replied, "It was no matter of any great consequence to him what a man's principles were, if he was but earnest in promoting a good work."[54] In other words, Hilton was arguing that it was not that important how orthodox a preacher's theology was. What was truly significant and what really mattered was whether, like Alline, one had indeed experienced the New Birth and could therefore bring about lasting conversions.

2 William Black (1760–1834): Methodist New Light?

During Nova Scotia's First Great Awakening, the young Methodist itinerant William Black was almost as influential as Henry Alline. But largely because of the preoccupation of so many scholars with Alline, Black has been pushed to a distant corner of contemporary historiography dealing with religion and the American Revolution.[1] Moreover – and this point is sometimes forgotten – by the late 1790s, Black himself was eager to play down his role in the Awakening, since by then he regarded his former New Light religious enthusiasm as an evil manifestation of "fanaticism" which automatically led to "infidelity."[2] In the early nineteenth century, Black found himself endorsing, with enthusiasm, anti–New Light and anglophile pro-establishment views. According to Black, Maritime Methodists, unlike the New Light Baptists and Congregationalists, were much "esteemed by those in authority for their quiet and orderly lives, good morals and strict loyalty."[3] In 1822, Black uncritically endorsed the view of the British-born Methodist minister Robert Elder, who stated, "Because we oppose their enthusiastic excesses I do not permit people to rise up and speak, alias to rant and rave in our solemn assemblies . . . They [the New Light radical evangelicals] would endeavor to persuade our people that they are in bondage."[4] In this cogent statement made by Elder in the 1820s and in Black's comments uttered a few decades earlier are to be found the reasons why, by the third decade of the nineteenth century, the Methodists had been displaced by the Baptists as the most significant evangelical denomination in Nova Scotia and New Brunswick. By rejecting so much of their First Great Awakening legacy, the Maritime Methodists, at a critical juncture in the religious history of the Maritime region, had enabled the Baptists, both Calvinists and Free Christians, to overtake them in terms of numbers and societal influence.[5] Even though the Methodist leadership and many of the rank and file had by the 1820s espoused the cause of British Methodist respectability, some of the rank and file emphatically had not. These men and women were proud of their New Light heritage and did everything in their power to ensure that it remained at the centre of their belief system and their collective worship. Denominational loyalty kept them within the Methodist fold despite the powerful "primitive belief" that drew them in the New Light direction.

A native of Yorkshire, William Black, in 1775, at the age of fourteen, emigrated with his family to the Chignecto region of Nova Scotia. His most recent biographer, Goldwin French, describes him as a man of "average height," somewhat rotund by middle age, with "a round rosy face ... a benevolent smile and a sweet voice."[6] In 1760, some fifteen years before Black's arrival in Nova Scotia, a twelve-year-old Henry Alline had emigrated with his family from New England to the Falmouth region, some 100 miles to the south of the Chignecto. Black was part of a large-scale movement of British immigrants from the Yorkshire-Cumberland region to Nova Scotia in the early 1770s, just as Alline had been part of the Yankee emigration to the colony a decade earlier. Black was influenced, it is clear, by his parents' Yorkshire Methodism, and of course Alline had been brought up in a strict Calvinist Congregational atmosphere.

In the early months of 1775, a few months before William Black actually landed in Nova Scotia, Alline experienced his New Light–New Birth. Four years later, Black experienced his, which was apparently just as traumatic and just as emotionally charged. Like Alline, Black wrote a journal; an edited version of it covering the years 1775–88 was published in the British Methodist journal, the *Arminian Magazine*, in 1791. "An Account of Mr. William Black" never had much of an impact on Maritime religious life, largely because, soon after it was published, Black seemed to be embarrassed by its contents. If Black had died in 1791, his Awakening legacy might have been as important and influential as that of Alline. But his virtual abandonment of the movement and his bitter criticism of it during the latter half of his life meant that internal and external forces merged to marginalize him and to do so with a vengeance. Black and most of the Maritime Methodist leaders were determined to exaggerate their extreme British loyalty and their ordered respectability as well as their anti-Americanism. As a direct result, tens of

William Black, 1760–1834
Maritime Conference, United Church Archives, Halifax
(artist unknown; photo by Stéphane Thomassin)

thousands of Maritimers began to look to indigenous New Light Baptist preachers – people like themselves, who understood a rural, religious culture and the continuing appeal of the Allinite, radical Methodist gospel of ecstatic, personal salvation.

During the early years of the American Revolution, Black "grew in wickedness," at least according to his journal account, "turning the grace of God into lasciviousness; spending whole nights together [with his friends] in the ridiculous practice of shuffling spotted pieces of pasteboard, with painted kings and queens on them; and dancing for four or five nights in the week."[7] The Chignecto region of Nova Scotia, where Black lived, was attacked in late 1776 by a motley Patriot expedition from Machias, Maine. The invading American force, made up of about a hundred men, attempted to capture the tiny British Fort Cumberland, but was routed and forced to retreat to its Maine base. The siege of Fort Cumberland destabilized the region, turning many of the older Yankee inhabitants against the newly arrived Yorkshire immigrants. Black could not escape all of the Patriot-Loyalist tensions unleashed by the siege and its ramifications. However, the establishment of British military power over the region late in 1776 meant that Black and his family were protected from some of the worst Patriot ramifications of the expedition.

The early years of the revolution as well as the uprooting emigration experience had obviously disoriented the teenager. Finding little solace in his "worldliness," Black discovered in "the spring of 1779" that "the Lord" was beginning "to work upon" his mind in "a most powerful manner." He heard about a Methodist class meeting where some were "being awakened, and several set at liberty." Feeling guilty about "card-playing, dancing, Sabbath-breaking, etc.," he "covenanted" with his brother John "to attend the meetings, to read and to pray, etc." At one of his first class meetings, led by a John Newton, Black broke into sobs even before the first hymn was sung: "The tears began to gush out of my eyes, and my heart to throb within me: so that in a little time most of the company did so too." One of the women was "set ... at liberty" and "her soul was brought out of dismal darkness, into marvelous light. O! how did her soul exult in the Lord her Redeemer, and magnify his holy name!"[8]

The revival house-meetings continued for "some months" – almost daily – from "sunset ... until midnight" and sometimes "until day light." Black "wept, fasted and prayed," and his constant cry was "Give me Christ! Give me Christ! Or else I die." He could "bear to hear of nothing beside Jesus and him crucified; and was amazed to see men, endowed with reason, and capable of enjoying God's love in time and eternity, spending their precious moments in the most trifling and unprofitable conversation."[9]

Then "one night coming from a religious meeting," while "the Northern lights began to wave backwards and forwards in the air," Black suddenly was frightened, feeling strongly, as had Alline, that the "day of judgment" was indeed imminent. He immediately threw himself on the ground and "cried to the Lord to have mercy" on his "poor, wretched, sinful soul." While lying there, he experienced a divine "thought" being powerfully "impressed" upon his mind. "The

curse of God," the words were firmly pressed into his inner consciousness, "hangs over prayerless families: God is not worshipped in
a public manner in your family: this is your sin." Almost immediately,
Black and his brother began to have "family prayer," both of them
fearing that if they did not heed the "voice of God," they would be
eternally damned. But family prayer did not resolve Black's inner
turmoil. Next, he heard an exhortation in which were uttered these
words: "Sin and repent, sin and repent, until you repent in the
bottomless pit." These fear-inspiring words went "like a dagger" to
his heart:

"Lord," (he thought) "I am the very man. I sin and grieve, and then I sin
again, alas! What will such repentance avail! I must be holy or I cannot be
happy." Now my sins were set in array before me. I saw and felt myself guilty,
helpless, wretched and undone. I went about from day to day, hanging down
my head like a bullrush, whilst streams of tears rolled down my cheeks, yet
still I found no deliverance. However, I was determined never to rest, until
I found rest in Christ. None of the externals of religion would now satisfy
my awakened conscience. I saw that if ever I was saved, it must be by grace,
through faith; and that this faith was the gift of God; but alas! I had it not;
nor was I yet brought wholly to trust in the Lamb of God, that taketh away
the sins of the world.[10]

The Wesleyan-Methodist emphasis on "free grace" through faith
was evidently haunting Black. It had permeated the discussions of
the class meetings and the many emotionally charged exhortations
he had listened to, exhortations that seemed to be particularly and
directly aimed at him. Despite his almost frenetic search for salvation,
Black found himself "further from deliverance than ever." His sins
were now "an intolerable burden," and like Alline he actually heard
the devil whisper in his ear, "Go and hang thyself." "But God of his
infinite goodness preserved my soul from self-destruction," noted
Black. A "wounded spirit," "melancholy," and experiencing acute "distress," Black felt "an abiding sense" of his "lost condition" for two
days. Then, at the Oxley home, where the local Yorkshire Methodists
were meeting, the seventeen-year-old finally experienced the New
Birth:

We tarried ... singing and praying for about two hours when it pleased the
Lord to reveal his free grace; his fulness and his suitableness, as a Saviour:
his ability and willingness to save *me*. So that I was enabled to venture on
the sure mercies of *David*, and claim my interest in his blood, with "I am
thine, and thou art mine": while our friends were singing

"My pardon I claim,

For a sinner I am,

A sinner believing in Jesus's name"

Now I could lay hold of him, as the hope set before me: *The Lord my righteousness*, My burden dropped off: my guilt was removed: condemnation gave place to mercy: and a sweet peace and gladness were diffused through my soul. My mourning was turned into joy, and my countenance, like *Hannah's* was no more heavy. After tarrying some time, and returning public thanks, I went home with my heart full of love, and my mouth full of praise.[11]

A few hours after being converted, and after returning home, Black confronted disconcerting doubt. Once again the devil spoke to him: "You are deceived; you are puffed up with pride" – and Black almost believed him. He rushed from his home "into the field, and throwing [him]self on the ground, cried to the Lord for help." The Almighty heard Black's prayer: "He saw my distress; filled my soul with love, and bade me go in peace." Black discovered that "no sooner does the storm come on, the wind blow, the waves run high; than I begin to doubt, and the more I doubt, the more I sink." At the precise moment when he was convinced that he would "perish altogether," God "didst ... reach to me thine arm, as thou didst once to sinking *Peter*." The devil's "temptations" had been more than matched by the godly "proportionate comforts" that always followed them. "If my difficulties were great," Black was relieved to find, "my deliverance was greater." The teenage convert's heart "glowed" within him, "while the fields broke forth into singing, and the trees clapped their hands."[12]

Like Alline, Black was not satisfied merely with being converted. He wanted very much to share his Wesleyan-Methodist evangelical message with other Nova Scotians during the disorienting years of the American Revolution. Black preached his first sermon in the spring of 1781, and after turning twenty-one on 10 November of the same year and feeling that he was now free of his family responsibilities, he began to itinerate. "From the outset, apparently," Goldwin French, his biographer, has pointed out, "Black was not simply an itinerant evangelist but a Methodist preacher."[13]

For less than two years, the itinerating careers of Black and Alline overlapped in Nova Scotia. The two evangelists had a great deal in common, far more than may have separated them. Both considered the emotional New Birth to be the pivotal Christian experience. Both were powerful opponents of Calvinism, and both (despite what some of Alline's disciples practised and preached) were concerned with living the simple, holy, and Christ-centred Christian ascetic life. In the period 1781–83, both men were widely perceived as being unusually gifted preachers who were able to communicate to their often huge congregations what many considered to be a divinely inspired message. Both men were also able to translate their intense physical and sexual energy into charismatic power. They effortlessly connected, in a very real sense, with the hundreds who crowded to hear them, offering them emotional release, simple black and white answers to complex problems, and an almost palpable sense of renewed *communitas*.

Of course, the two men had their differences. In his view of the creation, the perseverance of the saints, and the atonement, among other doctrines, Alline was certainly not orthodox, and Black often stressed this fact. Furthermore, Alline was a New England planter, with a Yankee twang in his voice, who always regarded New England as home. Black was a Yorkshireman with a Yorkshire accent, and anyone who heard him speak recognized his deep commitment to Great Britain, its institutions, its heroes, and its way of life.

It is noteworthy that the Nova Scotians who actually heard Alline and Black in the latter years of the American Revolution, and who recorded their impressions, believed that the two evangelists in fact preached precisely the "same gospel." According to the Liverpool merchant, general factotum, and diarist, Simeon Perkins, who was not a New Light enthusiast, the four sermons of Alline's that he heard in November 1782 were "very good," "very ingenious," "very good," and sounded "very well."[14] In fact, Perkins did not write one negative word about Alline. On 16 February 1783, he expressed what he knew the Liverpool consensus about Alline to be:

Mr. Alline Preached both parts of the day and Evening. A number of people made a relation of their Experiences after the Meeting was concluded & Expressed Great Joy & comfort in what God had done for them. Mr. Alline made a long Speech, Very Sensible, Advising all Sorts of People to a Religious Life, & gave many directions for their outward walk. This is a wonderful day & Evening. Never did I behold Such an Appearance of the Spirit of God moving upon the people Since the time of the Great Religious Stir in New England many years ago.[15]

It is clear that, for Perkins, Alline's revival had all the appearance of New England's First Great Awakening. This is the connection he and many of his Yankee contemporaries were to make not only in the 1780s but right into the nineteenth century.

A little more than three months after Alline left Liverpool for the last time, Black arrived. Perkins noted in his diary on Wednesday, 28 May 1783, "Mr. Black, a Methodist or New light preacher belonging somewhere up the Bay of Fundy Arrives from Halifax and Preaches at the Meeting House at Evening."[16] On 29 May, Black preached twice. "The People that followed Mr. Alline," Perkins observed, "seem very fond of him."[17] On Tuesday, 3 June, Perkins described "the Very extraordinary Stur among his hearers, great Crying-out etc.," and on Sunday, 22 June, he once again commented favourably on Black's preaching: "He performs very well."[18] Soon after 22 June, Black left Liverpool only to return late in April 1784. By this time, largely because of forces beyond his control, Black confronted a serious split among Liverpool New Light evangelicals – specifically, between the New Light disciples of Alline and the Methodists.

What is particularly noteworthy about Perkins's response to Alline and Black in 1782 and 1783 is that he was certain that they preached the very same evangelical gospel. The Yorkshire and New England residents of the Chignecto area evidently strongly agreed with this assessment in 1782, after Alline's first visit to the area. Alline's brother-in-law, John Payzant, who knew the area well, maintained that after Alline's first sojourn in the Chignecto, "New Lights and Methodist[s] joined together."[19] The radical evangelical united front was shattered soon after Alline left, it was reported, because of the antinomian preaching of one of Alline's disciples, apparently Thomas Chipman. As long as Alline was in the region, however, the New Light–Methodist coalition held together – his powerful, charismatic personality providing the glue.

Alline died in 1784 at the height of his career, leaving behind a considerable literary and oral legacy. It is not surprising, therefore, that for his contemporaries, as well as for so many twentieth-century scholars, Alline's noteworthy preaching career captured the essence of Nova Scotia's response to the American Revolution. He is the prism through which so much, perhaps too much, of late-eighteenth-century Nova Scotia history is viewed. Black, on the other hand, probably reached the apex of his religious significance in the 1780s and experienced an inexorable decline of influence as the eighteenth century blurred into the nineteenth. When he died in Halifax on 8 September 1834, Black seemed to have been pushed firmly to the margins of the province's religious life. The publication in 1839 of his *Memoir* did little to add shape or substance to his legacy. Black had almost lived too long; the eighteenth-century Black was a powerful, some would say charismatic, preacher; the nineteenth-century Black seemed to be far too concerned with British order and respectability and with the accumulation of "worldly possessions." In abandoning his New Light heritage, Black, in an ironic twist of historical development, significantly strengthened Alline's reputation as the "Whitefield of Nova Scotia."

Alline and Black responded to one another in different ways, and this may also help to explain why twentieth-century scholars have treated them so differently. In his *Journal*, published originally in Boston in 1806, Alline never even mentioned Black by name. Alline first visited the Cumberland-Chignecto region in July 1781, and for almost six weeks he saw "many sinners ... groaning under the burthen of their sins, and pleading for mercy, and for the blood of Christ with unspeakable agonies of soul."[20] Often preaching three times a day, he noted that the "hearers were so numerous" that he was "obliged to preach in the fields."[21] Because of the "power of the Holy Ghost that was among the people,"[22] Alline was able to persuade scores of Yorkshire Methodists and Yankee Congregationalists to join together to form a New Light church. On 16 August 1781, after visiting present-day Sackville, Alline noted in his *Journal*:

This day the church met and about twenty were added to it. It was a blessed day to my soul, especially at about eight o'clock in the evening: when speaking to the christians, my whole soul was so ravished with the love of Jesus, that I could scarcely speak; yea, my very heart seemed melted with love. O the love, the infinite love of my God! How is my soul on the wing when I have but one glimpse of that sacred love: and if one glimpse is so great and transporting what will it be to swim forever in the infinite ocean, and nothing to annoy. O my Jesus, shall I ever be so happy, shall I one day awake in perfect joy with thee? O it is all I want, and all I need. Give it to me, O my God, and thine be the glory forever. Amen.[23]

When Alline left his Cumberland followers on 21 August 1781, he felt that they were "all wrapped up in unity of the Spirit and bonds of peace." "When I left them," he explained, "I could hardly speak, although not with grief, for I could leave them freely, but was so affected with what I saw and felt of God's love and goodness; and to think I should one day meet them in glory, to love and praise my God to all eternity, bore my soul above the world."[24]

When Alline returned to the Cumberland area in early June 1782, he discovered "some Christians alive to God; but some had got into darkness (& Bondage) by disputing about principles."[25] The basic dispute principle was, without question, that of the perseverance of the saints – a key Allinite doctrine bitterly attacked by the followers of John Wesley. Doctrinal squabbling, however, did not stop hundreds from thronging to hear Alline "proclaiming the name of Jesus."[26] On 9 July 1782, Alline left the region, never to return.

Black's journal for the 1780s gives a different picture of Alline and also of Black's role in Nova Scotia's First Great Awakening. According to Black, Alline poached on the Methodist class meetings in Cumberland during both visits, persuading scores of recent Methodist converts to become ardent Congregational New Lights.[27] This Allinite poaching seems to have worried Black much more in 1782 than it had in 1781. The evidence suggests that Black's itinerating, which began in November 1781, was in fact inspired by Alline's example. Black's 1781 journal, moreover, reads very much like Alline's more famous *Journal*. For example, on 25 November 1781, Black observed: "Preached in the evening with much liberty; and many were refreshed. Part of this day I was in a lively frame, but experienced much dulness the remainder of it. O Lord, revive my soul, and quicken me, a poor unworthy creature; unworthy to eat the crumbs that fall from my Master's table!"[28] Black was certain that he could "see, or feel, or taste God, in everything."[29] He loved to preach and pray and exhort. "We seldom met together," he proudly observed, "but the shout of a king was heard in our camp." He found: "The Lord graciously stood by my weakness, and his spirit helped my infirmities; so that many times, though my body trembled, and my knees smote one against another, yet God delivered me from these fears, so that I could speak with confidence, freedom and tender affection."[30]

For the first few months of his itinerating ministry, Black preached in the Chignecto-Cumberland region – the area he knew best. In May 1782, though barely twenty-two years old, he felt compelled to make his way to the Allinite heartland – to Windsor, and then to Cornwallis and Horton, and even to Falmouth. On 3 June, at "a Mr. Johnson's" in Horton, Black "gave out a hymn, and engaged in prayer." "Mrs. Johnson," he pointed out,

was so over-powered with the love of God that she could scarcely stand under it. She broke forth in raptures of praise, and declared, in language I little expected from her, the wonderful goodness of God. She exhorted, with variety of expression, all present, to make their calling and election sure; and then, with inexpressible transport, cried out – "O! that I had wings like a dove, for then would I fly away and be at rest." Several present were deeply affected, and continued for two or three hours praising God, and imploring mercy.[31]

The following day, at a time when Alline was on board a vessel destined for Cumberland, Black preached at Falmouth, where "many felt the power of the word." "Several of Mr. Alline's friends were present," Black proudly wrote. "They rejoiced greatly, declaring, it was the very Gospel which they had heard – the power of God unto salvation."[32]

On 7 June, Black returned to Windsor and then made his way to Halifax, where he preached, as he bluntly put it, "to a stupid set of people." "O what a town for wickedness is this," he complained. "Satan has here many faithful and steady servants."[33] On 30 June, Black was back in Cornwallis, and at this time he was at the heart of an intense religious revival: "I preached at Cornwallis in the morning, on 'By grace are ye saved,' and in the afternoon, to the largest congregation I ever saw collected in any part of the country, or perhaps anywhere else on 'The Spirit of the Lord God is upon me; because the Lord hath anointed me to preach good tidings unto the meek; he hath sent me to bind up the broken hearted, to proclaim liberty to the captives.'"[34] Once again emulating Alline, Black emphatically associated himself with Isaiah; the "Spirit of the Lord God" was upon William Black, God's special prophet to Nova Scotia. Black's growing confidence in his God-given power was obviously affecting many Nova Scotians, who saw him as Alline's equal and not his Methodist inferior. Consequently, news about Black's Cornwallis revival swept down the Annapolis Valley and beyond, and his "pretty general notoriety ... led to the expression of a desire, from various quarters, of a visit from him."[35]

In early July, Black travelled to Annapolis and slowly made his way up the Annapolis Valley to Cornwallis where, on 9 July, he preached yet another memorable sermon. "O what a noise and shaking among the dry bones," he enthused. "My voice could scarcely be heard."[36] "Many saw the necessity of inward religion," he noted, "and with strong cries and tears besought the Lord for mercy."[37] Five days later, Black had returned home, where he discovered that seventy more Methodists had joined Alline's New Light church. According to an angry Black, Alline had "thrown all into confusion – broken-up the classes, and introduced a flood of contention, the consequences of which I dread."[38] Almost immediately, Black began his Methodist counter-offensive, and in the process his earlier positive view of Alline was replaced by an increasingly negative one. Moreover, by attacking the Allinites and by stressing the religious superiority of the Methodists, Black exacerbated the ethnic and religious divisions that were to be found near the surface of Cumberland life.[39]

In the early days of 1783, Black's journal reflected a morbid introspection underscored by the conviction that he had in fact been defeated by Alline and his New Light disciples. Eagerly searching for support, encouragement, and advice, Black began to write to John Wesley. On 20 February 1783, Wesley replied, urging Black to further his theological education in England at the Kingswood School. Wesley also warned Black about Allinism. "Of Calvinism, Mysticism, and Antinomianism," he cautioned, "have a care; for they are the bane of true religion."[40] Despite Wesley's warning, and despite the fact that the Allinites were creating serious problems in the Cumberland region, Black endeavoured in July 1783 to "maintain if possible a friendly intercourse with Mr. Alline, from a persuasion that with all that was exceptionable in his doctrinal views, there was associated sincere love to the Saviour, and an ardent zeal for the extension of his kingdom."[41]

On 4 July 1783, Black penned the following remarkable letter to Alline, who, despite his serious case of tuberculosis, was preparing for his fateful voyage to New England. The letter was most certainly received by Alline, who did not leave Windsor for Maine until 27 August 1783. It began "Dear Brother."

I hear you are very ill in body, but I trust happy in soul, rejoicing in the sweet Lord Jesus. Since I saw you I have been at Liverpool, proclaiming the love of Christ to lost sinners; and blessed be God we have had happy and delightful days. On my first arrival they appeared dull, having been without preaching for some time. But soon the fire began to kindle. I know not that I ever heard more heart-piercing cries, as well from the young as the old. The people of God too, more exceedingly happy, praising him for his wonderful goodness to the children of men. Their cries and praises ascended for hours together, so that sometimes our meetings did not break up till one in the morning. Truly the Lord rained down the manna of his love in gracious showers, and several declared with joy that they found the pearl of great price.

Then Black went on:

The people at Liverpool are all well, and most of them happy. They long to see you again; and I assure you I rejoice to find that the Lord has owned your labours amongst them, and I trust he will continue to do so until he calls you hence. Although we differ in sentiment, let us manifest our love to each other. I always admired your gifts and graces, and affectionately loved your person, although I could never receive your peculiar opinions. But shall we on this account destroy the work of God? God forbid! May the Lord take away all bigotry, and fill us with pure genuine, Catholic love! Wishing you God's speed in every work to which the Lord calls you, I conclude with, when it is well with thee, remember me.[42]

How does one account for Black's conciliatory letter? Obviously, seeing Alline face to face in the Chignecto region and actually feeling a deep Christian "affection" for the dying evangelist was a key factor. In addition, Black's remarkable Liverpool revival, which was perceived by its participants as a natural outgrowth of Alline's earlier ones, drew the two men together. This process was further strengthened by the growing conviction in Black's mind that, despite their differences, the Almighty was indeed using both of them to direct what Black referred to as the "power of God ... upon the [Nova Scotia] people."[43] Once he found himself in Alline's Yankee heartland, away from his Cumberland home base, Black seems to have been more willing to accept that Alline's gospel, despite its "peculiar opinions," was an integral part of "the work of God" in the colony. In July 1783, Black seemed to feel almost as close to the Falmouth preacher as he had in the summer of 1781. But before the friendship could be consolidated, Alline left the colony never to return.

Alline's death, however, did not thrust Black forward as Nova Scotia's foremost evangelist. In fact, a year after Alline's death in 1784, Black found himself relegated to the outskirts of the revivalist movement in the colony by a fellow Methodist, Freeborn Garrettson.[44] Although the Maryland-born Methodist preacher spent only twenty-six months in Nova Scotia, his influence in the colony was remarkable. Black continued to preach his Methodist gospel until his retirement in 1812, but he was never able to re-establish his First Great Awakening revivalistic ascendancy. The responsibilities of marriage, sickness, a growing suspicion of New Light revivalistic techniques, the expanding conservative influence of British Methodism – and, most important, a longing for respectability – all combined to draw Black away from his Awakening moorings. Although his achievements were rather "modest," according to his most recent biographer, Black "would have wished to be remembered" by posterity "affectionately as one who at great peril and at great cost to himself brought a new hope and assurance to thousands of people, many of whom were beginning a new life in an alien and inhospitable land."[45] When Black died on 8 September 1834, he left a considerable estate behind, together with what a leading Halifax Methodist minister referred to as a "universal mourning sympathy."[46] "Bishop" Black, as he was affectionately called, was widely regarded by his contemporaries as the "Father of Methodism" in the Maritime provinces. He is largely forgotten, however, by contemporary Canadians, especially those who worship in the United Church of Canada, the church that in theory, at least, embodies his own peculiar version of pietistic Methodism.

Yet William Black probably deserves more than this from posterity, from the Canadian Protestant tradition, Canadian evangelicalism, and the historical profession. From the vantage point of Nova Scotia's First Great Awakening, Black was not only an important evangelist but also a person who, almost despite himself, significantly shaped the New Light–New Birth paradigm – which became the religious prism through which the entire Canadian evangelical experience was viewed and interpreted not only during its formative stage but well into the nineteenth century and even beyond.

3 David George (1743–1810): Black Nova Scotian New Light Baptist

David George's New Birth in 1774, like that of Alline and Black, was the central and defining experience of his life – an amazing religious life and ministerial career in what are now the United States, Canada, and Sierra Leone. For George, born a slave in Virginia in 1743, "the work of conversion was wholly God's," because this kind of conversion was his own intense, personal, and unforgettable encounter with the Almighty, and he therefore felt compelled to underplay significantly in his preaching the importance of what he referred to as "the use of means" such as "the instruction of children and family religion."[1] The means, according to the first black Baptist minister in Canada and the "first Baptist pastor (white or black) in Africa,"[2] perniciously replaced the pristine divine with the manipulative human to create deadly "Pharisaism" permeated by an arrogant emphasis on the written word rather than on the inwardly felt and experienced word.[3] George's New Light Baptist faith was significantly shaped in South Carolina, before the outbreak of the revolution, by a direct and indirect Yankee, New Light, Separate Baptist influence;[4] and in Nova Scotia, from 1782, when he arrived as a Loyalist, to 1792, when he left for Africa, by the indigenous New Light and radical evangelical movement that owed so much to the charismatic Henry Alline.[5] David George would take with him to West Africa in 1792 a peculiar antinomian blend of American Southern and Nova Scotian New Light popular evangelicalism. When George died in Sierra Leone in 1810, a spent religious force, he was still, despite a myriad of setbacks, a New Light.

When David George was approximately fifty years old, he wrote a brief but still fascinating autobiography, which was published in the first volume of the British *Baptist Annual Register*. He began what he titled "An Account of the Life of Mr. DAVID GEORGE" in the following somewhat stylized manner:

I was born in ... Virginia, about 50 or 60 miles from Williamsburg, on Nottaway river, of parents who were brought from Africa, but who had not the fear of God before their eyes. The first work I did was fetching water, and carding of cotton; afterwards I was sent into the field to work about the Indian corn and tobacco, till I was about 19 years old. My father's name was John, and my mother's Judith. I had four brothers, and four sisters, who with myself were all born in slavery: our master's name was Chapel [James Chappell] – a very bad man to the Negroes.[6]

To refer to Chappell as "a very bad man to the Negroes" was to understate significantly the reality of his vicious and bloody racism. Chappell frequently whipped George's oldest sister, Patty, so that "her back has been all corruption, as though it would rot."[7] His brother Dick, after an attempt to run away from the plantation, was "hung up to a cherry-tree in the yard, by his two hands, quite naked, except his breeches, with his feet about half a yard from the ground." Then "they tied his legs close together, and put a pole between them, at one end of which one of the owner's sons sat, to keep him down, and another son at the other. After he had received 500 lashes, or more, they washed his back with salt water, and whipped it in, as well as rubbed it in with a rag; and then directly sent him to work in pulling off the suckers of tobacco."[8] David was also "whipped many a time on my naked skin, and sometime, till the blood has run down over my waistband." His "greatest grief," however, came not from the violence directed at him or his siblings but that directed at his mother – "to hear her, on her knees, begging for mercy."[9]

Because of Chappell's "rough and cruel usage" George escaped, making his way southwards into Creek Territory and then, early in 1765, farther west to the "Nauchee [Natchez] Indians."[10] While with the Natchez, he was purchased by an Indian trader, John Miller, for his superior, George Galphin, who was located at Silver Bluff, South Carolina. By 1766 George was permanently employed as a personal servant at Galphin's handsome brick house. Soon after the birth of his first child in 1771, George began to take an increased interest in things religious. In his autobiography he enthusiastically abandoned his description of his "bad life" at Silver Bluff to discuss the morphology of his conversion. A black friend from Charleston – a man named Cyrus – warned George "one day in the woods, that if I lived so, I should never see the face of God in Glory (whether he himself was a converted man or not, I do not know.)" This warning "disturbed" George and gave him "much concern." He began to recite, over and over again,

the Lord's prayer, that it might make me better, but I feared that I grew worse; and I continued worse and worse, as long as I thought I would do something to make me better; till at last it seemed as if there was no possibility of relief, and that I must go to hell. I saw myself a mass of sin. I could not read, and had no scriptures. I did not think of Adam and Eve's sin, but I was sin. I felt my own plague; and I was so overcome that I could not wait upon my master. I told him I was ill. I felt myself at the disposal of Sovereign mercy. At last in prayer to God I began to think that he would deliver me, but I did not know how.[11]

What is noteworthy is that at this stage of George's spiritual pilgrimage, he knew something about basic Christianity, not necessarily about the "how" but about the "what." He must have picked up some of this information from his sporadic attendance at the Anglican Nottaway Chapel situated near Chappell's plantation.[12] Moreover, he could have learned something about Christianity from his many white associates and perhaps from his work in the Galphin household. Of course, he also might have received some information about the Christian faith from slave believers other than Cyrus. Whatever the case, the thirty-year-old George, almost despite himself, was obviously seeking to be saved – in the radical evangelical Christian sense of the word.

In his autobiography, George stressed the fact that even before he had heard his first New Light sermon, he saw that he could not be saved "by any of my own doings, but that it must be by God's mercy – that my sins had crucified Christ; and now the Lord took away my distress." He was, he proudly declared, "sure that the Lord took it away, because I had such pleasure and joy in my soul, that no man could give me."[13] It was certainly fortuitous for George that "soon after" this intense spiritual crisis he "heard George Liele preach." Liele was a black New Light Baptist deacon who, soon after his conversion in 1773, had received permission from the white Baptist church in which he worshipped "to instruct [his] own color in the word of God."[14] Encouraged by his white owner, Liele visited the nearby plantations "whenever friendly plantation owners would permit."[15] Galphin was one of these plantation owners. It is interesting to note that George had known Liele "ever since he was a boy"[16] and was immediately drawn to the itinerant preacher. "His sermon was very suitable," George observed, "on 'Come unto me all ye that labour, and are heavy laden, and I will give you rest.'"[17] The Liele sermon was a form of New Light exhortation; and as Mechal Sobel has perceptively observed, there were many black exhorters who were very emotional in their preaching and who effectively used "'imagination and invention' – metaphors, parables, and allegories based on life rather than book learning."[18]

It would be an understatement to observe that Liele's exhortation/ sermon from Matthew 11:28 struck an unusually responsive chord in his close friend David George. George felt the huge load of his guilt pressing on his quickened conscience and welcomed the opportunity to have it finally and gloriously lifted. After Liele had finished exhorting his congregation, George rushed forward "and told him I was so; That I was weary and heavy laden, and that the grace of God had given me rest." Indeed, George stressed that Liele's "whole discourse" had been providentially directed right at him.[19] George's conversion was confirmed soon afterwards by the "very powerful preach[ing]" of the Reverend Wait Palmer,[20] who "came frequently" to the Galphin plantation to ensure that Liele's converts would not abandon their faith.[21]

Palmer has recently been referred to as "a most interesting and energetic preacher and evangelist,"[22] and, without question, he significantly influenced George's New Light and Baptist theology and practice. A native of Connecticut and an enthusiastic Separate New Light Baptist who had been deeply affected by the First Great Awakening, Palmer had been ordained in 1743. Soon afterwards he moved to Virginia and then to North Carolina, where he played a key role in the establishment of "the Sandy Creek Association of Baptist churches known for their revivalist, serious, evangelistic zeal and establishing new churches."[23] Palmer placed tremendous importance on the New Birth and on the Almighty's crucial role in precipitating conversion. As far as he was concerned, the Holy Spirit suddenly penetrated the soul of the converted individual; good works had nothing to do with true conversion, nor did education – only God's free grace, as shown in the death and resurrection of Jesus Christ.

The first time George heard Palmer preach, he felt so exhilarated that as the Baptist minister "was returning home Lord's-day evening," George went with him "two or three miles, and told him how it was with me." This testimony convinced Palmer that the new convert was ready for baptism by immersion and also for church membership. Other slaves, including George's wife, had been converted, and therefore, following New Light Baptist practice, Palmer "appointed

a Saturday evening to hear what the Lord had done for [them], and
the next day [he] baptized [them] in the Mill-stream."[24]

"Some time afterwards," George felt a powerful "desire for nothing
else but to talk to the brothers and sisters about the Lord."[25] This
desire was realized when Palmer organized the baptized slave converts "into a church ... at Silver Bluff." According to George:

Then I began to exhort in the church, and learned to sing hymns. The first
I learned out of [a] book was a hymn of that great writing man [Isaac]
Watts, which begins with "Thus saith the wisdom of the Lord." Afterwards
the church advised with Brother Palmer about my speaking to them, and
keeping them together; I refused, and felt I was unfit for all that, but Brother
Palmer said this word to me, "Take care that you don't offend the Lord."
Then I thought that he knew best, and I agreed that I would do as well as
I could so I was appointed to the office of an Elder and received instruction
from Brother Palmer how to conduct myself. I proceeded in this way till the
American war was coming on, when the Ministers were not allowed to come
amongst us lest they should furnish us with too much knowledge. The Black
people all around attended with us, and as Brother Palmer must not come,
I had the whole management, and used to preach among them myself.[26]

With his new responsibilities, the illiterate George felt compelled
to learn how to read the Bible. He approached the white children
"to teach me a,b,c." They "would give me a lesson, which I tried to
learn, and then I would go to them again, and ask them if I was
right? The reading so ran in my mind, that I think I learned in my
sleep as really as when I was awake; and I can now read the Bible,
so that what I have in my heart, I can see in the Scriptures."[27] This
sentence from George's autobiography cogently and simply summarized the essence of his New Light gospel and his entire radical
evangelical belief system. Reading the word had merely confirmed
what to George was the miraculous moving of the Spirit. Despite
having "received instruction from Brother Palmer" and despite his
reading of the Bible – and even despite the preaching of Liele and
Palmer – George was absolutely convinced that God had traumati-
cally converted him sometime between the conversation with Cyrus
and the coming of Liele.

Some twenty-five years after his conversion, when George was in
Sierra Leone, he discussed some of his basic religious views with
Zachary Macaulay, an evangelical Anglican (and future member of
the "Clapham Sect") who was governor of the new British colony.
Macaulay believed that George and most of the Nova Scotia immi-
grants were antinomians who placed far too much stress on the

importance of subjective "religious feelings" coming directly from the Holy Spirit and not enough on Christian morality and Christian discipline. Like many disciples of Henry Alline in Nova Scotia and New Brunswick in the post-revolutionary period, George and his followers, having experienced the "ravishing of the spirit" and the "rapture of the New Birth," could not imagine how they could lose their salvation; and their confidence, spiritual hubris, and certainty of redemption was such that they became increasingly indifferent to sin, especially to Christian sexual moral standards.[28]

In response to Macaulay's first and very difficult question about what George actually regarded as "the rule of our faith and practice," George seemed to place equal emphasis on "the written word" and "the spirit within us." Probing further, Macaulay asked the black Baptist minister to tell him whom he "considered entitled to the name of Christian." George's brief response reflected a certain sense of surprise: "Those that are converted to be sure."

"But what is conversion?" Macaulay asked.

"A man must know when he's converted," George replied, explaining that this certainty could come only through "inward feeling."

An angry Macaulay denounced this expression of Christian nihilism and insisted that conversion "involved a turning from sin to holiness, and that every other evidence was vain." According to the evangelical Anglican governor, a "voice supposed from heaven" was really "the delusive internal feelings of a corrupt imagination."

"What then," an exasperated George asked his interrogator, "you won't allow feelings to have anything to do with religion?"

"So far as the Bible allowed it," Macaulay answered. "The feeling there said to belong to converted persons, were love, joy, peace, meekness, gentleness, and where these were really felt, there was true conversion." The governor was condemning radical evangelical enthusiasm in general, and New Light spirituality in particular. He especially denounced the "inexplicable mental impressions and bodily feelings" that characterized the black Loyalists' religious life in Sierra Leone. In reply, George contended that the Holy Spirit worked in mysterious ways, often through "mental impressions" and "bodily feelings," and that "the work of conversion was wholly God's" and owed nothing whatsoever to "the use of means." "Prayers and instruction," he said, "can't convey grace."

Macaulay had heard George preach "unscriptural" sermons permeated by what the governor called "abominable doctrine." As Macauley recorded in his journal, George had declared, "It is not for every little sin as being overtaken by drunkenness, or some temptation, that a Child of God is to lose his interest in x + [Christ] ... once in x +, always in x + ... whom he [God] loves, he loves to the end." George also remembered these words, and in his discussion with Macaulay he could only raise the plaintive question: "But is not God unchangeable, how then can he withdraw his love from his Children?" Even though, according to Macaulay, George had finally admitted that "his eyes" had been "opened," the governor realized that no fundamental change had really taken place with respect to George's convictions. "The antinomian scheme," Macaulay perceptively observed "is a most seductive one: No means to be used, no exertions to be made, no lusts to be crucified, no self denial to be practiced." He saw it as the logical outgrowth of the "ruinous notion ... of instantaneous conversion" and its radical evangelical and New Light corollary, "that the genuineness of the work depends on some sensible impression made on the imagination at the time."

Macaulay's twelve-hour discussion and debate with George was not soon forgotten by the governor, who seemed haunted by the experience for days. In his journal he continued to attack George's theological views, which "attach[ed] to the moment of conversion a kind of mystical feeling whereby the person is made to know assuredly that at that very moment, God delivered him from his sins, justifying him by his grace." If any Nova Scotia black believer was asked "how he knows himself to be a child of God," the response would be "pretty much in the stile of David George." "I know it," George had declared, over and over again, "not because of this or the other proof drawn from the word of God but because (perhaps) twenty years ago I saw a certain sight or heard certain words or passed thro a certain train of impressions varying from solicitude to deep concern and terror and despair and thence again thro fluctuations of fear and hope to peace and joy and assured confidence."[29]

Despite his basic lack of sympathy and empathy for David George's theology and the gospel he preached, Macaulay's description, the best and most detailed available, seems to cut very close to the heart of the matter. It is clear from his interrogation of George as well as from his sermon tasting in Sierra Leone that Macaulay had peeled off the various complex layers that gave shape and some substance to the evangelical Christianity brought to Sierra Leone in 1792 by the Nova Scotia black Loyalists. Not all the black Loyalists were Baptists – there were scores of Methodists as well, disciples both of John Wesley and the Countess of Huntington.[30] Despite their not insignificant denominational differences, these Methodist and Baptist men and women shared a New Light heritage that probably owed more to Henry Alline and Freeborn Garrettson and their New

Brunswick and Nova Scotia disciples than it did to their American slave experiences. There is therefore a real ring of truth in the contention of the influential scholar of Christian missions, Andrew Walls of the University of Edinburgh, that the Allinite New Light legacy probably had a more significant short- and long-term impact on West Africa than it did on present-day Canada.[31]

It is sometimes forgotten that the American Revolution was the means whereby thousands of black slaves from the southern colonies were liberated, eventually making their way as Loyalists to what is now New Brunswick and Nova Scotia. George and his family were part of this remarkable exodus. After a brief sojourn in Halifax, the capital of Nova Scotia, George made his way in June 1783 to Shelburne, some 125 miles to the southwest. At this Loyalist centre, George immediately began to preach his unique brand of Christianity, and soon he had "about fifty members" in his church.[32] White opposition intensified in the community when George's preaching began to have an impact on some whites. According to George:

We then returned to brother Holmes's [in neighbouring Jones's Harbour], and he and his wife came up with me to Shelburne, and gave their experiences to the church on Thursday, and were baptized on Lord's day. Their relations who lived in the town were very angry, raised a mob, and endeavoured to hinder their being baptized. Mrs. Holmes's sister especially laid hold of her hair to keep her from going down into the water; but the justices commanded peace, and said that she should be baptized, as she herself desired it.[33]

The public baptism by immersion of a white woman by a black preacher infuriated many Shelburne inhabitants and "the persecution increased." Scores of "disbanded soldiers" destroyed George's house and those of his followers and threatened to burn down the church building. "But I continued preaching," George reported, "till they came one night, and stood before the pulpit, and swore how they would treat me if I preached again. But I stayed and preached, and the next day they came and beat me with sticks, and drove me into a swamp."[34] Soon afterwards, George and his family decided to move to the black settlement of Birchtown, to the southwest of Shelburne. But the persecution of blacks there eventually forced the reluctant George to return to Shelburne. By the latter part of the 1780s, George, once again based in Shelburne, was making contact with Allinite New Light congregations in Liverpool, Ragged Island, and Annapolis in Nova Scotia. In June 1786 the general factotum of Liverpool, Simeon Perkins, observed in his famous *Diary*, "A Black man from Shelburne, said to be a Baptist teacher holds forth at the

New Light Meeting House. He speaks very loud and the people of that meeting, I understand, like him very well."[35] In order to be "very well" liked by Liverpool New Lights, a preacher had to resonate faithfully with the spirit of Henry Alline's evangelistic message.

By 1791, George had begun to itinerate farther and farther from his home base. He visited black believers in Saint John, New Brunswick, on at least two occasions, baptizing fourteen men and women there, and he also baptized three in Fredericton, the capital of the colony. About his second visit to Saint John, George wrote in his autobiography: "When I was landing ... some of the people who intended to be baptized were so full of joy that they ran out from waiting at table on their masters, with the knives and forks in their hands, to meet me at the water side. This second time of my being at St. John's I staid preaching about a fortnight, and baptized ten people. Our going down into the water seemed to be a pleasing sight to the whole town, White people and Black."[36]

What did the Nova Scotia and New Brunswick followers of Alline think about David George? We know that Simeon Perkins, no friend of the Allinites in the late 1780s, had a favourable picture of the Baptist preacher, a picture refracted through the memories of some of the Liverpool merchant's New Light friends. It is certain that Harris Harding, an ardent disciple of Alline and the future "patriarch" of the Maritime Baptist denomination, regarded George in a most positive light. Harding starkly contrasted the worldliness of Shelburne whites against the spirituality of George and his black followers. "David's church," Harding once observed, "appears at times like a woman clothed with the sun."[37] A short time earlier in 1791, after worshipping in George's church in Shelburne, Harding wrote one of his typical letters to his sister.

Yesterday morning I attended David's Meeting, where as soon as I came I found about twenty or thirty made white in the blood of the Lamb – singing hosannahs to the Son of David. Several of them frequently was oblidg'd to stop and rejoice, soon after David began prayer, But was so overcome with joy was likewise oblidged to stop, and turn'd to me with many tears like brooks rolling down his cheeks desiring me to call upon that worthy name that was like Ointment pour'd down upon the Assembly – My soul was upon a Mount Zion.[38]

To be on Mount Zion with Harris Harding was to be an Allinite indeed.

A nineteenth-century Nova Scotia Baptist leader, William Chipman (1781–1865), met George during the latter's brief visit to Horton in 1791. Although only ten years old at the time, Chipman would never forget the visiting black Baptist minister. "I well remember his appearance," Chipman later noted, "rather tall and slender":

His modesty, humility, and very deep solemnity struck me with awe. I felt terror-striken, [he had never seen a Black person before] and could but draw the conclusion that he was a man of very deep piety: Oh what veneration I felt for him as a man of God! I envied him his happiness, and I was confirmed in my opinion of his piety by his whole demeanor. When he was asked to eat at the same table with Mr. Marchington [a wealthy resident] he modestly declined, saying, "No Massa, God has made a distinction in our colour; give me my food alone."[39]

It is difficult to reconcile George's "No Massa" response with his standing up to the white mobs in Shelburne and with his eagerness to baptize whites and blacks together, despite the hostility this often generated. Perhaps he felt uncomfortable eating with the Marchington family. Perhaps he carried with him from his slavery days a belief that there was nothing wrong about eating in the kitchen. There were certain real advantages in eating with other blacks or by oneself, especially if one was intimidated by polite and condescending white dinner conversation or by the complex world of etiquette and good table manners. The "No Massa" response may embarrass a reader in the 1990s; it obviously did not embarrass George, and it may have been a powerful statement underscoring his own independence and sense of identity and his shrewdness.

Despite his ministerial success in Nova Scotia and New Brunswick, George decided in the fall of 1792 to play a key role in encouraging other Maritime blacks to emigrate to West Africa under the auspices of the Sierra Leone Company. Having had enough of white racism, the Baptist minister had come to the conclusion that the black Loyalists had a far better future in Sierra Leone than in "Nova Scarcity," where so many whites were "very cruel to us, and treated many of us as bad as though we had been slaves."[40]

It has been estimated that close to 1,200 blacks left Nova Scotia for Sierra Leone ("the largest free migration of Blacks in history"),[41] amounting to one-third of "the total black loyalist population of Nova Scotia and New Brunswick."[42] With David George sailed most of the leaders of the Maritime black Loyalists – leaving behind a dispirited and largely leaderless black Loyalist population of some 4,000. It would take the Maritime black community decades to recover from this decapitation.

Sierra Leone was not a land flowing with milk and honey. George and many of his Baptist followers experienced religious declension in their new homeland. And when George died in 1810, he was a mere shadow of the man he had been in South Carolina and Nova Scotia. The sharp edge of his New Light enthusiasm had been worn down by the harsh realities of his new environment and by his own inner spiritual struggles and the weakening influence of the "divine impressions" – which had always been the essence of his Christian faith. Nevertheless, his legacy lived on, not only in Sierra Leone but also in Nova Scotia and New Brunswick. In the nineteenth century most Maritime blacks became Baptists, and their religiosity was very much the New Light variety, influenced at least partially by George and his disciples.[43] The New Birth, shaped by "dreams," "impressions," and a powerful personal and emotional relationship with Jesus Christ remains, in the 1990s, the key coordinate in the evolving religious system of those thousands of black Maritimers who faithfully worship in their African United Baptist churches.

4 Freeborn Garrettson (1752–1827): A Methodist New Light

A little more than a year after Henry Alline's death in New Hampshire on 2 February 1784, an intense religious revival swept through many of those same Yankee settlements in Nova Scotia that had, a few years earlier, been significantly affected by the First Great Awakening, which owed so much to the New Light Congregationalist Alline and the New Light Methodist William Black. This aftershock of the First Awakening owed a great deal to an extraordinarily able Methodist preacher from Maryland, Freeborn Garrettson.[1] The revival helped revitalize a rather moribund radical evangelical movement in the region, and it also provided the movement with a coterie of young, energetic, and gifted evangelists, the most outstanding of whom were Harris Harding, Edward and James Manning, and Joseph Dimock – all future patriarchs of the Maritime Baptists. Even though Garrettson explicitly and vehemently attacked the Allinite New Lights, he not only pumped spiritual life back into the Allinite New Light movement but he also strengthened the Methodist component in it.

Soon after landing in Halifax in late February 1785, Garrettson became the most influential Methodist in the colony. He had little difficulty in elbowing William Black aside and pushing him to the edges of the new denomination. Garrettson was regarded, with some justification, as a "man of varied resources, a powerful preacher and capable organizer, of genuine piety and holiness of life, who left an abiding impression on the whole life of the province."[2] His influence in Nova Scotia, according to J.M. Buckley, author of *A History of*

Methodism in the United States, "was almost equal to that of Wesley in Europe and Asbury in the United States."[3] "It may be fairly questioned," claimed his biographer and close friend, Nathan Bangs, "whether any one minister in the Methodist Episcopal Church, or indeed in any other Church, has been instrumental in the awakening and conversion of more sinners than Garrettson."[4] The Maryland Methodist itinerant was unquestionably an unusually gifted minister; he was a powerful and, some would say charismatic, preacher. Moreover, Garrettson was an indefatigable itinerant and a Methodist almost obsessed with – as he once expressed it – "rising higher and higher in the divine image."[5] He spent only twenty-six months in Nova Scotia, but it has been persuasively argued that he "left an abiding impression on the whole life of the province."[6] Next to Henry Alline, the evidence suggests, the Maryland Methodist was regarded by his contemporaries as the most able and influential preacher in late-eighteenth-century and early-nineteenth-century Nova Scotia.

Garrettson was born on 15 August 1752 in Hartford County, Maryland, near the mouth of the Susquehanna River. His father, an active Anglican, was a wealthy slaveholder, and he was also opposed to Methodism, considering it to be an especially evil manifestation of sectarian enthusiasm. Although keen to please his father, Garrettson fell under the influence of various itinerant Methodists soon after his twentieth birthday. Then, in 1775, at approximately the same time that Alline was being "ravished by the Spirit" in Nova Scotia, Garrettson was experiencing his own New Birth – an experience very much like that of the "Whitefield of Nova Scotia" and of William Black and David George. Moreover, like Alline, Black, and George, Garrettson wrote a journal, one that was published in Philadelphia in 1791 under the title *The Experiences and Travels of Mr. Freeborn Garrettson, Minister of the Methodist Episcopal Church in North America*.[7] Garrettson's *Experiences* shows convincingly that his "conversion to the Christian faith" was the "focal point" of his life "by which all that preceded could be interpreted and all that followed could be understood."[8] This New Birth emphasis added yet another layer of meaning and experience to the radical evangelicalism of Henry Alline and William Black and, later, to the New Light gospel of such preachers as Harris Harding and David George.

From May 1772 until his conversion in June 1775, Garrettson "felt the drawings of God's Spirit, and in a measure saw a beauty in Jesus." But, as he noted, "I did not know that my sins were forgiven; neither was the plan of salvation clearly open to me."[9] The death of his father in 1773 (his mother had died many years earlier) meant that the twenty-one-year old Garrettson was now solely responsible for "his

Freeborn Garrettson (1752–1827)
Drew University

father's business" – including the supervision of a number of slaves.[10] The added responsibility, together with "an expectation of accumulating the riches of the world,"[11] further exacerbated Garrettson's ever-present sense of religious guilt. Then, early in 1775, "one day being at a distance from home," he met a "zealous [Methodist] exhorter." The Methodist enthusiast asked Garrettson the quintessential evangelical question: was he born again? Garrettson simply and honestly replied, "I had a hope that I was."

"Do you know," his interrogator then asked, "that your sins are forgiven?"

"No," was the somewhat embarrassed response, "neither do I expect that knowledge in this world."

"I perceive," responded the Methodist, "that you are in the broad road to hell, and if you die in this state you will be damned."

"The Scripture," Garrettson angrily replied, "tells us that the tree is known by its fruit; and our Lord likewise condemns rash judgment. What have you seen or known of my life that induced you to judge me in such a manner?" Then Garrettson spat out the words, "I pity you," and turned his back on the Methodist. But as Garrettson strode away, he discovered, to his intense discomfort, that he "could not easily forget the words of that pious young man, for they were as spears running through me."[12]

Garrettson maintained that he endured this state of conviction "till June 1775." His spiritual journey, like Alline's, was significantly affected by the powerful force unleashed by the sudden transformation of colonial resistance into the American Revolution. Then, on a "blessed morning" in June, at a "day break" he would "never forget," he heard an eerie, loud, penetrating voice aimed directly at him: "Awake, sinner, for you are not prepared to die." This frightening and cogent message was, he was absolutely certain at the time and in retrospect,

as strangely impressed on my mind as if it had been a human voice as loud as thunder. I was instantly smitten with conviction in a manner I had not seen before. I started from my pillow, and cried out, Lord have mercy on my soul! As it was about the commencement of the late unhappy war, and there was to be a general review that day near my house, I had promised myself much satisfaction; for I was a professed friend of the American cause: however, instead of giving my attendance, I passed the morning away in solitude; and in the afternoon went out and heard a Methodist sermon.[13]

Torn between the Patriot secular message of liberty and freedom and the Methodist gospel of spiritual liberty and freedom,

Garrettson found himself "for several days" strangely disoriented and engulfed by a sense of acute sorrow. "None but those that have experienced the like exercises, can form an idea of what I underwent," he sadly observed.[14] As Garretson described it, "The devil, and the enmity of my heart seemed to rise higher and higher," immobilizing Garrettson and thrusting him deeper and deeper into an intense and disturbing depression. By the "Tuesday following," having heard the Methodist itinerant Daniel Ruff preach, Garrettson found himself "so oppressd that I was scarce able to support under my burden." After dark he mounted his horse, "in much distress," and rode homewards; finding himself even more depressed on his journey, he dismounted "in a lonely woods and bowed [his] knees before the Lord." There Garrettson confronted not only the Saviour but also the devil, in a disturbing Manichaean-permeated experience:

I sensibly felt two spirits, one on each hand. The good spirit set forth in my inmost mind, the beauties of religion; and I seemed almost ready to lay hold on my Saviour. Oh! unbelief! soul damning sin! it kept me from my Jesus. Then would the enemy rise up on the other hand, and dress religion in as odious a garb as possible; yea, he seemed in a moment of time, to set the world and the things of it in the most brilliant colours before me; telling me, all those things should be mine, if I would give up my false notions, and serve him. His temptations of a truth might be compared to a sweeping rain.[15]

While still on his knees "a considerable time," Garrettson found himself surrendering "to the reasoning of the enemy" – the devil cloaked in Patriot garments and spewing forth Patriot rhetoric. Quite suddenly, Garrettson's "tender feelings abated" and his "tears were gone," his "heart was hard" and he merely continued on his knees "in a kind of meditation." Then "at length" he summoned up enough courage to try to make some kind of deal with his maker:

Lord spare me one year more, and by that time I can put my worldly affairs in such a train, that I can serve thee. (It seemed as if I felt the two spirits with me.) The answer was, "Now is the accepted time." I then plead for six months, but was denied – one month – no – I then asked for one week, the answer was, "This is the time." For sometime the devil was silent, till I was denied one week in his service; then it was he shot a powerful dart. "The God," said he, "you are attempting to serve, is a hard Master; and I would love you to desist from your endeavour." Carnal people know very little of this kind of exercise: but it was as perceptible to me, as if I had been conversing with two persons face to face. As soon as this powerful temptation came, I felt my heart rise sensibly (I do not say with enmity) against my Maker, and immediately I arose from my knees with these words. "I will take my own time, and then I will serve thee."[16]

Garrettson then mounted his horse, "with a hard unbelieving heart unwilling to submit to Jesus." (Seventeen years after his unforgettable face-to-face confrontation and discussion with God and the devil, Garrettson could only declare, "Oh! what a good God had I to deal with! I might in justice have been sent to hell.") After riding only "a quarter of a mile," Garrettson at last found himself experiencing, in one telescoped moment, the beginning of the New Birth: "The Lord met me powerfully with these words, 'These three years have I come seeking fruit on this fig tree; and find none.' And then – the following words were added, 'I have come once more to offer you life and salvation, and it is the last time: chuse, or refuse.'"[17]

"Chuse or refuse" – these powered projections from an unfolding cosmic drama reverberated, over and over and over again, in Garrettson's innermost being. While he reeled from the divine verbal bombardment, he found himself "instantly surrounded" with a divine power: "Heaven and hell were disclosed to view, and life and death were set before me." He was absolutely certain that he was both actually hearing and actually seeing the essential Christian gospel – not through some human conduit, but directly from the Almighty. Garrettson was sure that if he "rejected this call, mercy would [be] forever taken" from him. He now was beginning to realize:

Man hath power to chuse, or refuse in religious matters; otherwise God would have no reasonable service from his creatures. I knew the very instant, when I submitted to the Lord; and was willing that Christ should reign over me: I likewise knew the two sins which I parted with last, pride, and unbelief. I threw the reins of my bridle on my horse's neck, and putting my hands together, cried out, Lord I submit. I was less than nothing in my own sight; and was now, for the first time, reconciled to the justice of God. The enmity of my heart was slain – The plan of salvation was open to me – I saw a beauty in the perfections of the Deity, and felt that power of faith and love that I had ever been a stranger to before.[18]

After finding "this pearl of great price," Garrettson's "soul was so exceedingly happy" that it seemed as if he "wanted to take wing and fly away to heaven." He began to sing with his powerful voice "the praises of [the] dear Redeemer," and as he neared his farm, the slaves heard him, and came to meet him at the gate "in great surprise."[19] Some must have wondered whether their master was drunk; but soon after he dismounted, they realized that Garrettson had experienced the early birth pangs of the New Birth, something he was determined to share with them – the fact that his "soul was so happy in God."[20]

When Garrettson went to bed "about midnight," he was absolutely certain of his conversion. But when he awoke "about day break," he heard, not the voice of God but that of the devil. "Where is your religion now?" asked the voice. "It was only a dream." Garrettson was "pained ... to the heart" and beset by doubts: "not feeling as I had done." This "temptation" compelled him to return immediately "to the fields and woods," where, "under deep distress," he threw himself to the ground. Then: "My beloved Master visited my heart with his love ... as great a manifestation as at the first." Bombarded by a powerful "impression," Garrettson returned to his house, mounted his horse, and set out to share his newfound faith with a group of Methodist friends. But instead of witnessing, Garrettson found himself unable to speak. "The cross was too heavy" and he "grieved the blessed Spirit," until, as he recalled, "I was brought under heavy trials; yea, deep distress of soul."[21]

It seemed, Garrettson observed, as if "the dear Redeemer" had "left me, or rather hid his face from me." Something – something very disconcerting – was pulling Garrettson away from his Saviour. Garrettson began to "wade through deep waters." He fasted and prayed until he "was almost reduced to a skeleton." Sinking "into desperation," he discovered himself to be "harassed by the devil, day and night!" "Ah," he heard the devil whisper in his ear, "where is your God now? You see you have been deluded; and if you will now take my advice, you will deny every pretention to this religion. The Methodists are a set of enthusiasts, and you have now a proof of this." Then Garrettson clearly heard almost the same words that Christ had been tempted by hundreds of years before: "All these things will I give you if you will deny that God you have been attempting to serve, and pray to him no more." A distraught and confused Garrettson

was sunk as low as I could possibly be; for my mind was encompassed with darkness, and the most severe distress. I was afraid my lips would be forced open to deny the God who made me. Glory, glory to my Lord! who again gave me a view of an opening eternity, and a sense of his dread Majesty; the sight of which brought me with the dust, prostrate with my face to the ground, where I lay for a considerable time with language similar to this, if I perish, it shall be at thy feet, crying for mercy. Thus I lay, till I recovered a gleam of hope that I should be saved at last.[22]

There appeared to be two major obstacles on Garrettson's rocky road to salvation. First, he was finding it very difficult to free himself from his father's bitter critique of the Methodists. To join the Methodists, as he felt his conversion compelled him to do, would, in a deep psychological sense, mean cutting himself free from the still powerful influence of his father. Second – and this obstacle owed something to the first – Garrettson began to realize that in order to be a true and committed Methodist, he would have to free his slaves. Doing so meant, among other things, abandoning his planter way of life and all that it represented. So "although it was the Lord's day," Garrettson did not worship at his local Episcopal church but instead gathered his slaves together for prayer. As he stood with his Anglican prayer book in his hand, this thought "powerfully struck" his mind: "It is not right for you to keep your fellow creatures in bondage; you must let the oppressed go free." It was as though "some person stood by me," he observed, and "appeared to be waiting for an answer." Garrettson was certain that this was indeed "that same blessed voice which had spoken to me before." Having not been overly concerned in the past about the Christian morality of owning slaves, Garrettson now

paused a minute and then replied, "Lord, the oppressed shall go free." And I was as clear of them in my mind, as if I had never owned one. I told them they did not belong to me, and that I did not desire their services without making them a compensation, and I was now at liberty to proceed in worship. After singing, I kneeled to pray. Had I the tongue of an angel, I could not fully describe what I felt: all my dejection and that melancholy gloom, which preyed upon me, vanished in a moment; a divine sweetness ran through my whole frame – O! in what a wonderful manner was my poor soul set into the depths of my Redeemers' love! Praise and glory to his name forever.[23]

Still motivated by "deep impressions," Garrettson was "determined to chuse God's people," the Methodists, as his people. From his first class meeting, where "a divine kindling ran through the whole house," Garrettson felt a "great freedom to speak," and he therefore began to itinerate. "I delighted in the cross of my dear Saviour," he exclaimed. "I was assaulted by many inward conflicts from the devil and the corruptions of my own heart; but Jesus was precious to me." Regarding the American Revolution as "the unhappy war," just as Alline had, Garrettson was determined to have nothing to do with it – despite considerable Patriot pressure.[24]

On 21 May 1776, Garrettson was licensed to preach, and he began his official Methodist itinerating career riding circuit in Maryland

and Virginia. His enthusiastic preaching brought about "a great agitation among the congregation"; one woman "clapped her hands in an ecstacy of joy" and "praised the Lord." Then "the divine presence appeared to run through the whole house: most of the people were melted into tears." In 1777 and 1778 Garrettson itinerated throughout Virginia and North Carolina, preaching to large gatherings of both blacks and whites. He noted in his *Journal* in October 1778, "Individuals thought me an enthusiast, because I talked so much about feelings; and impressions to go to particular places." "I knew," he went on, "the Spirit of God is the guide, and his word is the rule, and by it we are to try all our dreams and feelings." He was absolutely certain "that both sleeping and waking, things of a divine nature had been revealed" to him.[25]

Garrettson described "the flames" of Methodist revival which "the Lord" helped him spark in early 1779 in the Delmarva Peninsula of Delaware and later in the year in Pennsylvania and New Jersey. When Garrettson returned to Delaware in 1780, he was imprisoned – because of his "Methodist neutrality." After a brief incarceration in February 1780, he returned to his itinerating, "desirous of being lost and swallowed up," as he expressed it, "in the love of my dear Redeemer." He began to see visions and dream remarkable dreams about future events and about the heaven produced on earth by sanctification.[26] In the early 1780s, before his ordination as a Methodist minister at the Baltimore Conference in December 1784, Garrettson developed his reputation as an unusually gifted and often eloquent itinerant.

At the Baltimore Conference in 1784, the Methodist Episcopal Church of the United States formally came into being, and it was at this conference that Garrettson was instructed to make his way to Nova Scotia, the British colony that had remained steadfastly loyal to the cause of George III during the American Revolution. Garrettson was, it is clear, a man with a high energy level. This fact, together with his evangelistic zeal, helps to explain the impact he had on Nova Scotia in the 1780s. For more than fifty years, until his death in 1827, he preached his New Light–Methodist gospel from North Carolina to Nova Scotia, being responsible for thousands of conversions – over 20,000, some have claimed. The indefatigable itinerant once described to Bishop Francis Asbury, his American superior, a typical week spent in Halifax: "Sunday eight o'clock preach in our little chapel, which will hold about four hundred persons; ten o'clock preach in the poor house, where there are a hundred people ... at twelve o'clock in the preaching house; four o'clock in a private house by the dockyard; and by candlelight in the chapel. I preach every night in the week. Friday visit the prisoners."[27] Garrettson did not mention his frequent and many house visits, the time spent in keeping up his correspondence with fellow Methodists in Nova Scotia, New Brunswick, Great Britain, and the United States, his great "diligence and zeal" in studying the Bible, and his exemplary "prayerfulness and watchfulness." According to his biographer, he was widely perceived, and with good reason, as the antithesis of "the Slothful servant."[28]

During his twenty-six-month sojourn in Nova Scotia, Garrettson visited every major settlement except the Scots centre of Pictou. A year before his death, he summarized his Nova Scotia experience in the following manner:

I began to visit the towns, and to traverse the mountains and valleys, frequently on foot, with my knapsack at my back, up and down the Indian paths in the wilderness, when it was not expedient to take a horse; and I had often to wade through the mud and water of morasses, and frequently to satisfy my hunger from my knapsack, to quench my thirst from a brook, and rest my weary limbs on the leaves of trees. This was indeed going forth weeping; but thanks be to God, he compensated me for all my toil, for many precious souls were awakened and converted.[29]

Garrettson took full advantage of the earlier evangelistic work of his fellow Methodist, William Black, and also that of Henry Alline and his itinerating disciples – men such as Thomas Handley Chipman, Joseph Bailey, and also Ebenezer Hobbs, a teenage New Light exhorter.[30] Garrettson particularly cultivated the Yankee New Light heartland, stretching from Falmouth, down the Annapolis Valley to Granville, then to Yarmouth, and up the southern shore to Argyle, Liverpool, and Chester. He also broke important new missionary ground in Halifax, the capital, and in the Loyalist centre of Shelburne, which in the late 1780s was the largest British settlement in all British North America.

Garrettson, like Henry Alline, had a powerful voice, but unlike the Falmouth evangelist's, Garrettson's voice was rather "harsh and high-pitched." Apparently, it could easily be projected a distance of "a quarter of a mile."[31] In Nova Scotia, as in the United States, Garrettson's preaching "focused on Christ, Heaven and Hell,"[32] but always from an Arminian perspective (though one that in many important ways was shaped by a New Light enthusiasm). Because of his genteel background, Garrettson was very successful in aiming his message not only at the "middling and lower sorts," but also at society's leaders. And, of course, his message was permeated by a noteworthy emphasis on radical evangelical emotionalism. Generalizing from his own memorable conversion experience, Garrettson frequently pointed out that "to suppose a work of grace without the excitement of human passions, is as great an absurdity as it would be to expect a man to breathe without any movement of lungs."[33]

Alline and his New Light disciples, as well as the younger William Black and the black Baptist preacher David George, would have enthusiastically endorsed Garrettson's emphasis on the crucial and pivotal role of the New Birth experience; similarly, they and their hundreds of followers in the 1780s would have resonated with Garrettson's emphasis on "spiritual impressions," "dreams," "visions," and on actually hearing the "voice of God" and actually seeing the "Word of God" unfold before his eyes. It is not surprising, therefore, that Garrettson touched such a responsive chord in those regions of Nova Scotia that had experienced the white heat of the region's First Great Awakening.

Despite the opposition of a few of the more extreme Allinite Antinomians, whom Garrettson called "as deluded a people as I ever saw,"[34] the Maryland Methodist attracted large, attentive audiences in Nova Scotia in the spring of 1785. At Horton, the New Light centre, on Sunday, 22 May, more than a hundred people turned out to hear him: "The General Cry was after preaching – if this was Methodist doctrine it is agreeable to truth."[35] Later that same day, in Cornwallis, another New Light stronghold, there was "a Considerable moving on ye hearts of ye people," according to Garrettson. And on the following day, after a particularly emotional meeting, there was a uniform response: "If this is Methodist doctrine, I will be Methodist."[36] Scores of Yankees, a few of whom had heard George Whitefield and some of whom had been awakened by Alline or knew the evangelist very well, "after meeting ... continued some time hanging around each other, inquiring what they should do to be saved." Garrettson hoped that his revival would give the troublesome and embarrassing Allinite Antinomians a "wonderful Stab."[37]

Preaching a minimum of two sermons each Sunday, in barns, private homes, and Baptist and Presbyterian churches, and one each day of the week, Garrettson continued to itinerate up and down the Annapolis Valley from Windsor to Annapolis throughout June and July 1785. In late July he visited Liverpool and a month later made his way to Shelburne, where he particularly enjoyed preaching to the "black people" – Methodist and Baptist alike – who, to a person, were New Lights. While in Shelburne, Garrettson noted in his *Journal*:

Our dear Master began to carry on a blessed work; but the devil and his children were angry. They frequently stoned the house; and one night a company came out, and strove (as it stood by the brow of a hill on pillars) to shove it down. – Whilst I was preaching to near four hundred people by candlelight, they were beating underneath, to get away the pillars – In the midst of my preaching I cried out, *Without are dogs, sorcerers, whoremongers, idolaters, and whosoever loveth and maketh a lie*. The company ran off with a hideous yelling, and we were left to worship God peaceably.[38]

Garrettson continued: "During my stay in and around Shelburne (which was six weeks) numbers both white and black, were added to the society: and many tasted the good word of God, and felt the powers of the world to come."[39]

In the early autumn of 1785, Garrettson returned to Halifax and took charge of the large Halifax circuit, which meant regular visits to Windsor, Cornwallis, and Horton. In the spring of 1786, he once again visited Liverpool, where he observed in a letter to John Wesley that although "Alline's small party oppose us warmly, the greater part of the town attend our ministry, and the first people have joined our society."[40] After this success, especially among the Liverpool élite, Garrettson sailed to Shelburne, which was now in serious decline, and on to Barrington. At first the people of Barrington were unresponsive, having been warned by Thomas Handley Chipman (Alline's former right-hand man and now the New Light Baptist minister at Granville) that the Methodist minister was a "dangerous Arminian." Despite Chipman's warning – which owed a great deal to ministerial jealousy and what Freud has called "the narcissism of small differences" – hundreds turned out to hear the Maryland Methodist itinerant. "Between two and three hundred were awakened in a greater or less degree," reported a delighted Garrettson, who recorded that "their shyness and prejudices were all removed."[41]

Many of the Yankee inhabitants of Barrington, like those of Cornwallis, Horton, and Liverpool, were convinced that Garrettson's New Light message was identical with Alline's. The doctrinal differences were of little significance when the conversions were taken into account as well as other manifestations of the work of the Holy Spirit. They experienced firsthand with Garrettson, as they had with Alline, the glorious immediacy of Christ, as "the flame ran through the assembly." Garrettson reported: "It appeared as though there were but few present, but in a greater or less degree felt the flame."[42]

In the autumn of 1786 Garrettson returned to Halifax, and in the winter months of 1786 and 1787 he was largely responsible for coaxing into existence yet another revival in the Horton-Cornwallis region. Here, near Alline's home, the Yankee response was very similar to that occurring in the Barrington region. "I have had a blessed winter among them," Garrettson reported to Wesley on 10 March

1787. "If the work continues much longer as it has done, the greater part of the people will be brought in." In Horton, especially, "there had been a divine display; many convinced and converted to God." Garrettson also observed: "God is carrying on his work in a glorious manner ... the people flock from every quarter to hear the word ... The fields here seem white for harvest."[43]

Despite Nova Scotia's white fields all ready for harvest, Garrettson left the colony on 10 April 1787, having "received a letter from Dr Coke [one of Wesley's key lieutenants] in which he [Garrettson] was requested to attend the Baltimore Conference." Garrettson was not eager to leave. "It was with reluctance I came to this country," he maintained, "but I now feel a willingness to labour and suffer in the cause of God, among his people."[44] But he was never to return, not only because of his strong sense of being American and wanting to remain an American, especially once he was back in his homeland, but also because, as he once expressed it, "I was not clear that I had a call to leave the United States."[45] Moreover, Garrettson realized that there were so many more souls to be saved in the United States than in Nova Scotia, which was still only a peripheral colony in British North America.

Garrettson's departure from Nova Scotia in 1787 left a huge leadership void, which the Maritime Methodists were unable even to begin to fill. A little more than a decade later, the American flow of Methodist itinerants northeastwards to Nova Scotia and New Brunswick dried up. Bishop Asbury was not eager to send off his young itinerants to an alien land from which, he once noted, they returned to the United States full of Canadian-inspired hubris.[46] So the region would have to be satisfied with second- and third-rate British imports – Methodists who had little hope of becoming important leaders in the Old Country and who, moreover, were deeply suspicious of what they perceived to be dangerous, and anti-British, American New Light extremism. Their rejection of Garrettson-Allinite "enthusiasm" meant, among other things, that as the eighteenth century merged into the nineteenth, the Baptists would suddenly emerge as the leading evangelical and New Light denomination in the region.[47]

It seemed a remarkable coincidence that in the 1770s and 1780s two such gifted and charismatic preachers as Henry Alline and Freeborn Garrettson would have criss-crossed the same tiny "corner of Empire," preaching their own particular versions of the same radical evangelical New Light message. Both men had a great deal in common, despite certain obvious differences, including their views of Wesley, the Bible, and the Atonement. Both were American-born, both were converted at approximately the same time and both of their conversions were traumatic life-changing experiences. Both were ardent advocates of "free grace," and both believed enthusiastically in a religion of the heart. Both stressed the importance of all sensory perception in bringing the believer to God through Christ. Both were dynamic preachers, revivalists of the first order. They both, of course, believed in the centrality of the New Birth and in its primary importance in defining the essence of evangelicalism. Both of them encouraged their hundreds of followers, and the thousands who listened to them, to follow them to the mountain peak of religious ecstasy so that they, too, could share something of the marvels of Christ's love. And both men played key roles in establishing the New Birth paradigm that would become the evangelical norm for Maritime Baptists, for many Methodists and Congregationalists, and even for a few Anglicans. This paradigm would define evangelicalism and energize the movement not only in the Maritimes but throughout central Canada, especially during the period spanning the American Revolution and the outbreak of the War of 1812.

5 Harris Harding (1761–1854): An Allinite New Light Indeed

Harris Harding, like his hero Henry Alline, was "converted in a rapture," and "ever after he sought to live in a rapture"; and he "judged ... his religious condition" and that of all others by the intensity of their conversion experience.[1] The New Light–New Birth was also the central and defining event of Harding's long and fascinating ministerial and evangelistic career. In addition, like Alline, Garrettson, George, and the young William Black, Harding placed an almost inordinate "reliance on impressions, and often regarded them as direct intimations of the divine will, which it was his duty to obey."[2] For example, in 1790, while at Horton near Alline's home, Harding had a memorable dream, "which much affected, and made a singular impression" on his mind. "I dreamed," Harding informed his friends,

I was on board a small sailboat, with deacon Cleavland [a close friend of Alline], and a number of my dear Christian friends at Horton. Methought I stood upon the gunwale of the boat, having a spear in my hand. The sun shone with peculiar brightness. We were running before a pleasant breeze, at a little distance from a delightful shore. The water was also clear as crystal, and I could see the white and shining fishes at the bottom, while I was continually catching them with the spear. My friends, I thought, were sitting speaking of Christ's love to a fallen world, their cheeks bathed with tears, and apparently filled with peace and joy. I thought the deacon said to me, "You catch every fish you strike." I replied, "I miss none." Methought I fished until I had got the boat filled and then had a delicious feast with my fellow-disciples. I awoke in a joyful frame. I visited Yarmouth soon after.[3]

The dream, Harding was absolutely certain, was God's means of directing him to Yarmouth, in the southwest, "to fish for men."

Harding played a critically important role, especially in the first few decades of the nineteenth century, in imposing Alline's New Light revivalistic paradigm on the emerging Baptist denomination in Nova Scotia and New Brunswick, in particular. Harding was a strategically located link in the chain connecting Alline's eighteenth-century New Light evangelicalism with an important segment of nineteenth-century Maritime evangelicalism.[4]

According to the Reverend I.E. Bill, who knew Harding towards the latter part of his life, Harding's "pulpit talents ... intellectually considered, were never brilliant, but they were generally effective and useful." Bill followed this statement with a perceptive description of what he considered to be the strengths and weaknesses of this "Baptist patriarch":

In the strictest sense, he was an extemporaneous preacher ... He deemed it of far more importance that the *heart* should be burning with love, than the *head* should be stored with matter ...

If in addressing a congregation, he never dazzled with the splendour of his eloquence, he often touched their sympathies, and moved their hearts as he descanted upon the Savior's love ... At times there was a melting pathos in his utterances which was overpowering. While there was little method in his discourses, they were generally delivered with fervour, and interspersed with anecdotes illustrative of the topic he was discussing ... As regards religious zeal and activity, every day was devoted to God; and in this respect, his long life was one continuous Sabbath.[5]

But to one who knew Harding at the beginning of his preaching career, there was little of redeeming value either in the radical New Light's character or in his preaching style. Simeon Perkins contended in 1792 that Harding's "extravagant Jestures and wild motions of his Body and hands, etc., is, to me very disgusting, and the pain he seems to be in Breath, is distressing."[6] The influential Liverpool merchant later would argue that "a man of his [Harding's] character and principles" should never be permitted even near a pulpit.[7] According to Perkins, Harding was a dangerous Antinomian who practised, with considerable gusto, what he preached. As an example, Perkins reported that on 28 September 1796, Harding had been

Harris Harding (1761–1854)
Acadia University

forced to marry one of his most ardent disciples, "a young woman (Hetty Huntington) said to be pregnant by him."[8]

In the view of his biographer and co-pastor at Yarmouth, the Reverend J. Davis, Harding was "an erratic genius." He was "not in every sense a great man" and the "loftier reaches of argument and eloquence were beyond him," commented Davis. "His utterance was ready, quick, overflowing, apt to be loud and vociferous – in his earlier days accompanied with much gesticulation and movement to and fro ... deep also was his pathos, abundant his unction, while his tears were frequent ... His capital was not so large as that of some other men; but he kept turning it over and over perpetually, until it had yielded an ample increase."[9] One of Harding's close associates, the Reverend Theodore S. Harding, state that "as a preacher" Harris Harding was definitely "not methodical":

He dwelt most on the experimental part of religion, and greatly exalted in it. His great forte was "telling stories." He was full of anecdotes.

He was eminently useful in the conversion of sinners perhaps more so than any man in this country. He would sometimes seem to prophesy, and mark out people that he thought would be converted. He seemed to have an uncommon spirit of discernment that way.[10]

Harris Harding was born in Horton, Nova Scotia, on 10 October 1761, of Yankee planter and pre-Loyalist stock. Soon after his birth, his parents, like so many other Nova Scotia Yankees, decided to return to Connecticut. During the early part of the American War of Independence, though only a teenager, Harding supported the Patriot side. For his Patriot military efforts, he was captured by the British and was imprisoned for a time on a man-of-war. Then, in 1783, at the age of twenty-two, and despite his pro-American wartime activities, Harding returned to the Horton region, where he became a very popular schoolteacher.[11] Although very much "a stranger to experimental religion" and "famous for his love of fun and frolic,"[12] Harding began to attend local New Light services conducted by John Payzant, Alline's close friend and brother-in-law, and by Thomas Handley Chipman, the only ordained New Light preacher left in Nova Scotia since Alline had quit the colony for good in August 1783. Converted by Alline in 1779, Chipman had criss-crossed the colony with the Falmouth evangelist, becoming widely known as Alline's saintly associate. He had been legitimized by Alline's phenomenal success and by his close friendship, and this legitimization was emphatically confirmed after Alline's untimely death.

Although Harris Harding became Alline's most committed and probably most enthusiastic advocate, he had never actually met the Falmouth preacher. However, he knew Alline's family; he also knew intimately most of Alline's close friends and associates, and from these men and women he learned all he was to know about the

"Whitefield of Nova Scotia." But so much of this emerging oral tradition became exaggerated and distorted in the telling and retelling.

Harding not only attended New Light services; according to his sister, in 1785 he was also "much taken up with the Methodists in the region, especially Freeborn Garrettson."[13] Garrettson apparently stressed to Harding, in an explicit attack on Alline, that it was indeed necessary for the individual to make "strenuous efforts in seeking the Lord." "Men must do their part" in trying to be more Godly, he declared, "and God would do his." As a result, Harding tried everything in his power "*to work hard* for salvation instead of *believing heartily* for it." He prayed no fewer than twelve times a day and fasted every Friday, but despite all his efforts he could not "find his way into the heavenly kingdom." Instead of being part of "the great regenerating process," he found himself "plunged into despair."[14] (How often this phrase was used by the New Lights!) Harding felt himself spiritually immobilized – pushed in one direction by the Wesleyan-tinged and anti-antinomian evangelism of the gifted Garrettson and pushed in a radically different direction by the New Light legacy of Henry Alline.

One memorable "forenoon" in late 1785, on his way to his schoolhouse, Harding suddenly and unexpectedly "seemed all at once to obtain a view of Jesus." Instantly, he realized that Methodist "good works could not save him"; he could be saved only by totally surrendering himself "to the Saviour, just as he was, to be saved 'freely by his grace,' and by that grace alone." When Harding arrived at the school, after this unforgettable and exciting encounter with Jesus Christ, "joy and love transported his soul." His sister later recalled: "He forgot the children of his charge. Eternal glory was all before him, and he stood bathed in a flood of tears. His countenance was so altered, that the children gathered around him, they likewise in tears, and thought him dying. Truly there he began to live. When he came to his recollection he thought, by the sun on the window, that he must have been standing on one spot nearly an hour."[15]

Soon after his Allinite New Light conversion, Harding accompanied John Payzant to Chester, southwest of Halifax, where Harding exhorted after Payzant preached. Harding was obviously being tutored by Payzant. He was also being tested in the field – his effectiveness carefully weighed according to an Allinite scale. Payzant was concerned about the spiritual welfare of his young protégé when he saw that Harding had wandered off "with some of old acquaintance ... he had gone with a bad crew."[16] Payzant observed in his journal, "I saw what a danger he was in if he gave way to the enemy and Satan like a Roving Lion seeking whom he may devour."[17]

Harding was not devoured by Satan's forces, however, and he soon began to itinerate on his own: to Liverpool in 1787, to Chester in 1788, throughout Annapolis County in 1789, to Onslow, Yarmouth, and Amherst in 1790, and back to Liverpool in 1791; then to Shelburne, Barrington, Argyle, and Yarmouth. On his travels, Harding did everything in his power to emulate Henry Alline and even tried to look like Alline. According to one contemporary, he had a similar appearance: "slender, frail, and even ghostly."[18] Moreover, Harding preached "Mr. Alline's gospel," which he regarded as being "the mind of God" and virtually "infallible."[19] Simeon Perkins, who had often heard both men preach, noted that Harding's doctrines were "much the same as was propagated by Mr. Alline."[20]

Not only did Harding try to cultivate Alline's preaching style and physical image – to such effect that at times he gave the impression that he, too, was dying from "consumption" – but he also used many of Alline's evangelistic techniques, and he visited the areas where Alline had been particularly successful. He made excellent and extensive use of Alline's "hymns and spiritual songs," regarding them as being especially effective with children and young people. He also frequently used Alline's imagery and his very words. Furthermore, he wrote many letters to his friends throughout the colony and urged them to collect them for possible publication.[21] Like Alline, Harding wanted to author a book – for the spiritual benefit of his followers and the edification of posterity. In a typical Allinite letter, written on 14 May 1789, Harding observed from Annapolis Royal: "The mighty God of Jeshurun has girded his sword upon his thigh and is riding in the flaming chariot of Israel like a glorious Conqueror: his majesty and power are seen amongst the inhabitants of Annapolis. Some have of late felt his dying groans reach their despairing souls ... I see again the immortal shore that flows with milk and honey."[22]

Two years later, in May 1791, Harding wrote to his aunt in Horton, Dorcas Prentice, and to a young female convert, Keturah Whipple, about God's "gracious dealings" with his soul. "Yesterday I was walking across the field," he reported, "weeping and praying for the Dear Christians in Horton, when all of A Sudden, my soul view'd A bleeding Dying God – I lean'd over a fence and cry'd aloud for a Sinking Dying world – O my Dear, Dear Sisters if I had a thousand Lives I would wear them out Spreading the Everlasting Gospel – I know it is your Meat and Drink to see his Kingdom come."[23] A short time later, Harding excitedly informed Nancy Brown, another

Horton friend: "Jesus holds me in the Hollow of his Bleeding hand – Since I have seen you my Soul has rejoiced seeing how the Holy Ghost has (at times) fell upon the Assemblies; But I see some trying Moments too. Sometimes for an hour or two it seems as if all Hell arose to withstand me; but it is so far from moving that thro Jesus I tread them down with ease – for I know he shall Sling out my enemies as out of the middle of a sling, for I am bound in the bundle of Life with his dear Children."[24]

Harding was determined, as he put it in 23 August 1791, to "go in the name of brother Alline's God ... to New England."[25] From the declining Loyalist centre of Shelburne, he wrote on 24 August 1791 to Thaddeus Harris, a deacon of the Cornwallis New Light Church: "O brother, stand in that gospel that Henry Alline once proclaimed to your soul, and others in Cornwallis. That is the gospel that is the life of my soul, and if I am called to it will not only suffer for, but seal with my blood."[26] Two days later, once again trying to emulate Alline, Harding was planning to board a ship for New England. "Sometimes I can see a man stand and call, 'Come over and help us,'" he asserted. "I assuredly believe God has called me to preach the gospel on the other side of the flood."[27] But Harding never made his way back to New England. Instead, he had to be satisfied with (as he typically expressed it) the "shaking of the dry bones[28]" in the Nova Scotia "part of the Vinyard."[29] He informed Alline's brother in Falmouth:

The lowing of the milch kine is heard in this land. The angel of the Lord is riding on the white horse through Barrington. Three are converted; numbers under great distress, groaning for mercy; and almost every soul is shocked through the place. Jesus also spreads his blessed wings over Argyle; his kingdom is come into three souls in that place, of late, and several are waiting heavily under their guilt. The saints frequently in meeting are crying aloud. "The sword of the Lord and of Gideon," and righteousness breaks in like an overflowing flood into our Assemblies.[30]

Harding could hardly contain his intense delight when he was told by one Nova Scotian in 1791 that his preaching was precisely the same "Gospel that brought Salvation to my soul under Henry Alline."[31]

In common with many of his close friends from the Horton-Cornwallis area (young men such as Joseph Dimock and the Manning brothers, James and Edward, and the gifted female preacher Lydia Randall), Harding in the late 1780s "placed great reliance on impressions, and often regarded them as direct intimations of the divine

will, which it was his duty to obey."[32] Often he equated his strong
pangs of conscience with the explicit commands of the Holy Spirit.
It should not be surprising, therefore, that one of the most significant
manifestations of eighteenth-century New Light antinomianism in
Nova Scotia occurred in 1791 in the Allinite-Harding bastion in the
Cornwallis-Horton region. At the core of the movement was Mrs
Lydia Randall, widely regarded as "their head speaker"[33] and leader,
who vociferously and eloquently denounced "all the orders of the
church."[34] And guiding her, inspiring her, and, some would say,
manipulating her (often from a safe distance) was Harding. For some
of her followers, Randall was the Nova Scotian Anne Hutchinson:
charismatic, bright, articulate, and obviously a social and religious
revolutionary. Caught up in Harding's New Light restorationist movement of 1789 and 1790, she and some of her friends were determined
to establish their own unique version of radical New Light faith and
practice in Alline's home church – the Cornwallis and Horton New
Light church. The Reverend John Payzant, who was Randall's pastor,
described her role in the radical religious movement she was helping
to shape and direct:

The Second Sabbath of May [1791] it was the turn to have the Church
Meeting and Sacrament at Horton. Mrs. R[andall] rose against all the orders
of the church and [said] that they were but outward forms and contrary to
the Spirit of God. These novelties in the Church caused many to follow the
same examples, which made much trouble in the Church ... She told me
that she had seen by the Spirit of God, that Baptism and the Lord Supper,
with all the Discipl[ine], of the Church was contrary to the Spirit of God
and his Gospel, and that Marriage was from the Devil. That she was determined to live sapate [separate] from her Husband, for it was as much sin
for her to have children by him as by any other man and she saith that there
were many that would follow her in it, that there were many young women
that were converted, which she has as soon see them have children by any
man; [than] to Marry.[35]

In reply, Payzant "told her that she was involving herself in an
abstruse that she would find much difficulty to get out" and he
"begged of her not to advance such sentiments for she had not well
considered them for she would make herself an object of Redecule."[36]
But Mrs Randall, who stressed over and over again, as did her
spiritual mentor Harris Harding, that "she had seen" directly "the
Spirit of God," quickly countered by contending that "her mind had
gone farther on these things" than Payzant's.[37] Since Lydia Randall
had frontally challenged marriage and male domination of any kind,

Payzant and his supporters regarded her – with good reason – as a dangerous revolutionary.

By August 1791, Payzant's church was badly split; everything was in a state of utter confusion, and support for what Payzant called these "fantastical notion[s]" quickly "spread from town to town and many adopted this new scheme." The Church Covenant and Articles of Faith were denounced as being "not[h]ing but forms and wholly contrary to Religion." The followers of Mrs Randall even stopped Payzant from serving communion. "They pretended," reported a distraught Payzant, "that they were taugh[t] by the Spirit of God to go beyond all order, that they had great discoveries beyond whatever was known before, either by the primitive Christeans."[38] Absolutely convinced that they were divinely inspired agents of the Holy Spirit, they manifested an extraordinary zealousness and enthusiasm for what they called the "New Dispensation" – their peculiar version of Christianity. The evidence suggests that they had moved far beyond Alline's volatile mixture of Whitefieldian New Light orthodoxy and his mystical heterodoxy.

In order to establish his authority, Payzant decided, sometime in 1792, to impose "church rules" on his disintegrating congregation. This move was vigorously opposed by James and Edward Manning, who were enthusiastic supporters of Randall and Harding (and were later to become leaders of the Maritime Baptist denomination). They "came to the Church meeting, and begun to dispute, and condemn the Church Rules, and say that all orders were done away, and that the Bible was a dead letter, and they would preach without it and such like things." It seemed clear to Payzant that Edward Manning, in particular, "was insinuating these Eronious Sentiments in young peoples minds."

The New Dispensation movement continued to spread "from town to town and many adopted this new Sc[h]eme." Some began to "burlesque the Church" and contend that the New Dispensationalists "were the only lively Christeans." Lydia Randall, showing some Quaker influence, attacked "1st Marriages 2nd all order 3ly the scriptures 4ly Ministers proving their doctrine by the Scri[p]tures." She also, according to Payzant, maintained in Manichaean fashion "that God had made the Elect; and the Devil had made the non Elect"; and, moreover, that many "gave away to carnal desire, so that their new plan took a contrary effect, for instead of living so holy as they preted [pretended] to, they were light and carnal."[39] New Dispensationalism had become a Nova Scotia and New Brunswick version of antinomianism, and as it lurched madly away from community behavioural norms and from Alline's position, an understandable reaction began to set in.

Church meeting followed church meeting as the New Dispensationalists continued to attack their opponents. They maintained that they alone accurately interpreted the Bible, since they alone "were led by the Spirit of God and that their explanation of the Scriptures were all spiritual so that they were absolutely right."[40] There were endless discussions about the proper interpretation of certain key verses of scripture, and the persistent debate seemed to defuse somewhat the explosive issues confronting the church. Payzant continued to oppose the demand that the "preachers" of the New Dispensationalists, especially Randall, be summarily expelled; this, despite the fact that he realized his policy would lead to the permanent departure of many anti–New Dispensationalists from his church. But he naively hoped that "by gentle means" order and good sense and stability would return to his congregation.[41]

On 6 October 1792, the Cornwallis church met and finally decided that its members "would stand by the Church Rules, and that no person should have [the] liberty, to vote, to speak, in Church meetings but those that held to her Rules." At Falmouth, because of the strength of the New Dispensationalists and their continuing opposition to all rules, they "were merely denied ... the ordinance." In response, some asserted, in good universalist fashion, "that all the world would be Saved."

Some said, that there was no such man as Christ; and all the Christ that there was, was what we felt in ourselves; and therefore why should they hold to Baptism, and the Supper ... Others saith that the Devil made all Such as would be lost and that God made all them that would be saved. So that all that God made would go to him, and that all the Devil made would go to him, and these last sentiments they pretended to maintain from Serivture [Scripture].[42]

After Edward Manning had become what some of his critics spitefully referred to as the pope of the Nova Scotia Baptist Church, and an ardent Calvinist and vociferous critic of extreme New Light enthusiasm, he attempted to describe what he considered to be the heart of New Dispensationalism:

Mr. Alline's lax observance of divine institutions fostered in the minds of his followers such ideas as these; that the ordinances are only circumstantial, outward matters, and mere non-essentials; that the scriptures are not the only rule of faith and practice; and that no person is under any obligation to perform any external duty until god immediately impresses the mind so to do ... Several began to question the propriety of having anything to do with external order or ordinances, and soon refused to commune with the church ... As they had no rule to go by but their fancies, which they called "the Spirit of God," great irregularities ensued.[43]

Manning, who for the remainder of his life was to be embarrassed by his close association in 1790–92 with the New Dispensationalists, had deftly cut to the heart of the movement's ideology. Here was a man who had worked closely with Lydia Randall and Harris Harding in bringing the movement into existence and who had, moreover, significantly affected its evolution. If any single person understood New Dispensationalism and its appeal, Edward Manning did. As far as he was concerned, it was Alline's "lax observance of divine institutions" and his emphasis on the "spirit of liberty" and "individual illumination" that persuaded many of his followers to break out of the radical evangelical and New Light framework to enjoy what to many was regarded as "Quaker and Shaker" freedom.

There was a deep desire to experiment, to shatter existing religious values, to reshape fundamentally evangelical individualism, and to challenge frontally community norms. With the Spirit of God within them, having experienced the intensity of the New Birth, having been ravished by the Almighty, anything seemed possible and permissible. Their sin had been cancelled out, once and for all, by the sacrifice of Christ; and sinning, whether in the flesh or the spirit, could not distance them from their Saviour. Instead of turning towards ascetic behaviour, as Alline had preached and practised, many New Dispensationalists (especially a number of young and gifted women, driven by the "spirit of liberty," and in order to test the viability of their New Birth and to flaunt their spiritual *hubris* at their neighbours and challenge patriarchy) committed what Manning called "their extravagancies."[44] Their "great irregularities" obviously served a number of interrelated purposes. They were the means whereby one could both enjoy sin and appreciate salvation – no insignificant accomplishment in any age. "Antinomian excesses," moreover, enabled women in particular to express freely and creatively their innermost emotional and sexual desires and drives at a time and in an age when such behaviour was regarded as sinfully aberrant.

During 1791–92, while Randall and the Mannings were witnessing firsthand the rise and fall of their New Dispensation movement in the Allinite New Light heartland, Harris Harding was trying to spread his version of Allinism along the Yankee shore, from Liverpool to Shelburne and then to Barrington, Argyle, and Yarmouth. In December 1792, shortly after returning to Cornwallis, he informed Thomas Handley Chipman, a leading critic of New Dispensationalism: "The Lord has been passing thro this land in very deed, my Bro – And altho' many too many abuse their Liberty in the Blessed-Gospel; yet I have seen the Blood of Jesus sprinkled on the Door posts of many hearts – And verily believe as far as I can judge the true light now shines clearer than ever before, The last days of Glory is ushering in certainty upon God's People."[45]

Harding was trying to build a bridge between those who had "abus[ed] their Liberty in the Blessed-Gospel," people like himself, Lydia Randall, the Mannings, and Joseph Dimock, on the one hand, and, on the other, Chipman and Payzant; for they were all closely linked in the public mind with Henry Alline. It is noteworthy that throughout his long ministerial career, Harding always tried to avoid controversy, for instance, by refusing to make difficult decisions or often by escaping for months from his Yarmouth home to avoid conflict. Moreover, he was eager late in 1792 to downplay the divisiveness of the New Dispensation movement largely because he realized that it was a declining religious force in the colony but also because he was now being singled out as the "principal ... propagat[or]" of the antinomian doctrines in Liverpool "and other parts of the Province."[46]

In order to deflect criticism from his New Light New Dispensationalism – a movement, he had to confess, which had been pushed by Lydia Randall beyond the flexible boundaries of Allinism – Harding became preoccupied in the last decade of the eighteenth century and the first of the nineteenth with fostering a series of religious revivals. He played a key role in giving shape and substance to Nova Scotia's Second Great Awakening. In 1792, while in the Yarmouth area, a safe distance from Cornwallis and Horton, Harding observed the beginnings of a "reformation" – "a little cloud, like the bleeding hand of Jesus, in this part of the vineyard."[47] By the early spring, he proudly reported, "Near fifty ... are savingly born again."[48] When the revival fires were dampened in Yarmouth, Harding quickly moved to Liverpool; there were obviously many "souls to catch" all along the western shore. The following year, 1793, he was in the Cobequid region, near present-day Windsor, leading a revival there – a revival that led to his controversial ordination at Onslow. Harding's ordination was denounced by the two ordained New Light ministers in the colony, Payzant and Chipman. According to Payzant, Harding was not fit for ordination since he "had spoke much against ordination, against ordained Ministers, against the orders of the Church, and many such like Things."[49] In other words, despite Harding's special pleading and despite his revivals, he was seen by two men who knew him very well as an unreconstructed New Dispensationalist and as a man unworthy of being ordained a minister in Alline's struggling sect.

In 1795 Harding was on the move again; in 1796 he was back in Liverpool, and the following year back in Yarmouth. It is not surprising that on 19 May 1797, a distraught Onslow Church "ordered a letter to be sent to call Rev. Harris Harding home."[50] But Harding refused to leave Yarmouth. While in Liverpool, he had played an important role in bringing about what Simeon Perkins – no friend of Harding's – called "a remarkable Stir of Religious Concern among the people."[51] According to the prim and proper Perkins, there was an "Extraordinary stir among the Young People, principally the Females," and much "Swooning and Extices."[52] Harding was evidently exhilarated by the experience; he spent a great deal of time with the young people in the community, and a number of the empowered young women developed "a great natural fondness for him and thought all his tender expressions for their souls was the effect of natural passion."[53] At least some young women had felt the same way about Henry Alline, finding it very difficult to distinguish between his spiritual and his sexual appeal.

In Harding's relationship with one young woman, Hetty Huntington, he apparently confused the sexual and the spiritual, the profane and the sacred. According to Payzant, who since 1793 had been the minister of the New Light church in Liverpool, Harding was merely acting out his antinomian beliefs. Under strong community pressure, Harding publicly confessed that he was guilty of fornication and on 28 September 1796 he married Hetty. Six weeks later a child was born to the couple.[54] Many of Harding's supporters, who had been keen to have him replace Payzant, now quickly withdrew their support, and early in 1797 Harding accepted a call to the Yarmouth New Light church. He continued to preach in Liverpool in 1797 but only in private homes. Obviously, he still had his supporters, who were willing to forgive a man who was very much a sinner like themselves but who seemed to be a special instrument of the Holy Spirit and the means whereby Alline's gospel would be spread throughout the colony and beyond.

In Yarmouth, Harding "kept school for the support of his family."[55] Influenced by what seemed to be a popular groundswell of enthusiastic support for believer's baptism, Harding was baptized by his close friend James Manning on 28 August 1799. Yet another

Harding-inspired revival was sweeping Yarmouth; and Manning, the former New Dispensationalist who was now a New Light Baptist, had "been sent for to assist in the work."[56] Harding's public baptism added fuel to the revival fires and convinced many of his followers that he did indeed possess "a double portion of the Spirit."[57]

The revival of 1799–1800 owed something to Harding's preaching, but it probably owed more to the popular grassroots demand for baptism. The revival fires spread from Yarmouth and Shelburne up the Annapolis Valley, leap-frogging to the Cumberland region, the boundary area between Nova Scotia and New Brunswick, and then moving into the Saint John River Valley. This was obviously a Baptist revival, as those who participated in it and those who critically observed its remarkable growth realized. New Light preachers such as Harding, Dimock, and the Mannings were not leading the religious procession; they were running hard just to keep up, and some rather reluctantly were baptized themselves – realizing that if they could not lead by example, their followers would quickly find other more receptive leaders.

There was a great deal of truth in Bishop Charles Inglis's report to his Anglican superiors in London in which he warned of "the prevalence of an enthusiastic and dangerous spirit among a sect in the Province called New Lights, whose religion seems to be a strange jumble of New England independence and Behmenism. Formerly they were Pedobaptists, but by a recent illumination, they have adopted the Anabaptist scheme, by which their number has been much increased and their zeal enflamed."[58] Inglis was particularly concerned with Harris Harding's growing influence in the western half of the colony. According to the first Anglican bishop in what is now Canada, intelligence from the Yarmouth region had informed him that "several hundreds have already been baptized, and this plunging they deem to be absolutely necessary to the conversion of their souls."[59] Inglis also charged that the New Light Baptists were "engaged in a general plan of total revolution in religion and civil government."[60]

In order to impose some kind of administrative system and order over the emerging New Light–Baptist popular movement, in 1800 the Mannings, Dimock, and Thomas Handley Chipman, in particular, urged their ministerial counterparts, men such as Harris Harding, T.S. Harding, Joseph Crandall, and Payzant, to adopt a "close Baptist communion plan."[61] Such a plan meant that only the baptized could participate in communion and be full members of the church. Since only ministers belonging to the new association could baptize, and since the people only accepted baptism by an ordained minister, the baptized ministers were now effectively in a position to control the movement. Thus, among other reasons, in order to assert their power and control (especially over such women as Lydia Randall), these young men, excluding Payzant, espoused closed membership and baptism by immersion, even though Alline had considered both to be frothy "non-essentials" of no lasting spiritual significance.[62]

The newly constructed Baptist closed-communion yoke certainly never rested easily on Harding's shoulders, particularly as the yoke was soon loaded down with a thick sheet of Calvinism borrowed from the Danbury Association in New England.[63] Not wanting to leave the association, Harding resolved to steer clear of it, concentrating on his growing church and community; in 1805 and 1806 he was very worried that "the religious aspect in Yarmouth was sadly dark."[64] He must also have been concerned about the arrival of the Reverend Ranna Cossit, an Anglican minister from Cape Breton, who was widely known as someone who appealed to "the 'lower class' of people."[65] With the increasing influence of those he considered to have abandoned the gospel of Alline, Harding felt a great need for some kind of convincing proof that he was indeed doing God's work in Nova Scotia. For the first time since his ordination a decade earlier, he considered abandoning the ministry unless his "commission ... were sealed afresh with tokens of success."[66] He therefore decided to *will* into existence an Allinite "reformation" – without, however, the New Dispensation side effects. According to various eyewitness accounts, "under a strong presentment of approaching blessing, he ventured to employ language like this: – 'Sinners! I have long entreated you to repent and believe. But now I tell you God, by his Spirit, is coming to convince you of sin, of righteousness, and of judgment to come, and convert your souls. Fight against him much longer you cannot; or the Lord never spoke to me, nor by me – I am a deceiver, and deceived.'"[67]

Harris Harding, like his hero Henry Alline, was able to use the spoken word as a "bare and brutal engine"[68] against the "heart" (and rarely the "head") of those who heard him. His New Light evangelistic preaching, it was noted, "abounded with short pithy sayings, such as are apt to stick to the memory like burs."[69] At the start of a typical sermon, Harding's manner "was still and moderate." But gradually he became more and more agitated, and his mind and words began to lose any sense of cohesion. Then, suddenly, his voice became louder and louder and his "speech ... rapid and indistinct ... until at length little was heard but a sound, loud, confused and intensely earnest." Next there were "copious tears" and uncontrolled "unrestrained action and movement."[70] For Harding, the genuine New

Light spirit was gloriously at work; and for many of those who heard him, as had been the case with those who listened to Henry Alline years before, there was a powerful sense of understanding and of empathy with the preacher and the message. Like Alline, Harding was able to create an intense human involvement with the present, the here-and-now existence, as well as with the infinite, eternal future. His disjointed words, softened by a flood of tears and permeated with intense feeling, seemed to capture the essence of the New Light gospel – which for Harding was the rapturous New Birth experience. His words triggered a shattering psychological and spiritual experience in many who heard him; it was as if the entire New Testament and the person of Christ was being described in one long and convoluted Harding sentence. As powerful verbal and oral projections, Harding's words seemed to take upon themselves an aura of mysterious power.

In the view of his enemies, it was fitting that the man who, according to his biographer, "gloried to the last" that he was a New Light, first and foremost,[71] but who had found it so difficult to distance himself from New Dispensationism in the 1790s, should witness the undermining of his own reformation by men and women putting forward arguments that he himself had used a decade or so earlier. Harding's biographer has given a particularly evocative description of these radical New Light enthusiasts:

They had no regard for order or government in the church. Frills, ruffles, all adornments in dress, were their abomination: and they quarreled with Mr. Harding because he would not preach against such things. They brought their peculiarities into the conference meetings, and warm discussions were held upon them there. They attacked their minister in public, and openly contradicted him. They ascended the pulpit – even the sisters, in the heat of their inspiration – stood at his side – and commanded him to hold his peace. The worship of God was thus changed into confusion and hubbub. Then these people would collect their finery, and commit it to the flames. Some would even take their crockery and china-ware from their shelves, and bury them. They would enter into minute confession of their sins before promiscuous processions in the night, and parade the streets, exclaiming, "Behold the Bridegroom cometh! Behold the Bridegroom cometh!" Such were the demonstrations to which these people were led by the spirit that was in them, and which they fondly deemed to be the Spirit of God.[72]

Stung by the continuing attacks of the New Light Antinomians – men and women whose views he had significantly influenced – Harding withdrew his church from the Baptist Association in 1809, in order to keep his congregation. Attacking both the principle of "close communion" and the litmus test of Calvinism, Harding maintained that true ministers of Christ had to "rely entirely upon that divine influence with which the apostles were favoured when they were setting men apart for the work of the ministry, or building up the church of God"; he therefore "entreated" his ministerial friends, most of whom were now eager to play down their earlier New Dispensationalism, "not to be particular respecting external order or outward forms, which would all perish in the using."[73] In this brief statement, Harding was using the code words all would recognize, in order to underscore his primary commitment to the New Light views of Henry Alline.

It was not until 1828 that Harding's church was reunited with the Baptist Association.[74] In this development, almost everyone realized that Harding was returning to the fold not as a convert to the mainstream Baptist position but as an unrepentant New Light. When he died in 1854 his church had over 700 members; and a decade later it was calculated that there were more than 2,000 baptized Baptists in the Yarmouth region "under the care of eight pastors."[75] The 1871 census for Yarmouth County noted that there were 9,896 Baptists, adherents, and actual church members out of a total population of 18,550, of whom 5,301 were Roman Catholics. Thus, less than two decades after Harding's death, 62 per cent of the Protestant population and 55 per cent of the total population was Baptist.[76] These remarkable percentages owed more to Harris Harding than to any other Baptist leader; moreover, they emphasize the fact that the Allinite legacy lived on long after the death of Alline and Harding.

Harding's obvious success as a Baptist minister in western Nova Scotia did not make it any easier for the last Nova Scotian New Light preacher to face eternity. Harding's biographer and longtime friend observed that at his moment of truth, Harding could not "taste those raptures in which he had been wont to luxuriate, regarding them as special proofs of the presence and power of the Holy Spirit."[77] All the old New Light warrior could say on his deathbed was, "Good words! good words! But the Lord was not here – the Lord was not here."[78] Harding's cry of despair was permeated by a special pathos and sense of disappointment because he knew that when Henry Alline had died in Portsmouth, New Hampshire, in 1784, his last words – described as "the breathings of a soul swallowed up in God" – had been, "Now I rejoice in the Lord Jesus."[79] Instead of rejoicing in the very presence of his Saviour, all that the frightened and disoriented but honest Harris Harding could do was to blurt out, "But the Lord was not here – the Lord was not here."

PART TWO

The Evolving Radical Evangelical Ethos of Canada: From Nova Scotia to Upper Canada and Back

INTRODUCTION

The Allines and Garrettsons of this world obviously tell us a great deal about the complex ways in which the radical evangelical style developed in Maritime Canada at the end of the eighteenth century. Without question, these preachers played a critically important role in shaping the New Birth and the radical core of evangelicalism. But even though a very strong case can be made that a powerful symbiotic relationship linked these popular leaders to ordinary people – men and women so much like themselves – it is still necessary to probe, as best one can, into the rank-and-file religious mind of as many British North Americans as possible. Such an attempt, a kind of religious history from the bottom up – so easy to advocate but so difficult to do – will, one hopes, substantiate the central argument of what some might consider to be an otherwise élitist biographical approach. Moreover, by including central Canada for the first time in the descriptive analysis, a serious attempt will be made to try to demonstrate that a common radical evangelical thread did indeed connect evolving radical evangelicalism from Nova Scotia with central Canada during the formative stage of English-speaking Canadian Protestantism.

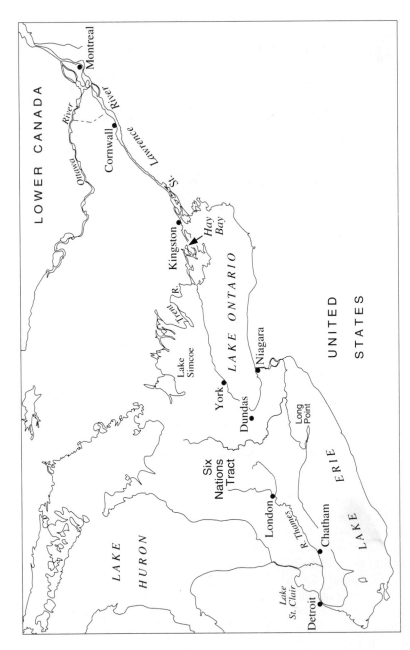

Map 2
Upper Canada, 1800

6 The Nova Scotia New Lights: From the Bottom Up, 1785–1793

During the decade after the American Revolution, scores of rank-and-file Nova Scotians, men and women who were thoroughly ordinary settlers, described, often graphically, the powerful and continuing hold that the New Light–New Birth paradigm had on their religious lives. For every Henry Alline or Harris Harding and for every William Black, Freeborn Garrettson, or even David George, there were scores of Sarah Browns, Charlotte Prescotts, George Boyles, and Betsy Blairs. These women and men represented the broad mainstream of the radical evangelical movement, and their voices complemented those of their New Light mentors and leaders – people disconcertingly like themselves.

There are more than a hundred extant letters, "spiritual songs," and autobiographical fragments written by these rank-and-file Maritime New Lights during the years 1785–92. These New Light letters and songs[1] – all unsanitized and unedited – throw a great deal of penetrating light on popular radical New Light evangelicalism in Atlantic Canada during its significant early phase. The absolute centrality of the Alline, Garrettson, and Harding New Light–New Birth experience is obvious in all of these documents, as is the Allinite New Light language. One of the most striking conversion narratives was penned by a twenty-three-year old Edward Manning in 1789.

Manning (1766–1851) was born in Ireland of Roman Catholic parents, but when he was still an infant, his family moved to Falmouth, Nova Scotia, near Henry Alline's home. At the age of ten, in 1776, Manning heard what he once described as "that man of God, the late Henry Alline," pray at his father's house. "I well remember his addressing me," Manning observed a number of years after the event, "though but a child, and the tears dropping from his face upon mine, while he exhorted me to flee from the wrath to come." Manning was greatly influenced by Alline's appeal, but as he later wrote, "To my shame [I] shook it off, and continued very thoughtless till the age of twenty-two." In his teens, Manning studied surveying and navigation, and was regarded as being a good scholar. But despite his preoccupation with "singing songs and jesting," he could not, he once observed, escape from Alline's "sting" which "was still in [his] mind" right up to his conversion in 1789.[2]

In late 1788 and early 1789, under the influence of Freeborn Garrettson, the town of Falmouth experienced what Manning referred to as a "spiritual awakening" and "reformation." Like others in the community, he was drawn to the revival meetings where "the Spirit of God would powerfully take hold of me." But Manning resisted – exerting, he said, "every power and faculty of my soul to keep from expressing myself before the congregation." After the meetings, he rushed to join his young friends in scoffing at the religious enthusiasm that was engulfing their community. But despite this oscillation, he found that by the early months of 1789 he was being particularly influenced by the preaching of Harris Harding, whom he described as being "an instrument in the hands of God alarming my mind." Harding was twenty-nine years old at the time, lively, intense, sensuous, and emotional; as has already been noted, he had been converted three years earlier. Manning was also affected by the preaching of Joseph Bailey, "an eminent Christian" who had travelled with Alline and who, though not ordained, was apparently an effective preacher. In 1789, Bailey was thirty years old – in the prime of his life – and he was able to project at Manning, with conviction, that Allinite gospel which had exerted such an impact on the region a decade earlier.

But the preacher who actually brought about Manning's conversion was the Reverend John Payzant, who in 1786 had been ordained minister of the Horton and Cornwallis New Light church. Payzant had been converted in 1775, at the same time as Alline, and was now forty years old and a tanner by trade. Some time in the middle of April 1789 he preached a sermon that Manning would never forget. There was more than a little irony involved in this development. In 1776 Manning's father, Peter, had been found guilty of the murder of Payzant's stepfather, Malachi Caigan, and had been hanged. In all likelihood, Alline's father, William, who in 1776 was a member of the "Jury of the Sessions of the Peace," was involved in both the

Edward Manning, 1766–1851
Acadia University

conviction of Peter Manning and his execution. Payzant spoke from an Old Testament passage, "where the children of Israel came to the Waters ... And could not drink ... by reason of their bitterness." According to Manning, Payzant "spoke with so much vision in opening the Scripture to my understanding that I was struck with Astonishment – I can't say that the fear of Hell or the Misery of the damned terryfd me much at this time," but "the World wore a different aspect," and there was, for the first time, no desire to neutralize religiosity with "frolicking." Manning resolved to find salvation. A concerned Christian neighbour, seeing how agitated his young friend was, gave Manning one of Alline's hymns which, Manning observed, "set forth my condition as it really was." The six verses eloquently captured the young farmer's spiritual predicament:

O hardened, hardened heart of mine
That loads me with distress
And doth like Iron fetters bind
My Soul from happiness.

O was there ever wretched on Earth
In such a State as I
Exposed to everlasting death
Unwilling yet to fly

Mount Sinai's Thunders doth not wake
Me from this Stupid frame
Nor can the love of Jesus brake
My Soul into a flame

The greatest grief that I indure
Or trials that I find
Is that I am destressed no more
With this unfeeling mind

I mourn because I cannot mourn
And grieve because not grieved
I think I long from sin to turn
Yet fear I am deceived

Great God Receive me as I am
And let me See thy face
And all my heart and soul inflame
With thy Redeeming grace

Manning had no trouble appropriating the first five verses of Alline's hymn as a description of his own spiritual state. But he could not say the last verse because, as he noted, "I know I was not willing to be converted." That evening a distraught Manning tried to sleep, but the fear of hell kept him awake, and for three days he was morbidly melancholy. At dinner at the end of this period, he "had such a sense of the State of [his] Soul" that he dropped his "knife and fork and left the house immediately." The giant of a man, six foot four inches tall, made his way to the nearby woods with the determination not to return until he had been redeemed. He tramped about 1,000 yards into the forest and knelt down to pray. "In the agony of [his] soul," the only prayer he could utter were the six words, "Lord have mercy upon my Soul." At that precise moment, Manning felt not only "a Hell in my own Breast Sufficient to torment me to all Eternity" but also a realization that God could and would save him. Yet conversion did not come; instead, further intense conviction, confusion, and then suddenly a morbid fear of death overwhelmed him.

Finally, on 26 April 1789, after Payzant's sermon and the exhortations of a number of young friends – exhortations specifically aimed at Manning – his "heart was broken." He "could not contain" himself and "wept aloud, and came to a decision to seek the Lord." Manning declared, for all to hear, "I am determined, if I am lost at last – I am determined to go to hell begging for mercy." But the New Birth still evaded Manning, who evidently for at least a day "endured much horror of mind." He clearly saw, he said, the "justice of the Almighty in my eternal condemnation" and realized that this was the result of "a most astonishing change having taken place in my view of that justice ... It appeared that I could not but love it, even though it [justice] proved my eternal damnation." Such a realization was "overwhelming" and eventually produced in Manning a disorientation so profound that he "was lost for a season to time-things." After he came to his "recollection," the Almighty and "all creatures appeared different ... from what they ever did before," and an "indescribable glory appeared in every thing." He later wrote that as near as he could recall, his New Birth occurred on 27 April.

It took Manning approximately a month to be absolutely sure of his salvation. On 25 May, at a special thanksgiving service for the recovery of George III, Manning was at last able to jettison his "melancholy bordering on despair" and replace it with "a great solemnity" on his spirits and a great concern for the spiritual welfare of all the unredeemed as well as a remarkable love for his fellow Christians. For example, when Manning even thought about Harris

Harding, he "immediately broke into a flood of tears and cried aloud." Manning felt an even more powerful emotional attachment to "an old christian man" whom he had "been acquainted with before," and this sense of "nearness" drove him to cry out "louder still." From the specific, in terms of relationships, Manning's thoughts moved to Christians in general and then to the Almighty: "Love kept increasing. My mind turned upon God; – an inquiry arose in my breast, whether it could be possible that God would be infinitely condescending, or could be possessed of such nature as to have mercy upon me. I immediately discovered, that it was possible. At this discovery my whole soul was set on fire."

Manning felt, just as Alline had two decades earlier, that his "soul was wrapt up in God's eternal love," and he cried out in joyous praise. Those who were riding with him on his way home heard the yells and wondered what was wrong. The ever-dependable Joseph Bailey rode up and asked, "Edward, what is the matter?" Manning replied, "O, Mr. Bailey, my soul is melted with love to God." Not having the strength to sit up in his saddle, Manning "leaned upon [his] horse's neck," as did Bailey who, in typical New Light fashion, was "rejoicing and praising the Lord." Manning was "intensely filled with supreme love to God," seeing "his glory in every thing." "It was not," he observed "a confidence of my own safety, nor merely a certainty of my own individual interest in his love that caused me to rejoice; but the glory and harmony of his perfections overcame me, and a satisfactory belief in my personal interest in his mercy followed as a consequence." In this manner, he "obtained liberty to [his] poor imprisoned soul"; and as might have been expected, his "happiness was unspeakable" and, as he put it, "full of glory."

Soon after "this memorable day," Manning became a member of Payzant's New Light church. His happiness as a member of the church, however, was "greatly interrupted by an almost continual impression" that he "must engage in preaching the gospel." This "impression" experience was, of course, common among the New Lights, as was their heavy emphasis on "witnessing" or "sharing the faith." Manning was first encouraged to pray in public and then to exhort, and he did so in Falmouth, Windsor, Newport, Horton, and Cornwallis. Praying and exhorting in public further whetted his appetite for preaching, and in September 1789 he resolved to accompany Thomas Handley Chipman "and one or two young men to Chester." Manning's preaching career had begun – a good and perhaps safe distance from his home in Falmouth.[3]

Within a year, Manning, greatly influenced by Harris Harding, became an integral part of the New Dispensation movement. But by the end of the eighteenth century, after his ordination in 1795 and his baptism by immersion in 1797, he became concerned about the antinomian excesses of his associates and began his relentless journey towards ministerial and denominational respectability – as a Calvinist Baptist. Despite this, the man who was often described by his contemporaries as "the Baptist Pope of the Maritime provinces" always considered his New Birth in 1789 as the defining evangelical moment of his long and often tortuous religious life.[4] A long-forgotten "spiritual song" composed by Manning at the time of his conversion conveys something of his original New Light enthusiasm:

1

I've found my Soul Deliver'd
My Joys are from on high
By God I'm highly favour'd
I feel his coming nigh
He's brought me from destruction
And undertook my Cause
From sin Death and Affliction
My ransom'd Soul he draws.

2

He draws me where or whether
I feel a warm desire
My Soul Aspires thither
Up in the Car of Fire
I see my Foes A Falling
My God he goes before
I hear his Spirit calling
Come tread the peacefull Shore.

3

I see all Heaven engag'd
And God within me Reigns
Which makes my Foes enraged
That I have left my Chains
I've left your Dismal world
And call my God my All
While your in Darkness hurld
Upon this Earthly Ball.

4

Within one theres A fire
That burns with Rapid flame
And with A Pure Desire

Cries Worthy is the Lamb –
Yea Worthy Thou art forever
For thou wast slain for me
And I obtain the favour
To know thy Love is free.[5]

One of Edward Manning's friends, and a person who probably sang this spiritual song enthusiastically, was Charlotte Prescott.[6] She was born in Halifax in October 1764 and died in Chester in March 1833. In 1786, soon after moving to Chester, a coastal community to the southwest of the capital, twenty-two-year-old Charlotte discovered that "the Lord was pleased to enlighten her understanding in the mysteries of redemption." Through the evangelistic preaching of John Payzant, she first experienced conviction and then the New Light–New Birth. It is noteworthy that Payzant had been converted directly through Alline's influence about a week after his brother-in-law's traumatic New Birth. According to Payzant, he had been encouraged by Alline that since "the Lord had appeared for him in a most wonderful manner," he was absolutely certain "that the Lord would appear for me." In his journal, the twenty-six-year-old Payzant cogently described his conversion in the following manner (without many of the New Light excesses and flourishes of his brother-in-law):

Sunday the Second day of April [1775] the Lord appeared for my Soul in [the] most wundal [wonderful] maner, So that I was Sure that Christ had paid that debt, which I had been trying to Pay with my good works. The joys and tranceport of my Soul, to think that I had been laboring So long for Something, and I did not know what. But now the Lord hath made himself known to me, as a complet Redemer, then I center my Soul on him for time and all Eternity. There came Such a thought in my mind, go, and tell what great thing the Lord hath done for you.[7]

Charlotte Prescott was one of many Nova Scotians who were destined to hear about the "great thing the Lord hath done for" Payzant. "My heart sunk within me under a load of guilt," Charlotte observed on hearing Payzant. "I knew that God would be just if I were sent to hell," she continued,

but how he could save me consistently with the claims of justice I knew not. Thus black despair brooded over my spirit. I thought if any person was an object of pity, I required it more than all, but none deserved it less. Often did I use these words of the poet,
    Shew pity Lord, O Lord forgive,
    Let a repenting rebel live.[8]

Charlotte Prescott could apparently "neither report, believe, nor pray." She observed, "My heart in rebellion refused the mercy I had sought, until those words came with power to my mind, 'By grace ye are saved through faith, and not of yourselves, it is the gift of God.'" Almost miraculously, for the change was instantaneous, the verse calmed her troubled mind: "All was peace; I beheld by faith the bleeding suffering Saviour, bearing my sins on the cross. I was delighted with the suitableness of the provision made in the gospel."[9] The New Light–New Birth had finally come to an exhausted and exhilarated Charlotte Prescott.

A few years later she married another ardent New Light, George Boyle, since being "unequally yoked together" was regarded as a blatant sin against the Holy Spirit. When she died in 1833, she asked her longtime New Light friend Joseph Dimock, who was Baptist minister at Chester, to preach her funeral sermon from the text "By grace are ye saved," a verse that she said had been especially "sweet to her through all her pilgrimage."[10] There is one extant letter written by George Boyle, an Irish-born schoolteacher, tavern owner, and merchant. Composed on 19 September 1790, it is permeated with New Light imagery:

I bid you A Thousand Welcomes to my Dear Jesus O Methinks I hear you tell he is altogether Lovely. O External praises to his Dear Name that ever so unworthy a Wretch as me was Brought to hear the Joyfull Sound of Salvation sounded in my Ears and apply'd to my poor Sorrowful Soul *O Glory to the Eternal God* that Brought and conducted my way to this part of the world to see a New Heaven and a new Earth … I Cannot express half my feelings, my Love, my gratitude to the Eternal prince of peace, who Condescended to Bow the Heavens and Come down to redeem poor wretched perishing Christless Souls from that Unfathomable Gulf of Woe and Misery they had plung'd themselves into *of whom I am Chief* …

But because of God's love and grace, Boyle declared that he could sing: "Room Enough in Realms above / Jesus Courts them in his love." In true New Light style, he proclaimed:

Bless'd be God a full fountain for all Judea and Jerusalem may Come And have their Blackest Sins and Iniquities Wash'd away in the all attoning and purifying Blood of Jesus.

Boyle concluded this Allinite letter:

O I wonder how any Soul can hold out or refuse such endearing Love as the dear Redeemer offers them, but alas they Cannot see any Beauty or

Comeliness in him – but you my Dear Sir that has found him to be precious invite intreat and beseech them to come and be Married to your Lord and Master. O Methinks I hear you do so in the Soft and Melting Language of your Soul.[11]

It was so easy for George Boyle to write in 1790, during the white heat of his New Light experience, about the "unspeakable Joys & Glories which will be our happy theme to all Eternity." Twenty years later there were few "Joys & Glories" when Boyle, who always remained a close confident of Harris Harding's, was charged and then acquitted in Liverpool "for an Assault on the Body of Ann Lesslie Juni, attempting Rape."[12]

A friend of the Boyles in Liverpool and a person who knew Harris Harding well was Nancy Lawrence DeWolf. Sometime in 1789 or early 1790 she experienced regeneration while living at Granville, near present-day Annapolis Royal. Nancy had been born in 1764 in Lincoln, Massachusetts, where her father, the Reverend William Lawrence (1723–80), a distinguished Harvard graduate, had been a leading Old Light (or non-evangelical) Congregational minister – a man very much opposed to any manifestation of religious enthusiasm. Probably in 1788, Nancy came to Granville from New England to visit her Loyalist brother William and sister-in-law, who had recently moved to the area. While in Granville, Nancy came under the influence of Harris Harding, whom she considered to be an inspired instrument of the Almighty. Her enthusiasm was equal to that seen in the letter which her friend Helen Grant wrote to Harding in March 1790:

Glory Glory to God for what he has done for the fallen race of Adam, Glory to God for what he has done, and is still doing, for Annapolis Sinners. *Glory to God* that ever I had a Name and portion among the Despised followers of *Jesus* I think it is the highest honour that he could be conferr'd on me to make me worthy of the Name of a New Light, Glory to God that ever my feet trod [the] Nova Scotia Shore that ever I heard the Sound of the Gospel – O my Dear Brother the Lord is on his way he is once more passing thro Annapolis Calling poor Sinners home. Three I trust in the last week was brought out rejoicing – there is a Number of Souls born to Jesus in this place since you left us.[13]

Immediately after Nancy's unforgettable New Birth (until her death in 1807, she remembered the precise time and place at which it occurred), she became an ardent New Light. Encouraged by Harding, she felt a deep inner need immediately to share her new-found faith with her friends and family – and it certainly was a New Light faith, centring on the New Birth and being significantly shaped by Henry Alline's theology as interpreted by his young disciple, Harris Harding.

Nancy was overwhelmed by "the riches of free grace" to such an extent that, without her mother's consent, she abandoned her spinster status in December 1790 for marriage to a widower, a much older man with three young children. Her husband was James DeWolf, a merchant from Horton near Henry Alline's home. He had, she explained, "a double claim" to her affections: "For he loves Jesus, we have a spiritual union that earth nor Hell can never dissolve which will outlive time and exist to all Eternity."[14] After briefly describing her "deceit" to her mother and requesting forgiveness in a letter written on 5 January 1791, Nancy DeWolf turned her attention to what mattered most to her – the salvation of her family and friends. Nancy's mother, a very traditional Old Light Congregationalist, must have been both angered and amazed to be instructed by her daughter to tell all their Lincoln neighbours that they must be born again, or Nancy would be "eternally separated from them." "Tell them," she informed her mother, "tis not for any merit or worthiness in me that the Lord hath chosen me, no tis free Grace, free Grace and it is free for them as me." She continued, "Give my love to Bulkly Adams and wife, tell him he must forsake all for Christ or He is lost for ever, remember me to all my friends tell them that the friendship of the world is enmity with God, that my soul loves and longs for their redemption."[15]

Nancy DeWolf, by her conversion and her marriage, had obviously declared her independence of her mother and her Old Light family. Although happily married, at least for the first few years, Nancy found herself estranged from her family, for her relatives were unable to condone either her religious enthusiasm or her secret marriage to an older man. There is a sense of despair and acute concern in the letter she wrote to her mother on 2 May 1793. "Tis a year and half since I received a line from the family," she complained, "and have only heard from you but once" since early 1790. "I want exceedingly to hear from each one of the family," she confessed, "sometimes my heart forebodes a thousand evils, and imagination points distress and horror around that dwelling where first I received the ellemental life." Eighteen months later, on 9 October 1794, Nancy informed her mother, "Tis now almost three years since I received a line from any of the family, I conclude you have entirely cast me of[f], but God is my refuge, my refuge, my fortress, high tower and exceeding great reward. He will not leave me nor forsake me." She still had not heard from her family on 17 April 1795. Meanwhile, in her few letters home, she bombarded her mother with Allinite statements, such as "O that you may have an interest in that Lamb which was slain from before the foundation of the world."[16]

Sometime between April 1796 and November 1798, the DeWolf family moved from Horton – the Allinite New Light heartland – to Liverpool. During this period, Nancy evidently lost much of her religious enthusiasm, having lost contact with her New Light friends and with Harris Harding. Her mind, she graphically observed, "was carried away, captive into Babylon" and her "harp was hung upon the lovely willows." She now never mentioned "experimental religion" in her letters to her mother. Rather, she complained bitterly about her poor health and her husband's frequent absences from Liverpool. "There is nothing but a sciety [anxiety] and trouble in this life," she moaned, "and tho we are prospered in our outward circumstances beyond our expectations yet it appears to me all is Vanity and Vexation of Spirit."[17]

All was vanity and vexation of spirit for Nancy DeWolf until Liverpool's "Great Reformation." Until the early months of 1807, she was evidently far more interested in Liverpool's economic prospects and her husband's many trips than she was in New Light and radical evangelical Christianity. Then she experienced a remarkable spiritual revitalization; she rediscovered the excitement of her earlier New Light faith. Like many other Nova Scotians in the first decade of the nineteenth century, Nancy DeWolf had experienced first the ecstasy of regeneration and then the slow and almost inevitable slide to religious apathy and indifference. Then came spiritual renewal, to be followed for many (but not for Nancy, who died soon afterwards) by a decline and then another outburst of religious revitalization.

In early February 1807, Nancy, together with hundreds of her Liverpool neighbours, was caught up in what the Reverend John Payzant described as "a wonderful moving [among the people] of the power of God." For almost two months she attended special revival meetings at least "four or five times a week," and by the first week of April she had, she was certain, rediscovered the magic of her earlier faith, during what she called "a day of Pentecost." She wrote to her sister:

It is thought their is five Hundred brought to the knowledge of the truth. I could write a volume but I am affraid I shall frighten you, for I was so far from enjoying religion when I was with you. My mind was carried away captive into Babylon and how could I sing one of Zion's songs in a strange land? My harp was hung upon the willows, but O my sister I can bless God their is a Glorious reallity in experimental Religion. I can say this night with the energy of truth that I am a living witness for the cause of Christ, that we must be born again or never enter the kingdom of Heaven, that we must be slain by the law and made or live by grace. O that it might spread from shore to shore that the knowledge of the Lord might cover the earth as the waters do the seas.[18]

For a two-week period, Nancy observed, no one worked in Liverpool, since everyone was caught up in the revival. The enthusiasm, energy, and confidence of the young converts struck a particularly responsive chord in Nancy as she remembered those days and months, some two decades earlier, when she, too, had been absolutely certain about the glorious reality of experimental religion. When she heard the young Liverpool converts witness to their faith, she heard her own voice echo from what seemed to be a distant past. She knew the words, she knew the phrases, and she understood the complex nature of the concern, for these had all once been hers. What reverberated through her mind, ricocheting wildly into the darkest corners of her guilt, were the familiar – the painfully familiar – reminders of a past when she was convinced that she had suddenly and marvellously, by the ravishing power of the Holy Spirit, been "reinstated in the Image of God." In March and April 1807, the present was collapsed into the past as Nancy DeWolf confronted the bitter depths of her backsliding. "God has redeemed my soul," she wrote, "He has taken me out of the Horrible Pit and mirey clay and put a new song into my mouth, even praise to God."[19]

Nancy DeWolf's experience was not unique. Around the turn of the eighteenth century, many other Protestant residents of what is now Canada experienced the ecstasy of conversion and then the prolonged despair associated with spiritual declension or backsliding. Like Nancy, they used the periodic revivals that pulsated through British North America to be "revived," not reconverted. What they succeeded in doing was to restore the New Light purity of their original conversion experience. There was more than enough New Light energy in the original regeneration experience to propel them into the future – but for how long, God only knew.

Some of the most strikingly interesting New Light letters were written by women, especially teenagers. These letters, including those of Nancy Lawrence DeWolf, provide the "thick evidence" supporting the contention that the New Light gospel percolated to all elements of the region's demographic mix. The New Light gospel was the antithesis of an élitist religion. It was evangelical populism in its pristinely pure form. To prove this key point conclusively, some of these letters must be examined further and quoted extensively.

Charlotte Prescott Boyle's younger sister Elizabeth was eager to emulate Charlotte's New Light spirituality. She always treasured the two letters Charlotte had sent her. One had assisted her in finding salvation, and the other had helped her confirm her fragile faith. The first[20] read:

December, 1789, Chester.

My Dear Sister,

Yes doubly so, I trust, for the blessed Jesus has had compassion on you, notwithstanding all your fears ... Dear Betsy, cast your burden on the Lord who has promised to sustain you. Does he not say "He that cometh to me I will in no wise cast him out." "His blood cleanseth from all sin." How impressive and endearing is his language. "Open to me my love, my dove, my undefiled, for my head is filled with dew and my locks with the drops of the night." My dear Sister, view him in the garden groaning under the enormous load of our guilt, until he sweat great drops of blood. When I think of his extreme suffering, and of the complete salvation he wrought [for] his own people, I am constrained to cry with Mr. Alline, "My soul, and what a God is this."

The second letter,[21] written soon afterwards, built upon the first:

Dear Sister, what a reason have we to bless and praise our Gracious Redeemer who beheld us in mercy, when we were cast out in the open field of ruin, to the loathing of our persons. He then did cast the skirt of his love over us: and did say to us live. This was a time of love indeed! may this fill our hearts with love to Jesus, may we remember what he has done for our souls, which will incline us to cleave to him and live near to him – then and then alone can we be happy.

I have been much depressed since I saw you, but blessed be God he says "Though sorrow continue for a night, joy cometh in the morning." He has this day afforded me the light of his countenance. He has this day fed me with the bread of life. I can praise his blessed and holy name. O that Jesus would behold in mercy those that are on the road to destruction. My heart feels for them who are out of the ark of safety. May you, my dear Sister, be much engaged in prayer. "They that wait on the Lord shall renew their strength." When you are near your heavenly friend, remember your unworthy sister,

Charlotte Prescott

Elizabeth was twenty-one years old in 1790 when she penned the following "not finished" letter to her religious mentor, Joseph Dimock:

Help a worm of the Dust to praise the Name of *Jesus*, He is precious yea he's worthy of all praise, & adorations O he is my Life, my Strength, and my Only Joy: I Want words to tell you his Goodness to me the most Unworthy of all his Creatures, he did Indeed pluck my Soul as out of the Jaws of the Devouring Lion, And from the lowest Hell, And hath Since been with me in the fiery furnace, in the Lion's Den, and in passing thro Deep Waters. I have been very Ill almost all Winter so as at times to be depriv'd of my reason, Yet I have enjoy'd the presence of *Jesus*. And often found his Love to transport my Soul Beyond itself, Yet was not without Many Dark and Distressing hours. But about 3 Weeks ago I was in the greatest distress of Soul that Can be imagin'd. The Enemy made me Believe I was past all recovery, He told me I had had my days. And had pass'd it; that I had been Exalted up to Heaven, and so with the greater Vengeance should be thrust down to Hell. He told me I had sold my Saviour, and denied the *Lord* that Bought me, that I had been Inviting others to Christ and Should myself be a Castaway, And that I Should be Eternally Banish'd *from the presence of the Lord*.[22]

One of Elizabeth's closest Chester friends, Hannah Webber, found it depressingly impossible to experience the New Light–New Birth. She desperately wanted to, but all she could do was write with a "heavy heart":

Pray dont think I mean to tell you my Experience NO NO. Because I have none to tell you for I never was Convert'd, therefore I have nothing to Tell, If ever I Should be So happy as to be brought into Liberty it would be well worth my while to write out all from the first to the Last.

Hannah thought she could hear God's voice, but then realized it was "nothing but a Delusion of the Devil." She knew the New Light language; she experienced the powerful appeal of the New Light fellowship of believers, and still she could not open herself to her "Saviour, Spotless innocent and pure." All she could do was feel intense and prolonged despair – and chastize her Christian friends for not being sufficiently Christlike:

Sometimes I think I must part all the Dear children of God. How can I bear to part from those that Call'd me so often and much More from Christ Thats always Calling of me I Love every Body in the World that I think Loves God, I think I can count Christians as the excellent of the Earth, Indeed they dont know What they Enjoy they dont tell of a Christ half as much as they ought to do, I think if I Could Say that Christ was mine it would be my Delight to tell of his Goodness to an ungodly world, But Little Hope of ever being One. Ah while I write I tremble for fear it will all be to my Condemnation. I think [of] all the race of Adam I am in the dreadfullest state. Once I could read I pray with delight, and so I Can now Sometimes, but very seldom, Sometimes I go out with this Intent, well I'll go and fall at the feet of Jesus I'll give myself up to him, but when I get there I have no heart. Well I think how can I give myself up to thee, I shall never be more willing to receive him than what I am and so I shall never obtain Mercy, then I try to pray but Cannot say one word then I go and take the Bible thinking to find Something there to comfort me But that like a pointed Dagger to my Heart; well there is not One promise there for me, this is the way I Spend the chief of my Days, in this Sad Melancholy State, mourn with me, pray for me.[23]

Charlotte Lusby of Amherst shared Hannah Webber's "sad melancholy state" of spiritual frustration. On 4 August 1790, she complained about having to be satisfied with "resting Short of Christ," despite Harris Harding's protestations to the contrary. She found herself frequently in tears – regarding herself as beyond Salvation: "What an unworthy Creature I am, of the least of God's Mercies, for it Never Can be that I Should be a Christian for I think I have the most Temptations and Trials and Trouble of any One on Earth; Sometimes I think I Shall be a Christian and at other times I think it is Impossible, for I have Greiv'd Gods Spirit so often that he will not have Mercy on me."[24] In November 1790, Charlotte was still complaining about her "unhappy" and "stupid" spiritual state and her "Heart as hard as a Stone."[25]

Betsy Blair of Onslow, however, had absolutely no doubts about her transforming New Light experience. On 17 August 1790, she wrote a fascinating letter to Charlotte Lusby's sister, who also was named Betsy. Betsy Blair's letter was virtually indistinguishable from scores of those written by her spiritual mentor, Harris Harding. There were three powerful paragraphs in the brief letter, all of which made noteworthy use of Allinite language and imagery:

Dear Sister

Thro' the Goodness of God I am what I am, Bless'd be his name who hath Caused me to rejoice in his Unchangable Love And Shall have ever to adore his Bless'd Name, for his infinite condescension to one of the most

Unworthy of all his Creatures: But O I can Say he is my God, He is my Shield and Everlasting defence against the Ungodly world; Tho Sinners Rage, and Devils Blaspheme, I find a Determination to stand for that Bless'd Cause, And am willing that my Name should be Cast Out as evil, for I know that all them that is truly his must suffer persecution, And Bless'd Bless'd are they that is found worthy.

Then Betsy continued, in an particularly mystical fashion:

I have Cause to bless and adore him for what he is in himself infinitely Holy in all his ways and Righteous in all his Judgements. O go on in the Strength of your Lord and Master Stand in that Bless'd Cause which is Stronger than Death, For Methinks The happy day hastens when our Souls shall be disentangled from the Clogs of Mortality and we Shall awake in his Likeness And be Satisfied – O Can it be possible that Worms of the dust will be so ravish'd with his Beauty – Thou art fair my Love, Thou hast doves Eyes. O Soul Transporting Word, *God Man Mediator* "The Bright and Morning Star that leads the way" Methinks my imprison'd soul longs to be gone, But O why Should I think the time long when I feel his Love and will Carry me thro all my Trials, And how fair is my love, my Sister, my Spouse. When I feel his Smiles I Can Say he is my friend in time, and will be thro Eternity; And why Should I be Impatient to be gone for he has promis'd me never to leave me nor forsake me, O that he may Empty me out of Self, for I know this Bless'd Robe of Righteousness will And that, and that alone will stand when Heaven and earth shall pass Away.

The final paragraph was a marvellous example of New Light evangelism and fellowship through peer correspondence:

Dear Sister for so I trust to Call you by the Acquaintance Brother Harding has had with you, which gives me Boldness to write to you, hoping You will not take it amiss; and should be glad of a Letter from you the first Opportunity. O Dear Sister go on, if we never meet in time, we Shall Spend an Eternity together; Stand the Storms a few Moments more – And you Shall Safely Reach the happy Shore – There you shall reign in Everlasting Light – Your name is there in the bright Worlds above And theres your portion in Unbounded Love – *All Glory to the Lamb*. Give my love to all the lovers of *Jesus*. They seem near my heart who so are his followers. Tho I never saw none of your faces, I trust we are united in the Bond of the New Covenant never to be broken, I Can Say as the Angel to Mary, *Hail ye that are highly favour'd of the Lord*; for the Lord will crown you with Everlasting Joy, your peace will be as an Overflowing flood. Nothing to annoy you, Tho you might be tried in a furnace. *Daniels* God will deliver you and bring you off

Conqueror, O Amazing Condescension and wonder. O ye Saints of Joy, Shout the wonders of the redeeming Love – for Behold Oh Soon, I trust thro' Boundless Grace with you to bear my part in that immortal Note of praise. *"My Peace I give unto you, but not as the World giveth."* Must conclude and Subscribe your Unworthy Sister in Christ.[26]

In a letter to Joseph Dimock, written on 20 August 1790, Betsy Blair projected a powerful and sensuous Allinite message:

Dr Bro^r

Tho' we are absent in Body yet I find you near my Soul, O go on in the Strength of the Lord God of Abraham Isaac and Jacob, Go Spread Redeeming Love from Shore to Shore, and bid a Guilty World Welcome to Christ, Heal the wounded and feed the Hungry with immortal food, Go on with Joy to face a frowning world, turn not aside to Court the Worlds applause, But spend your Breath in the Redeemers Cause, Withstand the storm a few Moments more, And you shall Safely reach the peaceful Shore, There you Shall reign in Everlasting Day, – your name is there in the Bright World above – Theres your portion in Unbounded Love – And this is that Mystery of Mysteries God manifested in the Flesh And dwells with the Sons of Men – This the Eternal Word which became Flesh This is he that was made a Curse for us Who Hath born our Griefs and Carried our Sorrows This is he that had the Weight of the fallen World upon his Shoulders and was press'd as a Cart is press'd with Sheaves. This is he that groaned upon Mount Calvary and Shed his Blood for the Sins of the Ungodly to redeem Immortal Souls O this is he that will One Day appear in Glory to Judge both the Quick and Dead Saints And Sinners – Angels and Men The Only Name by which Salvation is found in, This is that Christ Which I Declare to my fellow Mortals until my Expiring Breath and this is the doctrine which by his Grace I am willing to Seal with my Blood Dear Brother go and the Lord Shall prosper Your ways O go on in the Strength of your Lord and Master Stand for that Cause that is Stronger than Death for methinks the Happy day hastens when our Souls shall be disentangled from the Clogs of Mortality and we shall awake in his Likeness.

She then went on in true Allinite fashion:

O Can it be that Worms of the Dust will be so ravish'd with his Beauty, Thou art Fair my Love, Thou hast doves Eyes, Thou hast Ravish'd my Heart with one chain of thy Neck I charge you O ye Daughters of Jerusalem If ye find my belov'd that you tell him I am Sick of Love My Beloved is mine and I am his Methinks my imprison'd Soul longs to be gone But O why Should I think the time long when I feel his Smiles, I Can Say he is my friend in time and will Carry me thro all my Trials. And why Should I be impatient to be gone, for he has promis'd never to Leave me nor forsake me, O that he may Empty me of Self, I know that his Bless'd robe of Righteousness will, O Tho' you might be tried as in a furnace, yet *Daniels God* will deliver you and bring you off more than Conqueror, O Amazing Condescension – My peace I giveth unto you but not as the world giveth – Least I Weary you must conclude and Subscribe Myself

Your Unworthy Sis^r in Christ
Betsy Blair[27]

Although only "a girl about 12 years old" in 1790, Susy Lynds, who had been witnessed to by Betsy Blair, her close Onslow friend, confidently corresponded with Joseph Dimock, though he was almost double her age:

Dr Bro^r

I take this opportunity of writing you, to let you Know that the Dear Lord is making up his Kingdom in this place. How is your mind at present? Are you determin'd to Stand for the Cause of Christ! O Stand for that Blessed Cause! And trust we shall soon meet one another face to face. Sometimes I long to take my flight out of this world into a world of Joy. My Dear Brothers And Sisters are yet in the Gaul of Bitterness and Bond of Iniquity. O pray for their Conversion And not for them only but the whole world. O Come poor Sinners Share a part, give this Bless'd Christ your heart, We will take you by the hand, Go with us to Canaan's Land. O poor Sinners take no rest untill the Lord appears for your Souls – O Be Encourag'd My Dear Brother we have but a few Moments more to Stand the Storms of this World, Then we Shall with Jesus Dwell in Joys Beyond what Tongue can tell

O may the Lord Send you here to proclaim the truth to your poor fellow Mortals[28]

Many New Light Maritime young women, during the decade following the end of the American Revolution, regarded themselves, despite their youth and lack of formal education, as the spiritual equals of the male leaders of the evangelical movement. For these women, this was true democracy – devoid of all republican cant. And these men, the evidence suggests, accepted this judgment without any reservations. In fact, Harris Harding and Joseph Dimock, at least until 1793, seemed to put their young female converts on a special pedestal, regarding them, as Harding once expressed it, as "Sisters ... in Zion ... Sitting together in Heavenly places."[29] Despite often bitter and vitriolic attacks, these New Light women could all enthusiastically endorse the statement made by one of their female leaders in 1793: "I care not what any says about me Christs name is good enough for us all to bear – O let me see righteousness Shine – The morning Stars shout for Joy. These words 'His ways are past finding out,' has roll'd thro my Soul of late discovering such a depth and height of wisdom, Love, Strength and power, as will forever ravish our Souls with silent astonishment ... We shall yet see the son of Man coming in the clouds of Heaven with pow'r In great Glory."[30] This belief in the imminent return of Christ, shaped in part by the events of the French Revolution, helped to energize the New Light movement in the early 1790s. Furthermore, the growing apocalypticism and millennialism was partly responsible for pushing some New Lights into often bizarre and heterodox positions and actions as they broke through the outer limits of New Light radicalism.

The New Light rank and file not only were the authors of many "spiritual and religious" letters, deliberately emulating the authors of the New Testament's Epistles, but they also composed a number of "spiritual songs." In doing so, they were following the example of Henry Alline as well as John and Charles Wesley. A few of these Spiritual Songs became almost as popular as those composed by Alline and were still being sung in some Maritime churches in the nineteenth and twentieth centuries. Most of them, however, were soon forgotten – even by their authors. The Allinite influence can be seen in Harris Harding's very forgettable composition:

Awake my Soul Come View the Happy Day
That hastens on to wipe thy Tears away
One shining Ray of that immortal Sun
I shall fill my Soul with Heavens Eternal One
Then shall I bow before the great I AM
And heavenly Armies Shout "All worthy to the Lamb."[31]

Thomas Bennett was another who was moved to compose hymns. A native of the Falmouth region, he was a key New Light leader, especially in the late 1780s and early 1790s. His "Chariots of Fire" almost matches Harding's hymn in creative quality!

In Chariots of Fire we'll soon Soar Away
Soon we'll awake in Heavens pure Day
Eternity, Rolling shall one thought Employ
Ravished and Soaring in One Scene of Joy.[32]

Joseph Dimock's two known hymns are of similar style. The first includes the following verses:

Joseph Dimock, 1768–1846
Acadia University

1

Once more the Dear Redeemer's Name
His Endless love his dying fame
Awakes my Soul with chearful voice
To invite you to the Heavenly Choice ...

6

And O poor Sinners, Come and Share
And you shall have a Mission there
There you Shall have a Glorious port
Wrapt in the Dear Redeemers Heart

7

O come and Share a Glorious prize
Of perfect Bliss that never dies
To triumph in Redeeming Grace
And See this Jesus face to face.[33]

Dimock began his second "spiritual song," with a notably Allinelike verse:

Thro Gloomy Hours and Happy Days
Tho Sore Distress, Tho pleasant Ways,
My Soul hath travelled in
A Miracle indeed I think
Sometimes I rise Sometimes I Sink
But Jesus is my hope

He concluded the hymn with:

And then my Soul by Sin Opprest
Goes Mourning for my wonted rest
My Christ is all my Cry
If Ere I meet my Blessed Christ
I'll hold him fast in my Embrace
And tell him all my Woe.[34]

Of far greater and more enduring significance as a New Light hymn writer was Benjamin Cleveland (1733–1811), a close friend and disciple of Henry Alline.[35] A native of Connecticut, he was an active member of the Cornwallis New Light Congregational church and a leading opponent of the New Dispensationalists and Baptists. Some of his hymns are still sung in some Maritime Baptist churches.

Perhaps the best known of these has as its first line "O could I find from day to day a nearness to my God." In the immediate post-Alline period, however, the farmer-hymnographer's most popular hymn was the one entitled "Longing For Christ":

1

Tho Undeserving of thy grace
I Long O Lord to see thy face
And bow Before thy feet.
I beg for food as for my Life
I cannot live without relief
Thou Didst the thirst Beget.

2

My panting Soul Aspires to be
Wrapt up in that unbounded Sea
Of my Dear Saviours Love
Then I Should Scorn all mortal things
Disdain A Share with Earthly Kings
My portion far above ...

4

I know my Journey soon will End
And I Shall See my Bleeding Friend
Ah See him face to face
Where all my Sorrows Shall be O'er
And Storms of Death shall Beat no more
But Everlasting Love

5

There to possess the free reward
Fill'd with the fulness of my God
And tho the Vessels Small
Ill Stretch to grasp the Boundless Sea
Enlarging to Eternity
Yet never fathom all.[36]

Cleveland's hymns, like those of Alline, connected with the religious experiences of many Maritimers. Cleveland was one of them, just as Joseph Dimock was – or Betsy Blair or Harris Harding or Charlotte Prescott. This democratization of Maritime evangelicalism during its crucial formative stage meant, among other things, that the gap between the so-called leaders and followers was virtually nonexistent. As Esther Clark Wright has so perceptively contended, the Almighty could be and was experienced directly, "without intervention of prophet, priest or king."[37] Each person was her or his own priest or prophet, and such a conviction, of course, was empowering. There seemed to be a symbiotic relationship between the New Light leader and the New Light led; if this connection was severed by the people, then the leader was without an audience and without power and influence. "Doing a work of God" became the only litmus test of New Light success during the formative period of the movement.

It would be wrong, of course, even to imply that this general democraticization process was somehow unique to Maritime religious life in the period following the American Revolution. During the same years, as the work of Nathan Hatch[38] and John Walsh[39] has so convincingly demonstrated, a similar evangelical tendency was to be found throughout the United States and Great Britain. For every Harris Harding in Nova Scotia, there were scores of Lorenzo "Crazy" Dows in the United States; for every Nancy Lawrence DeWolf, there were scores of Mary Ramsays and Sarah Middletons in Great Britain.[40] What gave Maritime radical evangelicalism its special quality was the original Protestant mystical impulse of Henry Alline and Freeborn Garrettson and the general demographic, political, and social environment in which it eventually evolved. There was – and this argument must emphatically be made – a great deal in common in transatlantic evangelicalism at the end of the eighteenth century. But it also must be stressed that Maritime British North America and also Upper Canada – what is now Ontario – were in certain respects strikingly different from contiguous regions of the United States and from Great Britain. The rejection of the American Revolution and much that it represented helped to emphasize some of these fundamental societal and geographical differences.

At the popular level, during the decade after the revolution, New Light radical evangelical religiosity, especially its emphasis on the New Birth and on "impressions" and intensity of "feelings," was obviously a mass religious movement of some consequence. It is virtually impossible to distinguish in the religious landscape between so-called élite and mass views; it may be argued that the two were identical, whether Methodist, Congregational, Baptist, or proto-Baptist. Moreover, one cannot see any real distinction between male and female views and practices. The type of "ecstasy of spontaneous *communities*" described by Victor Turner had clicked into fragile place as the New Light ritual process, and its language helped young and old alike, regardless of gender, to share an intense "feeling of endless power."[41]

Allinite influences, as well as some Garrettsonian ones, were to be found everywhere, inspiring and directing people – even propelling some – and providing them with the language to describe what seemed, to many, beyond finite description. A primitivist, restorationist impulse flowed into a preoccupation with the formative roles played by Henry Alline and Freeborn Garrettson, in particular, during the "awakenings." A kind of "Yankee holy whine," as some spitefully described it, became the New Light norm in Yankee Nova Scotia and New Brunswick. Eventually this "whine" and its special language were appropriated by many New Light Methodists, especially those who had not originally come from Cumberland and Yorkshire in Great Britain.

In Upper Canada some similar and also some very different forces were at work shaping the evangelical ethos of the region. Here there was a radically different cast of historical actors, and it was the American Methodist New Light version of evangelicalism that cut the pattern of religious development. As was the case in neighbouring New York State, an individualistic, democratic orientation was able to win out in the decades after the Revolution as an energized Protestant Christianity became largely concerned with its growing populist audience.[42]

7 The Canada Fire: Methodist Radical Evangelicalism in Upper Canada, 1784–1812

During the quarter century following the end of the American Revolution, radical Methodist evangelicalism grew at an even more dizzying rate in Upper Canada than it did in the United States. By 1810, actual Methodist church membership in the colony had risen to 2,603 from a mere handful of Palatine Loyalist Methodists in 1785. The total population of Upper Canada in 1810 was approximately 70,000, thus 3.7 per cent were Methodists (compared with only 2.5 per cent in the United States).[1]

When the War of 1812 broke out, an estimated 60 per cent of the Upper Canadian population were recently arrived American immigrants. Most were from New England, New York, Pennsylvania, and New Jersey, and most had flocked to the colony not because of its British form of government but because of the cheap, accessible land and the virtual absence of taxes. A further 20 per cent were British immigrants, many of them Roman Catholic Scottish Highlanders. Only 20 per cent of the population of Upper Canada were people of Loyalist background – the remnant and descendants of the 7,000 men and women who, because of their loyalty to the crown, had been compelled to seek exile in British territory to the north of the victorious American republic during and immediately after the revolution.

On 17 September 1792, Lieutenant-Governor John Graves Simcoe opened the first session of the new legislature of Upper Canada. Simcoe was determined to make Upper Canada, in every conceivable manner, the "image and transcript" of Great Britain. To counter the evils of American republicanism, the state was to encourage the "establishment of the Church of England," which was to be supported by "clergy reserves" (one-seventh of the crown lands in the colony) as well as by "the enhancement of rectories." According to Simcoe, "Every establishment of Church and State that upholds the distinction of ranks and lessens the undue weight of the democratic influence, ought to be introduced."[2] "I have always been extremely anxious," he observed, "both from political as well as more worthy motives that the Church of England should be essentially established in Upper Canada."[3]

In his first Speech from the Throne, Simcoe, a veteran of the Revolutionary War, declared to the new members of the elected Legislative Assembly and the non-elected but royally appointed Legislative Council, "I have summoned you together under the authority of an Act of Parliament of Great Britain" in order to carry out "great and momentous Trusts and Duties." He urged his listeners, "with due deliberation and foresight," to lay "the foundations of Union, of Industry and Wealth, of Commerce and Power" in this, the newest colony in the British Empire. Supported by George III, the Established Church of England, and, it was hoped, a landed aristocracy, Upper Canadians were to build a new British society in the midst of the North American wilderness, a society worthy of its king and its heroic Loyalist origins, a society and a country which, moreover, would continue to illustrate that "same manner of Patriotism" that so many of its leaders had so conspicuously demonstrated during the American Revolution.[4]

To a casual observer – and indeed perhaps even to some of those who had come to listen to John Graves Simcoe – this first meeting of the House of Assembly and the Legislative Council of Upper Canada may well have seemed singularly and disconcertingly incongruous. Only a few years before, most of those in attendance had been penniless refugees. Now, as respected leaders of their communities, they were re-enacting the formal proceedings of the British Parliament – ceremonies which, on the surface at least, were far more suited to the stately halls of London than to a simple log building hastily erected in the wilderness of North America. Yet some of those assembled at the colony's tiny capital of Newark, near Niagara Falls, saw nothing out of place in this momentous event. To these Upper Canadians, this first meeting of the colonial government represented the culmination of all they had striven so hard to achieve during the previous decade. It was a visible symbol of the essential unity that existed between the corridors of power in Westminster and the back-woods of Upper Canada. The sacrifices made by the Loyalists during the American Revolution had not been wasted or forgotten after all.

Nonetheless, this meeting did graphically illustrate the unique cir-cumstances of the residents of the province. Many colonists, as their representatives stated in their reply to the Speech from the Throne, were "sensibly flattered by the strong testimony of His Majesty's paternal tenderness for the new Province."[5] As subjects of the British Empire, they were firmly committed to King George III and the constitution. Yet influential Upper Canadians could not ignore the physical, demographic, and social circumstances of their new home. In 1792, and indeed for the next twenty-five years, Upper Canada was a frontier community; its residents, though British subjects, were also North Americans who had strong attachments to the land and its people. Certainly, those who gathered at Newark in the autumn of 1792 were sincere in their ardent addresses of allegiance to the crown. But the American Loyalists were, by birth or by choice, citizens of the New World. Although many had been forced to flee for their lives because of the revolution, a large number had clearly been unwilling to leave the land of opportunity they knew best.[6] Moreover, many Loyalists still had strong personal attachments to the new American republic and over the next twenty years would develop lucrative economic and social ties with associates there – relationships that would play an increasingly important role in their lives.[7] These ties were significantly strengthened by the tens of thousands of Amer-ican immigrants – the so-called and incorrectly labelled "Late Loy-alists" – who flooded into the colony in the last decade of the eighteenth century and the first decade of the nineteenth.

These American settlers would have been particularly struck by the incongruity of Simcoe's anglophile vision as it was projected onto the North American wilderness, for on resettling in Upper Canada, they found the colony to be far more American than British. This was particularly the case in the realm of religion. Simcoe and the British officials who succeeded him could glibly talk about the "essen-tially established ... Church of England ... in Upper Canada,"[8] but their anglophile theory was confounded by the religious and demo-graphic realities of the Upper Canadian situation. In 1800, for example, there were only three Anglican ministers in the entire colony. One of these was the Reverend John Stuart of Kingston, a very gifted minister – energetic, intelligent, sensitive, and eager to expand Anglicanism, even if it meant that he would have to learn to preach extemporaneous sermons. But despite Stuart's considerable ministerial strengths, he felt compelled to report in 1795, "I may be permitted to end my Days here in Quietness – provided always, that I ask or expect nothing from my parishioners."[9] In spite of the presence of the military and the strength of Loyalism in Kingston, Stuart estimated that only about 10 per cent of the inhabitants considered themselves to be even nominal Anglicans.

Stuart's Anglican nemesis was the Reverend John Langhorn, who had been sent in 1787 by the Society for the Propagation of the Gospel to serve the area just west of Kingston. Instead of making Anglicans, Langhorn's extremely eccentric behaviour and his "uncouth manners and illiberal Conduct" drove his parishioners into the welcoming arms of Methodists and other sectarians.[10] Langhorn composed and sang "vulgar and obscene"[11] songs attacking Methodists. Moreover, he stubbornly refused even to walk on the same side of the road as a non-Anglican, and he especially abhorred the recently arrived American immigrants. When Langhorn left Upper Canada in 1813, most Anglicans were relieved. When he died in England in 1817 at the age of seventy-three, no one in Upper Canada exhibited any sorrow.[12]

The third Anglican minister living in Upper Canada in 1800 was the Reverend Robert Addison, who ministered in the Niagara area near present-day Niagara-on-the-Lake. Addison was certainly not an ornament to his profession. One of his parishioners once described him as a "poor drunken card-playing minister of the Church of England, whom I sometimes heard mumble over his form of prayer so fast that I could scarcely understand a word of it, and then read his short manuscript sermon with the same indifference and haste."[13] Even the Reverend John Stuart had to admit that his friend Addison was a failure as a minister because of "his temper and qualifications."[14] By 1812, there were three other Anglican ministers in Upper Canada: Richard Pollard, who lived near present-day Windsor; George Okill Stuart, John Stuart's son, who was in Toronto; and the former Presbyterian, John Strachan, in Cornwall. The latter two possessed considerable strengths, but the former seems to have had limited abilities and an unusually low energy level.[15]

The Anglican ministers who were in Upper Canada before 1812 failed miserably to stem the tide of what one of them in 1810 referred to as the "great progress," especially of the Methodists. Stressing the "Orthodox faith of our Church," the Reverend Richard Pollard saw the need to strip off "the fascinating garb, of Superstition and Enthusiasm."[16] But in the battle with the "most illiterate teachers," Pollard found himself on the defensive. It was one thing to attack the "self-appointed Teachers" who propagated "pernicious error."[17] It was quite another to persuade those whom Stuart once referred to as the "generality of the vulgar" to reject the "emotional blandishments" of the Methodists.[18] The Methodist "Canada fire," it was observed, "spread like a conflagration over the Canadian circuits,"[19] and the tiny and motley collection of Anglican ministers could do little but watch the spiritual forest fire – through a lens clouded by a thick layer of bitter awe.

During the two decades preceding the outbreak of the War of 1812, a radical Methodism, tempered by what one Upper Canadian called "the flame of sanctifying grace,"[20] became the leading edge of evangelicalism in the colony. In fact, Methodism was the cutting edge of Protestantism – far more so than the Allinite New Light movement was in the Maritimes at approximately the same time. It seems clear that Freeborn Garrettson, in particular, would have felt very much at home in Upper Canada during these decades, as would Henry Alline and Harris Harding; and, to a much lesser extent, because of the prevailing racism, David George. The post-revolution William Black, on the other hand, would have been embarrassingly uncomfortable, regarding the American-influenced Methodists as dangerous revolutionaries.

Possibly the two most influential Methodist actors in the unfolding Upper Canadian religious drama in the 1790s and first decade of the nineteenth century were Hezekiah Calvin Wooster and Nathan Bangs – two very different (yet so similar) Methodist preachers and itinerants. Wooster dominated the 1790s; Bangs, the following decade. Both men were unusually charismatic preachers, and both were obsessed with Methodist evangelism and with sanctification. Wooster died a burnt-out shell of an itinerant in 1798, "in the 28th year of his age and the fifth year of his ministry."[21] Bangs, on the other hand, died in New York City in 1862 at eighty-four years of age, after an unusually successful career as itinerant preacher, "publisher, journalist, historian, and ecclesiastical statesman."[22]

Among Wooster's papers, found after his premature death on 6 November 1798, was the following brief spiritual biography:

Hezekiah Calvin Wooster was born May 20, 1771
Convicted of Sin, October 9, 1791
Born Again, December 1, 1791
Sanctified, February 6, 1792.[23]

Soon after his sanctification experience, Wooster became a Methodist itinerant. In 1796, together with Samuel Coate, he was appointed by the New York Conference "as a missionary to this distant field of labor" to the Oswegotchie circuit east of Kingston[24] (a position for which he had volunteered). After "enduring almost incredible hardship on their way, for they lodged no less than twenty-one nights in the wilderness," Coate and Wooster arrived in eastern Upper Canada just in time "to attend a quarterly meeting on the Bay of Quinte circuit" in Langhorn country to the west of Kingston.[25] Here they met the presiding elder, Darius Dunham, who had first come to Upper Canada from New York as a Methodist itinerant missionary in 1792. Dunham had accompanied William Losee, the pioneer Methodist itinerant to Upper Canada, who had first arrived in 1790.

Losee has been described, not unfairly, as a preacher belonging "to the exhorting dispensation, fluent, impassioned, fearless, denunciating – a veritable 'son of thunder.'"[26] In 1792 he had reported to the New York Annual Conference meeting in Albany, stressing the potential for Methodist growth in eastern Upper Canada and the "necessity of an elder to organize the Church, and give the sacraments."[27] Dunham, a blunt, direct man, who certainly earned his nickname "scolding Dunham,"[28] was made responsible for the Bay of Quinte circuit, while Losee moved farther east to the new Oswegotchie circuit. Within a year, the two men were at each other's throats – not because of theological differences but because they had fallen in love with the same young woman. When she chose Dunham, a bitter, disappointed, and disoriented Losee left the Methodist itinerary and returned to his home in New York.[29] He was never to recover from this failed romance.

Dunham had a reputation as a "hell-fire-damnation"[30] preacher, and in the early 1790s he was suspicious of extreme manifestations of emotionalism. He obviously knew very little about Wooster before the latter's arrival at the Bay of Quinte Quarterly Meeting. While Dunham "retired with the official brethren" to discuss matters of organizational consequence, the twenty-six-year-old Wooster began to encourage those who remained "in the house" to discover what he himself had discovered six years earlier: "full redemption in the blood of Christ." "The power of the Most High seemed to overshadow the congregation," it was noted, "and many were filled with joy unspeakable, and were praising the Lord aloud for what he had done for their souls, while others 'with speechless awe, and silent love,' were prostrate on the floor."[31]

On hearing the loud and persistent screaming and yelling, Dunham rushed into the house. His "wonder" on seeing his fellow Methodists writhing and moaning on the floor was suddenly transformed into indignation. After "gazing for a while with silent astonishment" at his friends and the newly arrived Wooster, the presiding elder fell on his knees and began to pray loudly "to God to stop the 'raging of the wild fire' as he called it." At precisely the same time, Wooster,

whose soul was burning with the "fire of the Holy Spirit," kneeled by the side of brother Dunham, and while the latter was earnestly engaged in prayer for God to put out the wild-fire, Wooster softly whispered out a prayer in the following manner, "Lord, bless brother Dunham! Lord, bless brother Dunham!" Thus they continued for some minutes – when, at length, the prayer of brother Wooster prevailed, and Dunham fell prostrate on the floor – and ere he arose received a baptism of that very fire which he had so feelingly deprecated as the effect of a wild imagination.[32]

The sanctification of Darius Dunham – a process whereby the Holy Spirit infused holiness in the individual – and the resulting "harmony in his prayers, feelings and views" sparked "the commence-ment of a revival of religion that soon spread through the entire province." Dunham played an important role "in spreading the sacred flame throughout the district, to the joy and salvation of hundreds of immortal souls."[33] But in 1797 and much of 1798, Wooster was the widely regarded special instrument of the Almighty in bringing about and spreading what contemporaries described as the "wild-fire Methodist revival." According to one contemporary, Nathan Bangs:

Calvin Wooster was a man of mighty prayer and faith. Frequently was his voice heard, by the families where he lodged, in the night season, when rising from his bed while others slept, he would pour out the desire of his soul to God, in earnest prayer for the salvation of souls. Such, indeed, was the strength of his faith in God, and the fervency of his spirit, as well as the bold and pointed manner of his appeals to the consciences of his bearers, and particularly to the wicked, that few of these could stand before him – they would either flee from the house, or, smitten with conviction, fall down and cry aloud for mercy – while in the midst of these exercises, the saints of God were shouting forth his praises.[34]

Dunham was not the only Upper Canadian Methodist preacher in 1797 who was directly influenced by Wooster to catch "the flame of divine love." Among the "many instances of the manifestations of divine power and grace" was an unforgettable incident in the Hay Bay Methodist Church. While a Wooster disciple preached a sermon regarding the centrality of conversion *and* sanctification, a young man "commenced, in a playful mood, to swear profanely, and oth-erwise to disturb the congregation." The preacher, "feeling strong in faith and the power of his might," suddenly stopped and "fixed his piercing eye upon the profane man, then stamping with his foot, and pointing his finger at him with great energy, he cried out, '*My God! smite him!*'" Immediately the young man fell, "as if shot through the heart with a bullet." Then "such a divine afflatus came down upon the congregation, that sinners were crying to God for mercy" from every direction "while the saints of God burst forth in loud praises to his name."[35] The extraordinary charismatic power unleashed by Wooster in 1797 was such that Nathan Bangs was absolutely convinced that "this great work may be said to have been, in some sense, the beginning of that great revival of religion which soon after spread through various parts of the United States." And at the core of the Wooster message, it was pointed out over and over again, was to be found his special emphasis on the Methodist "*baptism of the Holy Ghost.*" This single-minded preoccupation with the "Second Blessing," it was said, "fired and filled the hearts of God's ministers at that time, and ... enabled them so to speak that the people *felt* that their words were with 'demonstration and power,' and they could not well resist the influence of those 'thoughts which breathed,' and those 'words which burned.'"[36]

Wooster and "others of a like spirit" were able to use "such pointed language as made the 'ear to tingle' and the heart to palpitate." They encouraged those who accepted their gospel to draw a distinct boundary between themselves – "the righteous" – and "the wicked." The maintenance of this strict boundary helped immeasurably in creating a strong sense of Christian fellowship and community, though it often did so at the expense of family solidarity. Non-Methodist husbands, in particular, resented the powerful hold some Methodist preachers had over their wives. There were numerous examples of angry husbands rushing violently into prayer meetings, grabbing their wives by the hair, and dragging them home, kicking and screaming. There was at least one Methodist preacher who, while talking to a woman "under conviction for sin" in her home, was attacked by her husband, who cut a deep scar in the preacher's forehead. Such attacks, and the growing opposition of "the enemy," strengthened the resolve of the Methodists and also their conviction that they were indeed "the persecuted remnant of Israel." And the persecution, it is clear, helped fuel the revival fires.[37]

By the summer of 1798, Calvin Wooster, suffering from an advanced form of tuberculosis, resolved to return to his home in New York to die there. Even though he was in such a "feeble state" and was not able "to speak above a whisper," scores of people hurried to hear him before he left Upper Canada for good. His whispered sermons were reported to be "frequently attended by such a divine energy and unction, that sinners would tremble and fall under the announcement, while the people of God felt the *holy anointing* running through their souls. It is said, indeed, that his very countenance exhibited such marks of the Divine glory that it struck conviction into the hearts of many who beheld it."[38]

Just before Wooster returned to his family farm, probably in the early autumn of 1798, he had an unexpected visit from Lorenzo "Crazy" Dow, the infamous itinerant, who was then only twenty-one years old. "Pale, sallow, and somewhat consumptive in the appearance of his countenance," Dow "dressed in the plainest attire, with his single-breasted coat, often worn thread-bare." His "whole appearance" was such "as to awaken a high degree of curiosity and interest."[39] Wooster, however, was too sick and exhausted to be curious about his visitor, who evidently was far more curious about the dying man's gospel of the "Second Blessing." Dow had heard from a New York friend about "*Calvin Wooster*, in Upper Canada, that he enjoyed the blessing of sanctification, and had a miracle wrought on his body, in some sense." On eventually finding Wooster, the impetuous Dow went into the room where he was asleep. "He appeared to me more like one from the eternal world, than like one of my fellow mortals," recorded Dow. "I told him, when he awoke, who I was, and what I had come for. Said he, God has convicted you for the blessings of sanctification, and that blessing is to be obtained by the simple act of faith, the same as the blessings of justification [conversion]."[40]

A few days later, after one of Dow's sermons, Dow observed that Wooster "spoke, or rather whispered out an exhortation, as his voice was so broken in consequence of praying, in Upper Canada." While Wooster was whispering his exhortation, "the power which attended the same, reached the hearts of the people," Dow reported, "and some who were standing and sitting, fell like men shot in the field of battle; and I felt it like a tremor to run through my soul and every vein, so that it took away my limb power, so that I fell to the floor, and by faith, saw a greater blessing than I had hither to experienced." But Dow's sanctification process was not yet finished, for he felt "some of the remains of the evil nature, the effect of Adam's fall, still remaining." He could only "groan out" his desires to God, whereupon:

He came to me, and said, believe the blessing is now; no sooner had the words dropped from his lips, than I strove to believe the blessing mine now, with all the powers of my soul, then the burthen dropped or fell from my breast, and a solid joy, and a gentle running peace filled my soul. From that time to this, I have not had that extacy of joy or that downcast of spirit as formerly; but more of an inward, simple, sweet running peace from day to day, so that prosperity or adversity doth not produce the ups and downs as formerly; but my soul is more like the ocean, whilst its surface is uneven by reason of the boisterous wind, the bottom is still calm; so that a man may be in the midst of outward difficulties, and yet the centre of the soul may be calmly stayed on God.[41]

Dow had been so impressed and so inspired by Wooster that he, too, decided to spend some time in Upper Canada. This was to be a special pilgrimage for the sanctified eccentric. When he arrived in the Wooster heartland east of Kingston (probably in the summer of 1799), Dow apparently sparked a series of revivals by merely mentioning Wooster's name. As he noted in his journal, "On mentioning *Calvin Worster's* name, and the blessing he was to me, people who had here felt the shock of his labors were stirred up afresh, and some would even cry out, etc."[42] In his sojourn in Upper Canada, Dow made extensive use of his own version of Wooster's death. "His last words," Dow maintained, were "ye must be sanctified or damned." Then, according to Dow, Wooster cast a look upward and "went out like a snuff of a candle without terror."[43] Dow's second-hand story of the saintly Wooster's last seconds on earth was not the only one circulated in Upper Canadian Methodist circles in the late 1790s and the early years of the following decade. On his deathbed, when Wooster was asked by his father if "his confidence was still strong in the Lord," he apparently responded "with holy triumph, 'Yes, strong! strong!'" Then, just a moment before he died, Wooster distinctly whispered for all around him to hear, "The nearer I draw to eternity, the brighter heaven shines upon me."[44]

Wooster's remarkable success as a revivalist was traced to "the purity of his motives" and "the holy and burning zeal with which he pursued his vocations."[45] His magnetic personality and his almost limitless supply of spirituality and holiness significantly touched the religious lives of all who came in contact with him. "Whispering Wooster," who was regarded by his contemporaries as a preacher filled with the Holy Spirit and as a man who was obviously killing himself for his Saviour, personified radical evangelical Methodism in Upper Canada during its formative period. Clearly, it was he who established the exaggerated pietistic parameters of the movement. Because of Wooster's powerful impact on Upper Canadian radical Methodism, many of his contemporaries, including Nathan Bangs – no man's fool – were absolutely certain that the Second Great Awakening in the United States effectively began on British territory.

According to Bangs, "It became a proverbial saying among the people along the way from Canada to the seat of the New York Conference, that the northern preachers brought the Canada fire with them."[46] Dow was to make precisely the same point. As far as he was concerned, the "Canada fire" had overwhelmed him, radically transforming his life and his Methodist message.

According to one student of late-eighteenth-century American Methodism, there was an extraordinary explosion of Methodist numbers in New York during the years 1798–1805.[47] Obviously, this sudden and remarkable growth owed a great deal to the reality of the "Canada fire," which Bangs, Dow, and other principal Methodist leaders were absolutely convinced had burned furiously southwards and in the process had largely sparked the Second Great Awakening in the northern United States. Just as the Great Stir in northern New England during the latter years of the revolution had been traced to Alline's First Great Awakening in Nova Scotia, so too the Second Great Awakening in New York may have had its origins in neighbouring British North America. Wooster's "Canada fire" not only swept southwards through the heart of New York to Albany and beyond but also spread "up the shore of Lake Ontario, even to the head of the lake, to Niagara, and thence to Long Point on the northwestern shore of Lake Erie"[48] and to the region of present-day Windsor and Detroit. As the revival flames roared westward from the Bay of Quinte, they engulfed, among others, Nathan Bangs.

Bangs was born in Stratford, Connecticut, on 2 May 1778. His father was a "well-read blacksmith" and an Episcopalian who, like Garrettson's father, regarded the Methodists as dangerous fanatics.[49] Throughout his early life, Bangs was easily intimidated by his father, whose religious principles readily became his own. Bangs became a teacher and surveyor after moving to Delaware County, New York, with his family in 1791. Eight years later, in early May 1799, the twenty-one-year-old Nathan Bangs – a strikingly handsome man, "tall and slender, graceful in his manner, with the carriage of a gentleman born and bred"[50] – resolved "to move still further westward to Upper Canada."[51] He settled in the Niagara region in what he referred in his journal as "a strange land, beyond the limits of our native country."[52] Within a few months, having reacted negatively to the personality and lifestyle of the Reverend Robert Addison, the local Anglican minister, Bangs began to attend local Methodist services. He described Addison as "a card player and a drunkard" who "performed the liturgical service with indecent haste, following it with a brief, rapid, and vapid prelection." A strong contrast to Addison was the first Methodist whom Bangs met, a man he described as a "devout

Nathan Bangs, 1778–1862
The United Church of Canada/Victoria University Archives, Toronto

Arminian" whose Christian message "came like a dagger to my heart."[53]

All the Methodists whom Bangs met had in some way been permanently branded by the "Canada fire."[54] There was James Coleman, the Methodist itinerant who had first arrived in Niagara in 1794, coming from New Jersey by way of New England. He was said to be "a man of one aim and one business,"[55] which was preaching intense conversion and sanctification to all who would listen to him. Coleman was enthusiastically supported by two young New York itinerants, Joseph Sawyer and Joseph Jewell. These three young men, convinced that the Holy Spirit was determined to bring Nathan Bangs into the Methodist fellowship, singled out the young schoolteacher-surveyor for special spiritual attention. "In the kindest manner" they witnessed to him, encouraging him, wrote Bangs, for the first time in his life, to "fully disclose the struggles of my mind, acknowledging my doubts, my fears, and my desires."[56] Bangs wanted very much to be converted. Saving "his own soul," his biographer stressed, "was his absorbing anxiety." He pleaded with his Methodist friends "to show him the way to salvation." They enigmatically replied that "a clearer light" would eventually "dawn upon him" and he would soon "receive assurance – the witness of the Spirit."[57]

In order to help to short-circuit the conversion process, Bangs decided to adopt the simple and "severe" Methodist lifestyle. Up to this point, he "had prided himself on his fine personal appearance, and had dressed in the full fashion of the times, with a ruffled shirt, and long hair in a cue." On being received "into the Society of Methodists," he had happily cast off "all his ruffles" and "his long hair shared the same fate." Bangs's principal concern was, as he expressed it in his journal, "to make sure work of my salvation."[58] He described the "momentous work" which in August 1800 "wrought the regeneration" of his "struggling soul" in the following evocative manner:

After struggling hard, praying much, reading the Holy Scriptures, fasting, and conversing with religious friends for some days, he [God] showed to my mind a scene such as I had never fully seen before. All my past sins seemed pictured upon my memory; and the righteous law of God, so often broken by me, shone in overwhelming splendor before me; I saw and acknowledged the justice of my condemnation. Christ was then exhibited to my mind as having "fulfilled the law and made it honorable," "bearing my sins in his own body on the tree"; so that I, receiving him by faith, need not bear them any longer myself. This view humbled me to the dust. At the same time I felt a gracious power to rely upon his atoning merits by simple faith. Instantly I felt that my sins were canceled for Christ's sake, and the Spirit of God bore witness with mine that I was adopted into the family of His people. My mind was filled with awe and reverence. The wisdom, power, and goodness of God in devising such a scheme for the recovery of fallen man struck me with astonishment. With an ecstasy of holy joy did I lay hold upon the cross of the Lord Jesus as my Saviour. All boasting was excluded, except of the matchless love of God, who sent his Son to die for the world, that "whosoever believeth in him should not perish, but have everlasting life."[59]

When Bangs informed his father of his conversion experience, Lemuel Bangs was rather disparaging, contending that his overly emotional son had gone too far in assuming a knowledge of his personal salvation, "as knowledge supersedes the necessity of faith." Although taken aback at first by his father's lack of enthusiasm and support, Bangs was determined to preach the Methodist gospel – but not until he had experienced "sanctification." He knew that he was only halfway along the road leading to Wooster's "Canada fire." Bangs came under the influence of his class leader, Christian Warner, who was preoccupied with "the doctrine of sanctification as taught by Paul, expressed by Wesley and Fletcher," and preached in Upper Canada by Wooster and his growing number of followers. It was common knowledge, Bangs realized, that John Wesley had stressed that wherever sanctification was preached, "revivals usually prevailed." According to Wesley, sanctification, whereby the Holy Spirit pushed the believer towards Christian perfection, was indeed "the grand depositum which God has given to the people called Methodists; and chiefly to propagate this, it appears, God raised them up. Their mission was ... to spread holiness over these lands."[60]

Painfully sensitive to the "Christian purity" of Warner, "who professed the blessings of sanctification,"[61] Bangs finally experienced his spiritual breakthrough on 6 February 1801. He noted in his journal:

I went struggling on for some time, until, on the 6th of February, 1801, being that evening on a visit to a pious family with some Christian friends, we conversed till quite late on religious subjects, and then prayed, as with the Methodist custom ... Mr. Warner first prayed, and without rising, called upon me to pray. When I commenced, my emotions deepened, my desire for a pure heart became intense, and my faith grew stronger and stronger. My supplications were importunate, so that I know not how long I continued to pray. When I ceased, I sank down into an inexpressible calmness, as lying passive at the feet of God. I felt relieved and comforted, as though I had been "cleansed from all filthiness of the flesh and spirit." I had no extraordinary rapture, no more than I had often experienced before, but such a sense of my own littleness that I thought "what a wonder is it that God condescends to notice me at all!" All my inward distress was gone. I could look up with a childlike composure and trust, and behold God as my heavenly Father.

We staid all night, and the next morning in family prayer I seemed surrounded with the divine glory. I certainly was filled at that time with the "perfect love which casteth out fear," for I had no fear of death, or judgment. I could trust all things to my merciful God, through my infinitely sufficient Redeemer. Such a sense of God's ineffable goodness pervaded my soul, that I seemed to sink, confounded by his very love, into nothingness before him. I felt that I was the least of all saints, but had an evidence bright as the noonday sun that all my sins were taken away, and that without fear I could depart and be with Christ at any moment he should see fit to call me.[62]

The sanctification experience of 6 and 7 February 1801 was the defining moment of Bangs's religious life. It was far more significant and central than his earlier conversion experience. For Bangs, as it had been for Wooster, sanctification was the "sublime culmination" of "justification"[63] (as Wooster always referred to his conversion). Of course, sanctification was not possible without "justification." Sanctification was the necessary "purification of the believer subsequent to regeneration."[64] It was the essence of evangelical Methodism – its energizing principle, its defining movement, and the means whereby the Holy Spirit infused the movement's revivals and awakenings.

"Having been made a partaker of this great blessing," Bangs felt that he should "yield to the impression" that he was indeed called to preach. This "impression" manifested itself in a variety of ways. One day soon after his sanctification, as he was "walking the road, in deep meditation" about this calling: "A sudden ray of divine illumination struck my mind like a flash of lightning, accompanied with the words, 'I have anointed thee to preach the Gospel.' I sank to the ground and cried out, 'Here am I!'"[65] When he first exhorted, after a sermon preached by Joseph Sawyer (the "Boanerges" of Upper Canada), Bangs "shook in every limb," his "lips stiffened, and" he "could hardly speak." Then, by some miracle, he was convinced, his lips "were loosed, and the power of the Spirit descended on the assembly in such a manner that some sobbed aloud, some praised God audibly, and others fell to the floor as if shot dead." Bangs was obviously gifted with the "Canada fire." As a result, in August 1801 he "received license to preach, and immediately departed for a circuit." He carried with him the ingredients for spreading the "Canada fire" throughout Upper Canada, and especially in the western half of the colony.[66]

Despite some attacks of doubt and intense introspection, Bangs late in 1801 and early 1802 coaxed a number of local revivals into existence. Fortified by "impressions" (particularly dreams and visions), he was confident that these revivals would soon result in a colony-wide Great Awakening. But just when the Awakening seemed to be imminent, Bangs experienced what he referred to as "a severe trial."[67] He began to think that all conversions, all revivals, all experiences of sanctification were traceable "to morbid excitement of the imagination."[68] According to one of his biographers:

At the time [Bangs] was physically worn by excessive labors and wasted by frequent illness, and yet his conscience continued to lash his flesh to heavier tasks. His mind also had been strained to the limit of its tension, and his preaching every weekday in addition to the several services on Sundays permitted no relaxation. Furthermore, he was given to microscopic introspection, morbidly testing the genuineness of his spiritual experiences by the character of his feelings. No Medusa face will turn a man's heart to stone more surely than his own if he contemplates it long enough.[69]

Mentally, physically, and spiritually exhausted, Bangs had convinced himself in 1802 that "he had erred in the excitement which his labors had produced among the people, though he saw that their lives were reformed." He therefore resolved to preach differently and conduct his meetings in more moderation: "But the resolution filled me with dismay, and I sank confounded in an abyss of darkness, and began to fear that my own experience had been a delusion."[70] After preaching, he spent the evening with a Methodist family. Retiring to his bed "in indescribable distress," Bangs soon fell asleep. But then there came a bombardment of "awful alarms." He dreamed that a "throng of demons" stared at him: "When I saw them I exclaimed, 'I will not fear you. I know where to go for help.' But my prayers seemed like vapor and utterly without meaning. I had no access to God. I ceased praying, and the phantoms drew closer around me. I began again to pray, but with the like effect. When I again ceased, the demons rushed at me with increased violence, and I awoke in intense agony." Bangs jumped out of bed and fell on his knees, but he discovered, to his acute dismay, that "the heavens seemed to be brass over my head."[71]

Bangs rushed downstairs and informed the rather distraught "woman of the house ... a most amiable Christian": "I believe there is no mercy for me." Bangs was, as he expressed it, "tempted to open my mouth in blasphemy against God, and to curse the Saviour of men." On the "ensuing Sabbath" he had to preach twice, and he wondered how he could even face his congregation. His whole being was "filled with horrors." He ruefully observed, "No one but God, or such as have had like trials, can conceive of my wretchedness. I could hardly stand up; I felt that I ought not to preach, being as I feared, lost forever." But on the following day, at a special prayer meeting near Burford, Bangs "prayed for deliverance." He was profoundly relieved to be able to report: "God appeared in gracious power, dispelling the clouds which hung over my mind, removing my doubts and fears, and shining upon my soul with the brightness of his reconciled countenance. All within me rejoiced in God my Saviour. Never was the "cooling water brook" more refreshing to a thirsty man than Christ was now to my panting heart."[72]

Huge crowds now assembled to hear the Methodist itinerant, who seemed to be such a typical Upper Canadian – in everything except his intense spirituality and his preaching skills. Bangs, in 1802, was developing certain theatrical skills as well, skills that appealed to his entertainment-starved audiences. When one young man attempted to make "amusement" of everything Bangs said at an informal dinner gathering, Bangs asked the "thoughtless young man" if he would "have the goodness to return thanks to God for his bounties to us here today?" The group stood in silence waiting for the prayer, where-upon the confused young man shouted, "Sir, I beg to be excused" and ran out of the "public house."[73] On another occasion a gentleman tricked Bangs into holding an evangelistic meeting in his house and then, when scores of people had arrived, the man ordered the preacher to leave. "In the presence of all the people," and following the "directions of the Saviour," Bangs slowly and melodramatically took "a handkerchief from his pocket, and raising first one foot and then the other, he wiped the dust from the soles of his shoes, which they had collected on the ground of W., declaring at the same time he did it as a testimony against [him] for refusing the message of salvation."[74]

Early in October 1802, Bangs set off for the Bay of Quinte circuit, accompanied by the presiding elder, Joseph Jewell. On the journey from Niagara, Bangs observed along the way a remarkable "awak-ening among the people." He also noted, for the first time, that there was a "marked line of distinction between the righteous and the wicked, there being but very few who were indifferent or outwardly moral to interpose between them. All showed openly what they were by their words and actions, and either accepted religion heartedly or opposed it violently."[75] In this polarized frontier environment, Bangs was certain that a pious minority confronted "the great majority," and that most of those who came to hear him preach were "deter-mined opposers." He moved slowly from one isolated settlement to another, "preaching and praying with the people"; the "Divine Spirit was poured out upon them, and many were converted."[76]

Apparently, Bangs "pursued his labors"[77] in the Wooster heartland of the Bay of Quinte until December 1803, when he contracted typhus. He was confined to bed for almost two months, and another

month passed before he tried to preach, "and even then his voice
was so feeble that he could hardly be heard." Not realizing how
strained his voice was, Bangs forced himself "to speak loud enough
to be heard," and in the process developed what he called "that
double sort of voice." This "deep, tremulous undertone of his voice"[78]
was sometimes considered to be a Methodist affectation – something
like the New Light "Yankee whine" – though it was widely regarded
as a certain sign of divine unction. With its built-in echo effect, it
underscored the uniqueness of Bangs's evangelistic message.

By the early summer of 1804, Bangs had recovered sufficiently to
be able to return to New York to see his parents. On the way, he
spent some time "at the Mansion of Freeborn Garrettson, on the
Hudson, near Rhinebeck." Bangs had carefully "read and received
inspiration" from the published journals of the patriarchal itinerant,
and he "listened with deep interest" to the stories about itinerating
in Nova Scotia.[79] The two men had a great deal in common, and it
may be argued that Garrettson's sojourn in Nova Scotia indirectly
influenced Bangs's evangelistic strategy in Upper Canada a little
more than a decade after Garrettson's return to the United States.

At the New York Conference, held in New York City in June 1804,
Bangs was ordained a minister of the Methodist Episcopal Church.
This meant that he could now dispense the sacraments. When he
returned to Upper Canada, he made his way to the western part of
the colony, having received "a Macedonian Call"[80] to go there. On
his first visit to any new community, Bangs always began the service
in the same down-to-earth manner:

When a stranger appears [especially a preacher, he might have added] ...
the people are usually curious to know his name, whence he comes, whither
he is bound, and what is his errand. I will try to satisfy you in brief. My
name is Nathan Bangs. I was born in Connecticut May 2, 1778. I was born
again in this province, May, 1800. I commenced itinerating as a preacher of
the Gospel in the month of September, 1801. On the 18th of June, the
present year [1804], I left New York for the purpose of visiting you, of whom
I heard about two years ago, and after a long and tedious journey I am here.
I am bound for the heavenly city, and my errand among you is to persuade
as many as I can to go with me. I am a Methodist preacher; and my manner
of worship is, to stand while singing, kneel while praying, and then I stand
while I preach, the people meanwhile sitting. As many of you see fit to join
me in this way can do so, and others may choose their own method.[81]

Bangs then read a chapter from the Bible and led in the singing of
a Wesleyan hymn; he followed with a sermon permeated with the
theme "the Holy Ghost sent down from heaven." At the conclusion

of the service, Bangs would boldly command: "All of you who wish to hear any more such preaching, rise up." He would then tell all those on their feet that "in two weeks, God willing, they might expect preaching,"[82] and he would close the meeting with a benediction. A link in the Methodist circuit chain had been forged – hardened by the "Canada fire."

Bangs loved to itinerate in the western wilderness of Upper Canada. Not only did he persuade many of the unchurched to become Methodists, but he was also very successful in drawing Pennsylvania and New England Baptists into his evangelical Wesleyan fellowship.[83] A "Great Reformation," it was asserted, followed Bangs as he itinerated in the rural wilderness.[84] "My own soul," he emphasized, "enjoyed uninterrupted communion with God."[85] In late September 1805, having been moved to eastern Upper Canada, Bangs played a crucially important role in the famous Hay Bay Camp Meeting," located in the Bay of Quinte Conference.[86] At this camp meeting, which was attended by approximately 2,500 people (about 5 per cent of the total Upper Canadian population), Bangs successfully imposed the Wooster style of evangelical Methodism on the burgeoning movement's popular identity. "The impression of the Word was universal," he observed at the time, "the power of the Spirit was manifest throughout the whole encampment, and almost every tent was a scene of prayer."[87] Because of Hay Bay and because of Bangs's persuasive preaching powers, "a general revival of religion spread around the circuit."[88]

Bangs spent the remainder of 1805 and the early months of 1806 in the Cornwall region, where in April 1806 he married "Mary Bolton, of the town of Edwardsburgh, Upper Canada."[89] In the summer of 1806 he was sent to Quebec City, where the seed of Methodism fell on very stony soil. Within three months, because his congregation had dwindled to a single worshipper, Bangs made his way to Montreal, and he remained there until 1808, when he was transferred to a circuit in New York.[90] Although Bangs returned to Upper Canada as a visitor after 1808, he was never again a Methodist itinerant there. Bangs's most recent biographer has perceptively summed up Bangs's Canadian career as follows: "In his years as a missionary in Canada he had expounded the Methodist gospel from Detroit to Quebec City and had provided an enduring example of that self-sacrificing zeal which Methodism's success largely rested. Moreover, Bangs acquired a lasting reputation in Upper Canadian Methodism, a position that was strengthened by the nature of his subsequent career."[91]

Like many other Methodist preachers in other regions of British North America, Bangs was far more successful in the rural back-country than in the urban areas. Like New Light evangelicalism in Maritime Canada, Methodism, especially in Upper Canada, appealed particularly to frontier settlers who lived in relative isolation and had strong ties with contiguous areas of the United States. Moreover, the success of popular radical evangelicalism in British North America during the quarter of a century following the end of the American Revolution seemed to owe a great deal to the fact that it was being preached by young, vigorous, North Americans who struck a responsive chord with the populist values and aspirations of their congregations. Like all successful evangelical preachers, these dynamic "Spirit-soaked" itinerants were amazingly successful in pulling the Christian gospel from the realms of "ecclesiastical space" and powerfully injecting it into everyday frontier life.[92] This gospel was regarded by many urban inhabitants, particularly those with strong British ties, as pernicious and primitive religious emotionalism. But for the so-called ordinary inhabitants of the out-settlement, radical evangelicalism helped them make some sense of their lives; it provided firm and divinely sanctioned boundaries and coordinates in a society that was desperately searching for explicit boundaries and firm coordinates. For believers, moreover, there were new worship communities to which they could be attached – communities that provided fellowship, solace, and emotional support in times of crisis and disorientation.

The absolute centrality of radical evangelical Christianity in the lives of so many British North Americans owed much in the pre-1812 period to the fact that the Church of England was so weak. But radical evangelical Christianity probably owed more to demographic factors and the weakness of the British governmental presence in British North America. Moreover, the burden of taxation, government, and ideology was remarkably light, thus encouraging and facilitating British North Americans to be preoccupied with things religious – that is, when they had the time and energy left over from their pioneering exploits. In the frontier regions of British North America – from Windsor in Upper Canada to Halifax in Nova Scotia – during the years 1784–1812, religion was absolutely central and absolutely crucial, and it pushed to the dark periphery of colonial life political and ideological concerns. These concerns deflected surprisingly few frontier British North Americans from what they considered to be their primary concern: the salvation of their souls, and preparing for eternal life.

American Methodist leaders in the early nineteenth century calculated that every Methodist church member translated into ten adherents. One modern historian of early American Methodism has argued that the ratio was really one to eight;[93] another scholar has adopted in her work the ratio of one to fifteen.[94] If the lowest ratio, one to eight, is used for Upper Canada in 1810, it may be argued that there were approximately 20,000 adherents in the colony – 28 per cent of the total population. If the one-to-fifteen ratio is used, there would be an estimated 26,000 adherents out of an approximate population of 70,000 – 37 per cent of the population. Even if the total population of the colony in 1810 was 100,000 (an improbable figure), using the lowest ratio of eight to one, the Methodist percentage of the total population could have been 20 per cent. And if Baptist numbers are taken into account (some 400 members in 1810[95] – and the Baptists were just as evangelical as the Methodists, although far less successful in Upper Canada), the percentage of Methodist-Baptist adherents in a total population of 70,000, using the one-to-eight ratio, would have been 34 per cent.

In Nova Scotia in 1808 there were approximately 1,248 New Light Baptist church members and possibly 200 New Light Congregationalists.[96] There were also an estimated 600 Methodists. Using the same one-to-eight ratio, and considering the Nova Scotia population to be some 60,000 in 1808, the percentage of New Light Methodist adherents would have been 27 per cent – very close to the Upper Canadian figure. In New Brunswick, however, there were in 1810 no more than about 300 New Light Congregationalist and Baptist church members, and probably the same number of Methodists, out of a total population of 40,000. Thus, New Light and Methodist adherents made up about 12 per cent of the New Brunswick population.[97]

If other evangelical groups are taken into account, including evangelical Anglicans and Presbyterians, the Nova Scotia percentage of evangelical adherents in 1808 would amount to at least 33 per cent of the population; that of Upper Canada to 40 per cent; and New Brunswick to 15 per cent. Even at the most liberal reckoning, evangelical percentages of the total population of Prince Edward Island in 1810 and Lower Canada (where out of a total population of 300,000, less then 10 per cent were Protestant) were tiny – less than 3 per cent in both cases. (The population of Prince Edward Island in 1810 was approximately 5,000, and the New Lights, Baptists, and Methodists had a negligible impact on the infant colony.)

Of course, the population figures being used are very rough and must be regarded as such. But although they are rough estimates, when applied to the more conservative figures of church membership they are extremely suggestive. They seem to underscore the fact that by 1812 in Upper Canada and Nova Scotia (taking into consideration the large Roman Catholic population in both colonies), radical evangelicalism had become the major and most influential component of Protestantism. The War of 1812 and new immigration trends after 1815 were to weaken radical evangelicalism's hegemony over Protestant life in Upper Canada. But Nova Scotia and New Brunswick were largely unaffected by the anti-Americanism unleashed by the War of 1812, which equated American republicanism with religious enthusiasm, and in these colonies radical evangelicalism was to grow even stronger, especially in New Brunswick. Accompanying this growth was the inexorable expansion of "formal" or "orderly" evangelicalism within Presbyterianism and the Church of England.

8 "A Total Revolution in Religious and Civil Government": The Evolving Radical Evangelical Ethos of British North America, 1775–1812

In February 1805, some five months before the Hay Bay Camp Meeting, the eastern extremity of what is now New Brunswick witnessed the most violent and certainly the bloodiest manifestation of Maritime New Light antinomianism – one of the sometimes forgotten legacies of Henry Alline's charismatic ministry. This incident underscored some of the fundamental differences between Maritime and central Canadian radical evangelicalism during the interwar years and also some of the common compelling dynamics of the movement. In the spring of 1804 a religious revival had swept the region, a revival fuelled largely by the memories of Alline's and Black's remarkable First Great Awakening which had blazed across Maritime Canada a quarter of a century earlier. A few months after most of the revival fires had burned themselves out, a young woman, Sarah Babcock, encouraged by an itinerant New Light Baptist preacher, Jacob Peck, began to prophesy. Among other things, she confidently proclaimed that the end of the world was imminent – and that just before Jesus Christ returned, she, assisted by Peck, was to convert to her special version of Christianity all the local inhabitants, including the scores of French-speaking Acadian Roman Catholics.

Sarah's father, Amasa, was especially affected by her newfound spirituality; the evidence suggests that in fact her message may have helped plunge him into a form of insanity. On 13 February 1805, while grinding wheat in his handmill, Amasa took a handful of flour and sprinkled it over the kitchen floor, boldly declaring, "This is the bread of Heaven." Further encouraged by his daughter, he took off his shoes and ran outdoors into the deep snow, yelling wildly as he stumbled through the drifts, "The world is coming to an end, and the stars are falling." On returning to his house, the exhausted but ecstatic Amasa lined up his entire family – his wife and nine children, his sister Mercy, and his brother Jonathan – and ordered them to wait in silence while he honed his long "clasp knife." After he had sharpened the knife, Amasa walked towards his sister Mercy and ordered her to take off all her clothes and fall on her knees, and ready herself for immediate death and eternity. He then commanded Jonathan to strip; like his sister, Jonathan eagerly obeyed his older brother.

Amasa glanced nervously out of the window a number of times, apparently expecting to see his Saviour's face. Then, clutching his knife, he screamed, "The Cross of Christ!" and fatally stabbed his sister. As soon as Jonathan "saw the blood flow," he apparently regained "his senses" and rushed out of the door, naked. After hearing Jonathan's amazing story, a group of neighbours hurried to the Babcock house. On seeing them, Amasa cried, "Gideon's men arise!"[1] However, "Gideon's men" were not to be found, and Amasa was quickly captured. After having his arms securely tied, he was taken away, obviously deranged. Amasa was tried for the murder of his sister, and he was hanged on 28 June 1805. The Saint John, New Brunswick, *Gazette* of 24 June reported on the trial as follows:

It appeared in evidence that for some time before the trial, the prisoner with several of his neighbours had been in the habit of meeting under pretense of religious exercises at each other's houses at which one Jacob Peck, a well-known Baptist was a principal performer; That they were under strong delusions and conducted themselves in a very frantic, irregular and even impious manner, and that in consequence of some pretended prophecies by some of the company in some of their pretended religious phrenzies against the unfortunate deceased: the prisoner was probably induced to commit the horrid, barbarous and cruel murder of which he was convicted.

The "great ... concourse of the people at the trial" must have realized that in the *Gazette*'s account of the affair, neither Sarah Babcock's crucial role in what came to be known as the Babcock Tragedy nor the indirect influence of radical New Light evangelicalism had been given the attention they obviously deserved. Like so many early-nineteenth-century women, Sarah had been unceremoniously removed from the religious environment that she had largely created. Moreover, she was only one of many young Maritime women, in the immediate post-revolution period, who helped shape the contours of radical New Light evangelicalism in the region – especially its surprisingly strong and persistent antinomian variant.[2]

There were other New Light prophetesses in Maritime Canada and many, many female preachers, or exhorters. Perhaps the most widely known prophetess was Sarah Bancroft, who was from the Granville area of Nova Scotia near present-day Annapolis Royal. In 1791, Bishop Charles Inglis was very interested in this woman and was concerned about the threat she posed to good Anglican order in Nova Scotia in particular, and throughout the Maritime region in general. Inglis observed in his *Journal* on 24 August 1791: "Heard much of the prophetess Sarah Bencraft ... She lately told Mrs. Shaw and the family that it was a great honour to them to attend and wait upon her, *as she, the Prophetess, would be a pillar in Heaven.*" Despite the fact that a number of her prophesies were not realized, "the prophetess retained much of her credit and influence" among her "enthusiastic Sect called New Lights."[3] Many Nova Scotia women at the time were certain that God had spoken directly to Sarah, as he could to them, and were convinced that they were subject only to the Holy Spirit at work directly in their lives and not to the devil-encrusted regulations of the Old and New Testaments. They could not conceive of themselves as being merely "self-renewed and revived"; rather, they saw themselves as individuals whose contemporary inner selves had been "wholly eradicated and replaced" by the Almighty.[4]

The testimony of Inglis about the radicalism of New Light revivalism in the Maritimes is particularly important since, in an earlier phase of his career, he had witnessed firsthand the radicalism of the American Revolution. If, as Inglis implied, the religious radicalism of Nova Scotia was more extreme than the radicalism of the American Revolution, an illuminating contrast between evangelicalism in Canada and in the neighbouring United States comes into focus. It may be argued that although evangelicalism in the new United States was indeed shaped by its democratic and republican environment, Canadian evangelicalism – at least until the War of 1812 – may have been even more radical, more egalitarian, and more populist than its better-known variant to the south.

Even during Henry Alline's lifetime, as has already been noted, many of his most gifted followers had spun out his powerful New Light gospel in the direction of antinomianism. It was a development that he vehemently denounced.[5] For example, in his *Two Mites*, published originally in 1781, Alline maintained that "true redemption is raising the desires and life of the inner man out of this miserable, sinful, and bestial world, and turning it to Christ, from whence it is fallen.[6] Later, in *The Anti-Traditionalist*, first published in 1783, he contended that it was necessary for the Christian to "Turn from all, Deny all: Leave all." He continued:

I do not mean the outward and criminal Acts of Idolatry and Debauchery only: but any and every Thing in the Creature that in the least Degree amuses the Mind or leads the Choice from God. For even the most simple Enjoyments and Pleasures of Life will keep the Choice in Action, and therefore the Creature amused from God, and consequently sinking deeper and deeper in its fallen and irrecoverable State. Nor will you ever return to be redeemed until every Idol, Joy, Hope, or Amusement so fails you that you are wholly starved out, and there is not only a Famine, but a mighty Famine in all created Good.[7]

Carefully blended, Alline's perseverance and asceticism produced what he frequently referred to as "true zeal."[8] The former without the latter often led, of course, to antinomianism. Such an antinomian mix apparently prevailed in the Chignecto Isthmus region of western Nova Scotia in 1782 and in nearby Shediac in the first decade of the nineteenth century, and it was certainly a powerful popular movement throughout the Annapolis Valley in 1791 and 1792.

Some contemporary observers had firsthand opportunity to witness the evolution of antinomianism. William Black, on first meeting Henry Alline in the spring of 1780, described the New Light preacher as being "very zealous in the cause."[9] "He laboured fervently," commented Black, who stressed that Alline's coming to the Chignecto area "was made a great blessing to many."[10] But by the time Black visited Falmouth, Alline's home, in June 1782, their earlier friendship had soured. According to Black, Alline and his associates – men such as Thomas Handley Chipman and John Payzant, Alline's brother-in-law – maintained that the Methodist preacher "was no minister of Jesus Christ, soon after, he was no christian; and in a little while, down-right minister of Antichrist."[11] Black was also very concerned with what he perceived to be the pernicious growth of an antinomian, mystical, and primitivist gospel. In November 1782, an obviously distraught Black noted in his journal:

I rode over to *Tantramar*, [the present-day border region between Nova Scotia and New Brunswick] where I was sorely grieved to find *Mysticism* and the foulest *Antinomianism*, spreading like fire; and its deadly fruits already growing up on every side. The people were informed publickly, *That they had nothing to do with God's law: that David was still a man after God's own heart; when wallowing in adultery, and murder: that his soul never sinned all that time, but only his body*. Mr. Alline himself told several persons one day that *a believer is like a nut, thrown into the mud, which may dirty the shell, but not the kernel.* That is, we may get drunk, or commit adultery, without the smallest defilement, etc. etc.[12]

Three years later, on 22 May 1785, when Freeborn Garrettson was itinerating in Nova Scotia, he confronted in those areas of the colony that were settled by New Englanders in the early 1760s, what he referred to as "a people ... call'd Allinites."[13] "In general," he pointed out, "they are as deluded a people as ever I saw." He went on to observe: "They are most all Speakers in Publick. I was conversing with one of their head Speakers. She told me she thought death would Slay more Sins for her than ever was before. And as for Sin, said she, it Can not hurt one. No Not Adultery, Murder, Swearing, drunkenness, nor no other Sin Can break that Union between me and Christ. They have judged and passed sentence on me, as no Christian, Nor Call'd to Preach."[14] It is noteworthy that the shrewd and perceptive Garrettson underlined the key role played by the female "head speaker" in the movement. Garrettson also pointed out that the radical New Lights believed that they could "tell whether a person is a Christian at first sight" and that they were absolutely "sure of heaven as if they were already there, for sin cannot hurt them."[15]

Two Anglican ministers, the Reverend Jacob Bailey and Bishop Charles Inglis, also commented on what they regarded as the heretical views of some of Alline's more radical disciples and those of many of the New Lights. On 25 May 1789, the often acerbic Bailey wrote from Annapolis Royal that the New Light itinerants were creating "great confusion among the lower people" and were "of inconceivable damage to a new country, by drawing multitudes almost every day in the week, at this busy season, to attend to their desultory and absurd vociferations." Bailey went on: "These preachers, however, agree in rejecting the literal sense of the Holy Scriptures, and the Christian Ordinances. Their dependence is upon certain violent emotions, and they discourage industry, charity, and every social virtue, affirming that the most abandoned sinners are nearer to the Kingdom of heaven than people of a sober, honest and religious deportment, for such, they allege, are in danger of depending upon their own righteousness."[16] Bishop Inglis, a lapsed Methodist, endorsed Bailey's description and embellished it significantly, and in the process he emphasized the considerable influence that Alline's theology was still exerting on the Maritime evangelical mind a decade after his death in 1784. As far as Inglis was concerned, the New

Lights were "rigid Predestinarians" who believed "that all mankind were present, and actually sinned with our primitive parents." Inglis declared that "after conversion they are not answerable for any sins they commit, since it is the flesh and not the spirit which offends ... Many of them deny the resurrection, a future judgement, heaven and hell, though the Elect are to be happy and the Reprobates miserable after death. Their discipline is democratic. The right of ordination, dismission etc. lies entirely with the Brethren."[17]

A decade later, Joshua Marsden, a Methodist missionary in the border region between Nova Scotia and New Brunswick, noted that Alline's New Light–antinomian legacy was still being "industriously propagated ... by some new-light preachers." These men and women stressed four points:

1 "That a believer, though he sin ever so much is still pure; – God sees no sin in Israel."
2 "That the body of a believer only sins, and not the soul; as a nut thrown into the mud is only soiled in the shell, and not the kernel."
3 "That the body of a believer may get intoxicated and commit whoredom, but not the soul; that being spiritual is not affected by such fleshy lusts."
4 "That a sheep though he render himself filthy by going into the mud, and black, by rubbing against the stumps of burned trees, is a sheep still, as nobody ever heard of a sheep becoming a goat.[18]

Some might argue that a few key New Dispensationalist male leaders, such as Edward Manning, his brother James, and Joseph Dimock, had abandoned New Dispensationalism by the mid-1790s for two major reasons. First, they wanted to be settled ministers of the gospel, and they realized that antinomianism anarchy would undermine their leadership in the burgeoning New Light and Baptist congregations. To assert their power and control they therefore espoused Calvinist order and Baptist closed membership. Secondly, the evidence seems to suggest that by the middle of the last decade of the eighteenth century, some very gifted young male preachers, including the Mannings, Joseph Dimock, and Thomas Handley Chipman (all of whom considered themselves disciples of Henry Alline), were becoming increasingly concerned about the growing influence of such women as Lydia Randall, Sarah Bancroft, the Blair sisters of Onslow, Charlotte Prescott of Chester, and Betsy Parker of Nictaux.[19] In order to assert their male hegemony, the New Light men quickly marginalized their female competition, especially in the Annapolis Valley region stretching from Falmouth to Annapolis. In other New Light regions of Nova Scotia and New Brunswick, however, this male offensive faced opposition until at least the third decade of the nineteenth century. This, too, helps to explain the location and timing of the Babcock Tragedy.

The conservative reaction of the Mannings and their Baptist colleagues only highlights the radical character of the religion they opposed. By taking seriously the testimony from both proponents and opponents of the radical New Lights, we are in a position to begin a comparison with similar phenomena across the border in the new United States. It has been effectively argued that in the new United States "traditional structures of authority crumbled under the momentum of the Revolution, and common people increasingly discovered that they no longer had to accept the old distinctions," which had marginalized them into a widely perceived subservient and vulnerable status.[20] Gordon Wood, among others, has shown that during these years, popular evangelical Christianity seemed to be in a delicate state of spiritual tension, "poised like a steel spring by the contradicting forces pulling within it."[21] There was a spiritual quality, but there was also a secular quality; there was a populist bias but also an authoritarian bias; there was an emphasis on revelation but also an empirical tendency; and there was both a growing concern with individualism and a continuing obsession with the collectivity.

Nathan Hatch's *Democratization of American Christianity* expands our understanding of these powerful, conflicting forces that were first delineated by Gordon Wood in 1980. Hatch underlines the importance of the democratic impulse that permeated evangelical Christianity and transformed it according to the dictates of a new popular culture. This new evangelical culture, which fundamentally challenged élite orthodoxies and religious establishments, emphasized the vernacular in preaching and hymnody, and encouraged popular participation in religious rituals such as the camp meeting, the long communion, and believer's baptism. Popular evangelicalism questioned and even denigrated the values of the educated élite by defining cultural authority in terms of dramatic presentation and emotional persuasion, the hallmarks of the untutored and spirit-filled evangelical preacher. Ordinary folk were encouraged to place the emotional conversion experience on a much higher plane than either church membership or discipline. According to Hatch, "in this vast expanse of land" (the new United States) there emerged an individualistic, democratic American Christianity that was "audience centered, intellectually open to all, organizationally fragmented, and popularly led."[22]

Despite the fact that British North America, especially Nova Scotia, had rejected the American Revolution and American republicanism, a very good case can be made that in this even vaster expanse of land (the region that would become Canada), evangelicalism was more radical, more anarchistic, and more populist than its American counterpart. The Maritime brand of Allinite-Garrettsonian radical evangelicalism and the "Canada fire" of Wooster and Bangs certainly seem to lend credence to this contention. As noted above, unlike the new American evangelicalism, Canadian evangelicalism did not have to carry the baggage of civic humanism, republicanism, and the covenant ideal. Without these encumbrances, and avoiding the confusion created by "the interaction of conceptual 'languages,'"[23] Canadian evangelicalism was able to cut itself free from secular concerns – and this was the case for both men and women. Religious concerns were the only concerns; all other matters were, as Henry Alline once put it, "mere non-essentials."[24] When confronted by the world of "turnips, cabbages, and potatoes," is it surprising that the New Light followers of Alline's gospel chose instead the cosmic reality of the "One Eternal Now"?[25] And is it surprising that so many of the followers of Garrettson, Wooster, and Bangs were preoccupied with the blending of justification into sanctification to produce an ecstatic "oneness with Christ"?

It has recently been argued by Nancy Christie that "in both the Maritimes and the Canadas, popular evangelicalism was clearly dominant by 1812, with the New Lights, Baptists and Methodists clearly on the rise."[26] "Evangelical culture," according to Christie, "was recreating a social world in which spiritual authority was vested no longer in the outward man-made institutions of church and government, but in the inner spirituality of the individual resulting from the personal encounter between the converted and God."[27] At the core of this radical evangelical culture, especially in Maritime Canada, was what Anglican leaders such as Charles Inglis especially feared: "Not that 'the Evangelicals' might immediately incite political revolt or mob rule, but that the democratic spirituality of the evangelical ethos might unleash upon the embryonic society a host of newly assertive individuals."[28]

Throughout the 1790s, Bishop Inglis of Nova Scotia was absolutely certain that the New Lights, whether Congregational, Methodist, or Baptist, were "engaged in the general plan of a *total revolution in religious and civil government*."[29] "Ignorant men and women and even children under twelve years of age," he once reported, "were employed to pray and exhort, until the whole assembly groaned, and screamed, and finally ended with a falling down and rolling upon the floor of both sexes together." If this was not enough, "they added Dreams, Visions, Recitations, Prophecies and Trances."[30] Since his disconcerting tenure, during the revolution, as a Loyalist Anglican priest in New York (where he had seen the transformation of what he spitefully called "religious enthusiasts" into republican revolutionaries), Inglis, like other Anglican leaders of central Canada, had been concerned about the ways in which evangelical Christianity "dissolved" all forms of government and destroyed "all order and decorum."[31] Inglis's thesis, which underscored what he considered to be the disconcerting radical nature of Maritime evangelicalism, was enthusiastically endorsed by the scores of Anglican ministers in the region who regularly reported to their bishop about the state of religion in their communities. Evangelical anarchy, buttressed by the prevailing "democratic spirituality of the evangelical ethos," seemed to be the rule rather than the exception as Methodist, Baptist, and Congregational New Lights "undertook to prophesy, and to speak with new tongues, and to work miracles."[32] Various travellers deplored the "effects of fanaticism on the human mind" and the practice, especially along the Saint John River in New Brunswick, of scores of ecstatic worshippers "bawl[ing]" and "roar[ing]" out praise to the Almighty as they "went crawling about like wild beasts with others riding on their backs."[33]

Anglican critics of the New Lights, whether proto-Baptists, Methodists, or Congregationalists, even contrasted the "wild extravagances" they observed in Nova Scotia, New Brunswick, and the Canadas with the relative decorum of religious worship in neighbouring New England and New York. In drawing this contrast, the Anglicans and other critics of Maritime and central Canadian evangelicalism found themselves enjoying the enthusiastic endorsement of some of their New Light enemies. At least three former New Dispensationalist leaders who were to become influential leaders of the Maritime Baptist Church – James and Edward Manning and Joseph Dimock – visited New England and New York in the 1790s. The Mannings were a disruptive force in northern Maine, attacking all the ministers they met as anti-Christian hirelings; they did everything they could to persuade their hundreds of listeners to abandon "lifeless" versions of Christianity for the Maritime version of the true New Light truth.[34] The Mannings held that Maine Christianity and American republicanism had merged to produce an evil antithesis to the pristine Christianity that they preached and lived.

The Mannings' critique of American evangelicalism and all it represented was also expressed by Joseph Dimock. According to Dimock,

American audiences found him "so Disagreeable ... they can scarcely put up with it."[35] Confronting opposition, because of his "incorrect" preaching,[36] and often lacking "the inlargedness of ideas and freedom of speech" that he always experienced in Nova Scotia, Dimock was eager to return to "the people of thy choice" in his native province.[37] Dimock had found "the same God" in the United States as he worshipped in Nova Scotia. But he observed, "Still I find none that seem to have the life of God so pure in the soul as in Nova Scotia," and he concluded: "Much of the life and the power of religion here in the United States seem to withdraw and forms one constituted in the room thereof."[38] As has already been pointed out, similar comments were made by Methodist itinerants from New York after they had spent some time in Upper Canada. According to these men, the "Canada fire" burned with a far purer and more intense flame than anything they had experienced in the United States. They had no reason to exaggerate; if anything, situational pressures impinging on them encouraged them to do exactly the opposite. But they could not "bear false witness" and thus commit the unforgivable sin of denouncing the Holy Spirit.

Of course, it is possible that the Mannings, Dimock, Bishop Inglis, Crazy Dow, Nathan Bangs, and the others, including a myriad of present-day scholars, were, for a variety of reasons, distorting the uniqueness of Maritime and Upper Canadian radical evangelicalism. But how does one effectively explain away both the words and the actions of the influential American Methodist leader Francis Asbury? By the late 1790s, Asbury had become quite concerned about the questionable impact of the Maritime evangelical ethos on so many of his itinerants. He once observed that these young men returned to the United States "not so humble and serious as when they went."[39] Asbury was determined to do something about the New Light cancer, and he therefore decided not to send any more American Methodist itinerants to "Nova Scarcity" – shifting the responsibility to the Wesleyan leadership in Great Britain. One of the results of this decision was that the Maritime Methodists were quickly replaced at the leading edge of Protestantism in the region by the Baptist disciples of Henry Alline.[40] In Upper Canada, on the other hand, Methodism thrived because of the ministries of so many very gifted young American itinerants.

Another interesting critique of the Maritime evangelical ethos was expressed in print and privately by four Massachusetts Baptist ministers who visited the region in the first decade of the nineteenth century. Isaac Case, Daniel Merrill, Henry Hale, and Amos Allen were all disturbed by the New Light excesses that they witnessed in

New Brunswick and Nova Scotia.[41] They criticized openly and, sometimes, vociferously the religious anarchy that many Maritimers
equated with "spirit-filled worship," and they were determined to do
everything in their power to impose on the religious revivals which
accompanied their frequent visits a firm Calvinist Baptist organizational form – one that they eagerly appropriated from Massachusetts.
Despite their energetic efforts at organizational control, it was not
until the late 1820s and the 1830s that an effective Baptist denomination began to emerge in the region. The Maritime New Light
legacy, in short, could not be easily contained in standard New England organizational forms.

This argument about Canadian New Light revivalism and radical
evangelicalism may still be criticized for implicitly suggesting, as
Professor Tom Vincent has recently put it, that Henry Alline was the
"mystical, larger-than-life, proto-Baptist who could leap tall Anglicans and Methodists at a single bound, a veritable Paul Bunyan of
revival enthusiasm."[42] But even if Alline is pushed into the dark
oblivion of late-eighteenth-century Maritime historiography and
even if his religious legacy is perceived as nothing more than Bay of
Fundy fog, there is still more evidence to support the contention that
the Maritime and central Canadian evangelical ethos was, in most
respects, more radical, more populist, and more individualistic than
its New England or New York counterpart. How else can one explain
the remarkable career of the Reverend Jonathan Scott, Alline's most
perceptive Nova Scotia critic? Ordained a Congregational minister
in 1772, Scott remained in the Yarmouth region until 1794, when
he moved to Maine, where he died in 1819. In Nova Scotia in the
1780s, Scott was viewed as an Old Light – an ardent anti-Allinite.
But as soon as he started to preach in Maine, he was widely regarded
as a New Light – an evangelist who could even coax revivals into
existence.[43] Yet Scott did not change between 1793 and 1794; he
merely changed environments.

The essential question is how the two environments actually dif-
fered. Did the American environment of Massachusetts-Maine, for
example, encourage a certain religious style while that of neighbouring New Brunswick and Nova Scotia or Upper Canada encouraged a radically different one? Fresh research now makes it possible,
for the first time, to compare the different ways in which northern
Massachusetts and Nova Scotia developed generally in the period
1760–1820 and, more specifically, in the 1770s, 1780s, and 1790s.
In her ground-breaking comparative history, Elizabeth Mancke con-
tends that the two towns of Machias, Maine, and Liverpool, Nova
Scotia, although both settled by New Englanders in the early 1760s,

were "through experiences in two political systems, transformed into two distinct cultures."[44] Mancke shows that in Nova Scotia, unlike New England, towns as political entities actually ceased to exist. The Nova Scotia Yankees – who provided the core of the radical evangelical movement – had to be satisfied with two political privileges: "they could elect a representative" for the Halifax assembly, and "they could meet annually to levy a poor rate." "Beyond these privileges," Mancke points out, "a township's inhabitants had no political identity, as did their counterparts in New England, who elected town officers, levied taxes for town services, and could meet to discuss local, colonial, state or national issues."[45] The absence of effective local government and a dependence on Halifax and London naturally stunted political and ideological development in Nova Scotia. But the absence of an effective form of town government was responsible for far more, especially in the realm of religion. As Mancke puts it, the "divergent patterns in the collapse of Calvinist Congregationalism in Liverpool and Machias, and Nova Scotia and Maine, were not caused by significant differences in the impact of the forces of dissolution but rather by differences in the forces for maintaining cohesion and containing dissent."[46]

In New England, both before and after the revolution, the churches were very much supported by town governments and by legislative assemblies and, at times, by the courts. In Nova Scotia, on the other hand, the virtual elimination of town government had removed "a crucial source of local power for maintaining religious cohesion among Congregationalists and for channeling dissent into appropriate forms."[47] (It should also be pointed out that real local government did not exist in Upper Canada in the interwar years.) The differing political systems in the two regions "had the greatest impact on the course of the decline of Congregationalism, the social response to religious dissent, and the emergence of new sects."[48] For religious life at the local level in Yankee Nova Scotia, "difficulties were resolved by removing all group compulsion and allowing individuals complete freedom of choice." In other words, in Nova Scotia there was no "intermediate stage during which people could endow incorporated private religious societies with taxing rights buttressed by the government."[49] Ironically, in Nova Scotia greater individual rights characterized society, while in New England communalism still exerted a powerful influence. This individualism, fostered by a powerful localism devoid of the societal cohesion provided by town government, democratized Christianity and largely depoliticized religion. In New England, the First Great Awakening may have prepared the way for the American Revolution and for American republicanism and democracy. In Nova Scotia and New Brunswick, the emerging evangelical ethos, without the restraints imposed by an established Congregational Church, absorbed a powerful individualistic impulse and often stretched this well beyond the existing New England boundaries of even extreme religious behaviour.

In what is now Canada, the post-revolutionary movement to democratize Christianity and depoliticize evangelicalism was, in many respects, merely a continuation of Maritime Canada's ideological response to the American Revolution. Most of the thousands of Yankees who had settled in what is now Nova Scotia and New Brunswick during the early 1760s did not share with their friends and relatives in New England what John Adams once referred to as "the radical change in the principles, opinions, sentiments and affections of the people."[50] For the Yankees and other residents of Nova Scotia, "resistance to revolution" showed that they viewed events and personalities through a pre-1760 ideological lens rather than one from after 1765 – thus, through a basically religious lens rather than a secular one.[51] Nova Scotia Yankees did not conform to the general American pattern of ideological development, because their form of government and the nature of their society, with its special religious bias, prevented the development of what some contemporaries described as the "general enlightenment" and *éclaircissement* of key sections of the population.[52]

Nova Scotia's unique response to the revolution was the colony's First Great Awakening. It was basically a religious response – an evangelical social movement connecting events in Nova Scotia in the 1770s and 1780s with the New England of the late 1730s and 1740s. Henry Alline, in particular, was able to perceive a special purpose for his fellow colonists in the midst of the confused revolutionary situation. But his message was completely devoid of republican content, though it was truly revolutionary in its implications. The religious revival that swept Nova Scotia during the American Revolution was not merely "a retreat from the grim realities of the world to the safety and pleasantly exciting warmth of the revival meeting" and "to profits and rewards of another character."[53] Nor was it basically a revolt of the out-settlements against Halifax, the capital, or an irrational outburst against all forms of traditionalism and authority. The First Great Awakening of Nova Scotia may be viewed as an attempt by many Yankee inhabitants to appropriate a new sense of identity and a renewed sense of purpose. Religious enthusiasm in this context, a social movement of profound consequence in the Nova Scotian situation, was symptomatic of a collective identity crisis as well as a searching for an acceptable and meaningful ideology.

Resolution of the crisis came not only when the individuals were absorbed into what they felt was a dynamic fellowship of true believers but also when they accepted Alline's analysis of contemporary events and his conviction that their colony was indeed the centre of a crucial cosmic struggle.

The meaning of the unusual conjunction of events – of civil war in New England and an outpouring of the Holy Spirit in Nova Scotia – was obvious to Alline and the thousands who flocked to hear him. God was passing New England's historical mantle of Christian leadership to British Canada. In the world view of New Englanders fighting for the revolutionary cause, Old England was corrupt and the Americans were engaged in a righteous and noble cause. There was, therefore, some purpose to the hostilities. But to Alline, this "inhuman war" had no such meaning. Rather, along with all the other signs of the times, the Revolutionary War could indicate only one thing – that the entire Christian world, apart from British North America, was abandoning the way of God.

Alline's radical evangelicalism, as we have already seen, appealed to thousands of Nova Scotians and other Maritimers during and after the American Revolution. This radical evangelicalism had much more in common with the New England of the early 1740s than the New England of the 1780s and 1790s. It was a gospel that energized religious individualism and denigrated political solutions – whether radical or reactionary. This New Light legacy was to become the evangelical norm in much of post-revolutionary British North America. It also, of course, became the norm for the hundreds of black Loyalist Nova Scotians, who in the late 1780s and early 1790s were also affected by Allinite antinomianism.[54]

This is not to argue that some regions of New England, in particular, did not also experience outbursts of antinomianism, or "Christian primitivism," in the 1790s and the first decade of the nineteenth century.[55] But these outbursts may have owed a great deal (as Stephen Marini has suggested concerning the New Light Stir of 1778–1781) to events and personalities in New Brunswick and Nova Scotia.[56] Even so, even the Maine version of New Light antinomianism, taking everything into account, was somewhat more muted than the Maritime version; moreover, it was regarded by insiders and outsiders alike as being far more marginal. The Congregational Church and the Calvinist Baptists were far more successful in Maine than in the Maritimes in limiting the spread of Christian New Light primitivism. Moreover, much of radical evangelicalism in Maine was politicized and then channelled into what Allan Taylor has described as the "white Indians."[57] The influence of the Liberty Men and their republican/evangelical strategy in Maine demonstrated graphically not only the almost exaggerated religiosity of Maritime Christian New Light primitivism but also a fundamental distinction between the two societies.

Only in Halifax was the Anglican and governmental élite able to stem the tide of the radical New Light evangelicalism in the 1780s and 1790s. Effective use of the urban mob and the British army and navy prevented preachers such as Henry Alline, William Black, and Freeborn Garrettson from making significant inroads in the religious life of the community. In the Yankee out-settlements of the colony and even in much of Loyalist New Brunswick, however, the governing élite failed in its infrequent and futile attempts to impose British and Anglican order on an increasingly individualistic and radical evangelicalism. There was a similar tendency in Upper Canada, where most of the rural Yankee inhabitants (some 60 per cent of the population in 1810, it should be remembered) had succeeded in pushing Anglican order and decorum into the narrow confines of the region around York (present-day Toronto) and the commercial and military centre of Kingston. In an ironic twist of historical development, at the time the War of 1812 broke out, British and Anglican "peace, order and good Government" in Upper Canada and the Maritimes had been decisively defeated – not by American "life, liberty and the pursuit of happiness" but by the powerful forces unleashed by radical *and Canadian* evangelicalism. The War of 1812, along with the powerful forces of anti-Americanism and the pro-British feelings it unleashed, significantly affected central Canadian evangelicalism, in particular, and significantly constricted the broad spectrum of permissible belief and practice. But it should be emphasized that these forces did not succeed in completely eradicating radical evangelicalism from the central Canadian Protestant experience; and in the Maritimes, the War of 1812 had a negligible influence on the religious culture of the region.

In August 1824, nineteen years after the Babcock Tragedy and thirty years after Lydia Randall's antinomian movement had peaked, a final outburst of female protest took place not far from Henry Alline's home. A disconcerted Edward Manning described what happened at his regular Sunday morning service:

No sooner was I seated than a young Woman whom I know not, screamed out (from the gallery) and a number below, all females, a melancholy sound to me, because I thought there was such an extravagancy of Voice, and such uncommon gesticulations, leaving their seats, running round the broad [a]isle, swinging their Arms, bowing their Heads to the Ground, Stretching

their hands out right and left, then stretching them up as high as they could
while the head was bowed to the floor almost ... The young woman up in
the gallery came directly to me with an awfully dis-Figured face, screeching
verry loud, indeed calling me brother, O my brother O my brother! until
she was exhausted and then she turned away.[58]

This manifestation of what Manning referred to as Allinism must
have compelled the Maritimes' leading Calvinist Baptist minister to
remember ruefully his own enthusiastic involvement with New Dispensationalism three decades earlier. So much had changed with
him; yet so little had changed with respect to the disruptive power
of radical evangelicalism.

It may be argued that, unencumbered by the heavy burdens
imposed by American republicanism, Canadian radical evangelicalism was the religious equivalent of radical American republicanism. Almost despite itself, Canadian radical evangelicalism
"challenged the primary assumptions and practices" of British-
ordered society, "its hierarchy, its inequality, its devotion to kinship,
its patriarchy, its patronage, and its dependency." Canadian radical
evangelicalism offered, among other things, "new conceptions of the
individual, the family," and the community, and the bonds connecting
all three. In particular, it empowered women by stressing true
equality in the sight of God. In a profound sense, radical evangelicalism, whether in Nova Scotia or Upper Canada, and whether in
the 1790s or the first decade of the nineteenth century, "dissolved
the older and traditional ways of looking at reality" and presented
hitherto confined and disoriented men and women "with alternative
kinds of attachments" and "new sorts of social relationships" to balance the burgeoning individualism.[59]

Propelled by extraordinary demographic and economic developments in the interwar years, radical evangelicalism enabled thousands
of British North Americans to be "freed from customary connections
and made independent in new, unexpected ways."[60] According to
Gordon Wood:

In the decades following the Revolution, American society was transformed.
By every measure there was a sudden bursting forth, an explosion – not only
of geographical movement but of entrepreneurial energy, of religious passion,
and of pecuniary desires. Perhaps no country in the Western World has ever
undergone such massive changes in such a short period of time. The Revolution resembled the breaking of the dam, releasing thousands upon
thousands of pent-up pressures. There had been seepage and flows before
the Revolution, but suddenly it was as if the whole traditional structure,

enfeebled and brittle to begin with, broke apart, and people and their energies were set loose in an unprecedented outburst.[61]

British North America also, of course, experienced the breaking of the dam; but religious passion was, for the "ordinary" pioneers and planters, the essential, throbbing, thrusting stream of reality. For them, republicanism, pecuniary desires, and entrepreneurialism were worldly temptations provided by the devil and were to be assiduously avoided at all costs. They were battling for the Lord against "all principalities and powers" and all temptations. Their Christianity was to be uncontaminated by the world, even the promise of secular equality – what Herman Melville once referred to as "the great God absolute. The center and circumference of all democracy."[62]

From the vantage point of secular America in the late eighteenth and early nineteenth centuries, republican democracy unleashed by the revolution was truly radical. However, when viewed through a lens ground by the harsh realities of frontier life in British North America, it was Canadian radical evangelicalism that was the truly radical movement, since it dealt with the ultimate existential questions. In the context of the United States in the late eighteenth century and the late twentieth century, the American Revolution may indeed have been revolutionary – transforming American society. In the context of British North America in the late eighteenth and early nineteenth centuries, however, it may be argued that much of Canadian evangelicalism was just as revolutionary and populist a social movement – and perhaps even more so.

PART THREE

The Evangelical Rituals: Camp Meetings, Believer's Baptism, and the Long Communion

INTRODUCTION

Ecstatic conversionism and pulsating revivalism were not the only defining characteristics of radical evangelicalism in British North America during the period preceding the War of 1812. Radical evangelicals and their more moderate evangelical counterparts also experienced and expressed their intense religiosity by means of three amazingly popular Protestant rituals – the Methodist camp meeting, the Baptists' believer's baptism, and the Presbyterian long communion. Each of these rituals underscored the importance of community worship and individual commitment. Moreover, each took full advantage of the widespread rank-and-file belief in a form of peasant magic and mystery and a deep-rooted need for ritualized worship. Each also was uniquely shaped by the wilderness frontier environment, and each successfully anchored the cosmic in the rural reality of what is now Canada.

An empathetic descriptive analysis of these three Protestant rituals will, it is hoped, throw more light on how ordinary Canadian radical evangelicals and moderate evangelicals actually experienced their faith and expressed it in a ritual setting. Here is another opportunity to try to understand evangelicalism from the bottom up, and also from the top down – from the perspective of the ministers involved in the rituals. The contrast drawn between the camp meeting and believer's baptism, on the one hand, and the long communion, on the other, will help to underscore some of the basic differences distinguishing radical evangelicals from the more moderate evangelicals.

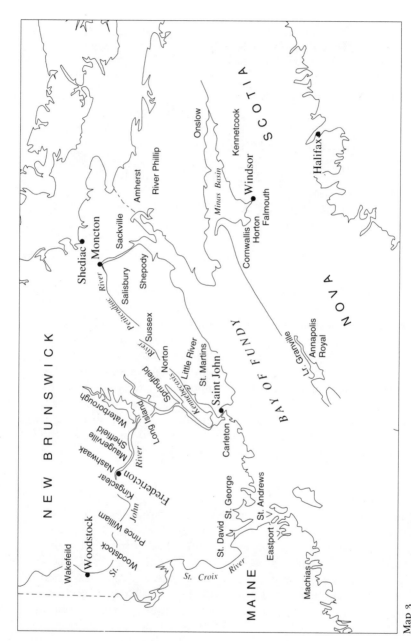

Map 3
The Rage for Dipping: New Brunswick and Nova Scotia in 1800

9 "A Powerful Means of Awakening and Converting Souls": The Hay Bay Camp Meeting, September 1805

At the 1805 annual conference of the New York Methodist Episcopal Church, William Case and Henry Ryan were appointed to the Bay of Quinte circuit, located near Kingston, in present-day Ontario. At this conference, these two young itinerants met Nathan Bangs and the other Methodist preachers from Upper Canada. Case and Ryan had already attended at least one camp meeting in New York and were eager to transplant the new instrument and religious ritual of Methodist evangelism in the fertile religious soil of British North America. They were certain that in the Wooster heartland, the Bay of Quinte region, there would be, as an immediate result of the first camp meeting, "a mighty display of ... awakening and converting," accompanied by the "sanctifying grace of God."[1] It did not take the two young men long to persuade Bangs that a camp meeting should take place sometime in late September. In Ryan and Case, Bangs discovered two very able Methodist itinerants – young men almost as gifted as himself. The three would make a formidable team, though in 1805 they all obviously regarded Bangs as the leader.

William Case was born in Massachusetts in 1780 and was converted to radical evangelical Methodism in 1803. His brother Isaac was to become a famous Maine Baptist itinerant who frequently visited New Brunswick and Nova Scotia and played an important role in bringing about the Second Great Awakening in the region.[2] Two years after his conversion, William Case was admitted on trial as an itinerant preacher by the New York Conference of the Methodist Episcopal Church. His first assignment, it is interesting to note, was to the Bay

William Case, 1780–1855
The United Church of Canada/Victoria University Archives, Toronto

of Quinte circuit. In the late summer of 1805, Case was twenty-five years old. He was rather short and in "every way well-proportioned," possessing a "pleasant ... countenance ... an air of solemnity," and a wonderful, melodious voice. "A thoughtful reader and student" in his youth, Case was, from the beginning of his itinerating career, an "assiduous and ardent preacher" who "first spell bound and then melted his auditors."[3] Often he would rush into his congregation, "shaking hands and speaking a word to each, perhaps throwing his arms around the necks of the young men, and entreating them with tears to give their hearts to God."[4]

As well as being a very successful Upper Canadian Methodist itinerant, Case was a committed missionary to the Mississauga Indians. His death in 1855, in Upper Canada, not only marked the end of a distinguished preaching career but also, in the words of his most recent biographer, "the end of the first phase of Canadian Methodism which was characterized largely by simple evangelical preaching and an intense determination to bring the gospel to every settlement in Upper Canada."[5] A woman who knew Case well during the pre-1812 period described him as "a very mild man," in order "to contradistinguish him from the great majority of Methodist preachers of that day, who were in general very boisterous."[6] One of the most boisterous of these preachers was, without contradiction, Henry Ryan.

Ryan was born in Massachusetts in 1775, of Irish Roman Catholic parentage. Sometime in the 1790s the former pugilist had become an enthusiastic Methodist convert. In 1800 he "was received on trial" by the Conference of the New York Methodist Church, and after serving on circuits in Vermont and New York he volunteered in 1805 to go, with William Case, to the Bay of Quinte circuit.[7] Ryan was the kind of "bold, energetic,"[8] giant of a man who was bound to become a legend in any frontier community. According to one contemporary, he was over six feet in height, "of large, symmetrical proportions, with prodigious muscular developments, and without doubt one of the strongest men of his age." His voice "excelled, for power and compass," noted a contemporary, "all that I ever heard from human organs."[9] "His energy, determination and pugnacity," his most recent biographer has contended, "were commensurate with his physical characteristics."[10] Ryan, it is clear, was not a person who turned the other cheek. When ruffians attempted to intimidate Methodist worshippers, he simply grabbed the offenders and threw them out of the building or "over the enclosures of the Camp grounds."[11]

A close friend, Elijah Hedding, described Ryan as "a brave Irishman – a man who laboured as if the judgment thunders were to follow 'his' every sermon."[12] His best-known and much-discussed exhortation, which he yelled out at the end of his usual hellfire and brimstone sermon, was "Drive on, brother! drive on! Drive the devil out of the country! Drive him into the lake and drown him."[13] A powerful and emotional preacher whom some described as spellbinding, Ryan soon became a "vigorous albeit overbearing"[14] Upper Canadian Methodist administrator. His abrasive personality and his attachment to the American variant of Methodism resulted in 1828 in a major denominational split, with the creation of his Canadian Wesleyan Methodist Church. Ryan died in Upper Canada in 1833, largely a spent force and a mere shadow of his earlier larger-than-life Methodist persona.[15]

In the summer of 1805, Ryan, Case, and Bangs made their way from the New York Conference to eastern Upper Canada. Even before their arrival east of Kingston, Bangs had apparently informed the Bay of Quinte Methodists and adherents that a camp meeting was being planned for the last weekend in September in the Adolphustown area, "where the first Methodist class of the province was organized in 1790 ... and its first Methodist chapel erected in 1792," and also where the Wooster "Canada fire" had first been ignited in 1797.[16] The choice of the actual location of the camp meeting, "on the land of Peter Huff on the shore of Hay Bay,"[17] not far from the Methodist Chapel, was pregnant with meaning. First, as the historian of religion Mircea Eliade stresses, when the infinite sacred actually thrusts itself into the finite world, a fixed point – a sacred/secular centre – is created. The truly religious person wants desperately "to be in the presence of the sacred, to live in that cosmic centre," even if this means a pilgrimage to potentially holy places "imbued with the power of the sacred."[18] Here, in the frontier region of Upper Canada, Methodist pilgrims attending their first camp meeting would be not only at the "cosmic centre" but also in spiritual fellowship with other potentially holy people, whose presence significantly added to the intense, collective sacred quality of the occasion. The Wooster heartland, it must be stressed, was regarded as a special Methodist holy place, where the Holy Spirit had once been powerfully active and where it was hoped she would return in late September 1805 with even greater transforming power. The Hay Bay Camp Meeting may, with some justification, be viewed as an Upper Canadian Methodist pilgrimage – a Protestant ritual of collective renewal and revitalization whose extraordinary appeal could be traced all the way back to European popular piety in pre-Reformation times.

There was a second and much more mundane reason for selecting Peter Huff's property – its geographical location. The farm was readily accessible "for waggons and foot passengers" as well as for those coming "in boats from up the Bay."[19] Furthermore, the Bay of Quinte circuit was the largest in the colony, with 510 members, and the contiguous Oswegotchie circuit was third largest, with 457.[20] There was, in other words, a large and available audience for the camp meeting, especially when one takes into account the one-to-eight ratio mentioned earlier. The holy place was there to attract the hundreds of pious Methodist pilgrims and the hundreds of merely curious frontier settlers who had heard about the strange and amazing occurrences in 1801 at Cane Ridge in Kentucky, where approximately 25,000 people had attended the memorable camp meeting.[21]

The extraordinary success of Cane Ridge and other camp meetings was the third reason for the Hay Bay Camp Meeting. Ryan and Case knew from personal experience what remarkable occurrences could actually take place at camp meetings, and Bangs very much wanted to be part of this "spirit-soaked" movement. He wrote with deep disappointment about having missed Cane Ridge, where "hundreds of hearers would fall as dead men to the earth under a single sermon" and where the "extraordinary scenes called the 'jerks' began." The "jerks," according to Bangs, were

rapid, jerking contortions, which seemed to be always the effect, direct or indirect, of religious causes, yet affected not only the religious, but often the most irreligious minds. Violent opposers were sometimes seized by them; men with imprecations upon their lips were suddenly smitten with them. Drunkards, attempting to drown the effect by liquors, could not hold the bottle to their lips; their convulsed arms would drop it, or shiver [shatter] it against the surrounding trees. Horsemen, charging in upon the meetings to disperse them, were arrested by the strange affection at the very boundaries of the worshipping circles, and were the more violently shaken the more they endeavored to resist the inexplicable power.[22]

The potential excitement triggered by a similar camp meeting at Hay Bay appealed to Bangs and his two Methodist companions, who were eager to try new and successful evangelistic techniques. The possibilities of actually seeing and experiencing phenomena like those that occurred at Cane Ridge proved compellingly attractive to the rural residents of eastern Upper Canada too. Would the "jerks" take place at Hay Bay? And would the Upper Canadian opponents of revivalism be unable to penetrate "the very boundaries of the worshipping circles" – the seemingly miraculous boundaries that protected the Hay Bay "cosmic centre"?

The Hay Bay Camp Meeting may be looked at in a variety of ways: as a Protestant ritual, as a manifestation of wild frontier religion, or as an example of an emerging sense of Upper Canadian community. Moreover, it can be looked at from within or from without and from the top down or the bottom up. The challenge is to combine a number of these approaches in order to throw a penetrating shaft of light on this memorable occasion. It is possible to use Nathan Bangs as a lens through which to see the Hay Bay Camp Meeting from a leadership perspective. His manuscript journal of the event begs such an approach.[23] It is also possible to try to understand the response of some of the participants in order to attempt to come to grips with the background, motivation, and experience of the many ordinary men and women who actually attended the meeting and were permanently branded by the experience.

Bangs was still only twenty-seven years old in September 1805 – already a well-known Upper Canadian Methodist itinerant with an impeccable and impressive record of evangelistic success. But he was also looking for new spiritual worlds to conquer, having virtually exhausted the potential of the one-day evangelistic enterprise. "Agreeable to appointment," Bangs began his manuscript account, "our Camp-Meeting began ... on the 27th of Sep. 1805 at 1:00 [P.M.] ... in an open field" on the Huff property. At the centre of the large open field, "a stage was erected and about 10 and 12 rods from this stage the tents were pitched in a direct line forming a right-angle." It was estimated that at Friday noon "there were about 250 people on the ground." The first worship service "was introduced with singing and prayer, "and a short sermon was preached by William Case on the text "Brethren pray." Despite "a number of Exhortations" following the sermon, there was "little movement among the People." After a hastily called "intermission of 20 minutes," Bangs stepped forward on the jerry-built stage platform and began to preach a sermon on "Christ our Wisdom, Righteousness, Sanctification and Redemption." The sermon and the accompanying exhortations began to have some impact on the audience sitting on the hastily constructed log benches – men on one side and the women on the other – "and the spirit of the Lord began to move on the minds of the people."

After a supper "intermission of one hour and a half," a special "prayer meeting was held by the whole congregation at the Stage." On their knees, as the sun began to set, they were bombarded by an exhortation by "one of the preachers" and then they began to pray again. Sometimes one person would pray, and at other times there would be a cacophony of prayers as the men and women competed for the Almighty's notice. As a result of this bombardment of prayer, "the power of God descended upon the Camp which soon raised songs of praise to God for salvation found." The intense and loud praying continued until ten o'clock, when yet another sermon was preached. Then, after a series of emotional exhortations, "a solemn awe rested upon our minds whilst the spirit of God prayerfully operated upon our hearts." At midnight "the majority," but certainly not all the participants, reluctantly "retired to their tents." The night had been "clear and serene," and the pine torches "glowing among the trees and above the tents" added an almost sensual atmosphere to the occasion as the "voice of prayer and praise mingl[ed] and ascended into the star-lit night."[24]

At five on Saturday morning, a "prayer meeting was held again at the stage and continued till eight"; then there was a sermon, followed by more exhortations. After a brief respite for lunch, Henry Ryan was given his first opportunity to address the growing audience, speaking on the text "My People are Destroyed from Lack of Knowledge." Soon after the sermon began, as Ryan directed his powerful voice at specific people in the congregation, "God made bare his potent arm." According to an amazed Bangs, "The Windows of heaven were opened and the bursting power of God descended upon the congregation in such an awful manner that it raised a general outcry among the People." All the preachers immediately "descended from the Stage and ran among the crowd exhorting the impenitent, comforting the distressed and encouraging the faithful, calling out Man and brethren help."

Leading the preachers in their offensive into the sobbing congregation was Nathan Bangs. During the Ryan sermon, Bangs had, he reported,

felt an unusual sense of the divine presence, and thought I could see a cloud of divine glory resting upon the congregation. The circle of spectators unconsciously fell back, step by step, until quite a space was opened between them and those who were seated. At length I sprung from my seat to my feet. The preacher [Ryan] stopped and said, "Take it and go on?" "No," I replied, "I rise not to preach." I immediately descended from the stand among the hearers; the rest of the preachers all spontaneously followed me, and we went among the people, exhorting the impenitent and comforting the distressed; for while Christians were filled with "joy unspeakable and full of glory," many a sinner was weeping and praying in the surrounding crowd.

Then Bangs went on:

These we collected together in little groups, and exhorted God's people to join in prayer for them, and not to leave them until he should save their souls. O what a scene of tears and prayer was this! I suppose that not less than a dozen little praying circles were thus formed in the course of a few minutes. It was truly affecting to see parents weeping over their children, neighbours exhorting their unconverted neighbours to repent, while all, old and young, were awe-struck. The wicked looked on with silent amazement while they beheld some of their companions struck down by the mighty power of God, and heard his people pray for them.[25]

In another version – the first unrevised version – of the Saturday events at Hay Bay, Bangs wrote:

The people of God were chiefly in a bunch by themselves when the camp took fire and the wicked formed a circle about where they stood with astonishment to see the exercise, whilst many of them were constrained to cry aloud for mercy. As soon as any were wounded by the spirit of God, they were immediately surrounded by a group of men and women who were earnestly engaged with God for their deliverance and such faith had they that five were left before they were enabled to sing the song of Redeeming Love. It might now be said of truth, the God of the Hebrews is come into the camp, for the noise was heard afar off. The groans and cries of the wounded, the shouts of the delivered, the prayers of the faithful, the Exhortations of the courageous penetrated the very heavens and reverberated through the neighbourhood.[26]

"This exercise," Bangs noted, "continued till about sunset," when a sermon was preached on "Behold He cometh with clouds." The sermon and the exhortations that followed it pumped life into an exhausted congregation, and "the exercise ran into a prayer meeting which continued all night without intermission." The intense public preaching and exhorting and the private witnessing and praying resulted in five conversions, "2 Backsliders reclaimed and 25 Sanctified." Many others, of course, were significantly strengthened in their already firm Christian commitment; others, the "unconverted," found themselves, almost despite themselves, beginning to ask embarrassing questions about the "state of their souls."

The description of the "circling" of the believers and the distancing of the so-called wicked is indeed fascinating. For many of the participants, the forces of righteousness were evidently battling the minions of the devil on holy ground – on sacred space. Both sides seemed to understand the cosmic power of boundary maintenance. Once on holy ground, conversion was possible; outside the circle, there was only eternal damnation; and to move from one area to another was in itself a powerful religious statement, a statement clearly understood by the participants.

Sunrise on Sunday, 29 September, witnessed still further "exhilarating Streams of divine light" that "illuminated our souls and the drops of Jesus's love gladdened our hearts." After breakfast, with an audience now estimated at 2,500, the Methodist "love-feast" began. "The interest and excitement were so great and the crowd so large," Bangs noted, that it was impossible to impose good Methodist lovefeast order on the people. "The impression of the Word," according to Bangs, "was universal, the power of the Spirit was manifest throughout the whole encampment, and almost every tent was a scene of prayer."[27] At noon, the Lord's Supper was administered. "We ranged the People," Bangs reported, "in a square body together and after the bread and water, the powers of God and man spoke feelingly and powerfully of the goodness of God, to their souls especially since they had assembled in that place." The "prayers of the faithful were so loud and incessant around the stage" during and just after communion "that preaching would not be heard." The people's prayers had overwhelmed the preacher's sermon. Consequently, Bangs made his way to a wagon situated at the edge of the large group of Methodists who were noisily praying, and there he began to preach on the text "Yea doubtless and I count all things but loss for the Excellency of the knowledge of Jesus Christ my Lord." Almost immediately "the noise ceased," and soon Ryan was able to begin to preach from the stand on the text "Many are called but few are chosen." Once again, Ryan's leather-lunged preaching triggered a wild outburst, as men, women, and children began "running to and fro, and from place to place to see what was doing," recorded Bangs, "for I suppose they saw stranger things today" than yesterday.

Bangs's description of the conversion of two young women who were sisters and a little boy "just after sacrament" – during what he called "this awful period" – captured something of the unforgettable excitement of the afternoon:

A young woman of high rank was struck by the power of God, and her sister seeing her weeping, came and took her away by force from the multitude. Some of the daughters of Jerusalem seeing the daughters of Pride running away with one of Christ's lambs, pursued after them, retook the brokenhearted sinner, and brought her back. The wolf who stole away the lamb, followed back and was soon shot with an arrow from the Almighty, which constrained her to roar aloud for mercy, and it was not long before God heard her cry and changed her furious nature into the lamblike nature of Christ. Anon the retaken captive was enabled to say the Lord has become my salvation therefore will I praise you.[28]

At about the same time as this furious Manichaean struggle was taking place between the "daughters of Jerusalem" and the "daughters of pride," a "little boy of 11 years old was struck under conviction in the camp, and converted on the spot." Bangs actually "saw them carry him away to the tent whilst his tongue was employed in lifting forth the praises of his Redeemer."

What is particularly striking about these conversion accounts, especially those concerning the young women, is the fact that they blend the spiritual and physical to such a remarkable degree. The young women are dragged this way and that way – to and away from the "sacred space" – by the representatives of God and the devil. A cosmic and a spiritual battle was thus incarnated on earth – in eastern Upper Canada – so that all who were there at Hay Bay could clearly see the sometimes violent struggle between the powers of light and those of darkness.

There was an even more remarkable incident that afternoon, one involving a Methodist "backslider who had become a maniac, and was in despair."[29] His symptoms were amazingly like those of the New Testament demoniac. "His distress was so great" that "he was delirious," thinking he had in some way "sinned against the Holy Ghost." Whenever a prayer was offered up on his behalf, he "would struggle with all his might to get away," often breaking away from a number of men who were pinning him to the ground near the stage on what he knew was sacred space. "The wicked Children of the Devil" (the men on the outskirts of the camp meeting) were "enraged" because the young man had been dragged into the inner circle. They "would have taken him away with violence" had not Bangs and his associates, including the muscular and pugilistic Ryan, "formed a ring around him 3 or 6 deep in order to keep them off." Here again the ring, or circle, was used in a spiritual and physical sense – as a barrier to protect a person against the forces of evil. Bangs and Ryan led the other believers in beseeching "God for Christ's sake to restore him to his right mind which was done." A miracle, they were certain, had occurred. The young man was at last able to "pray for himself, and tho he did not immediately obtain his faith of assurance, yet he was delivered from despair, and before the meeting broke up obtained the peace of God to his soul."

Sunday night was a night that would never be forgotten by those at Hay Bay, especially Nathan Bangs. As he looked around the camp site, seeing "the sable curtain of night" spreading "her dark mantle over us," Bangs experienced "an indescribable sense of the divine presence."[30] Overwhelmed by the physical beauty of the Upper Canadian environment, he felt a powerful urge to preach, circled as he was by "a number of soldiers of Christ with their hearts and voices raised in prayer" for the salvation of their fellows. "Others with streaming eyes and hearts uplifted to heaven while their bodies lay prostrate on the ground" were "chanting aloud the praises of Immanuel." "The Power of God descended" on Bangs "in such a manner that his shouts pierced the heavens; while his body was sustained by some of his friends." While, like the Old Testament prophet Joshua, he stretched out his arms, "as if to bless the weeping multitude, they stiffened and remained extended, and for some time he stood thus addressing the hearers, weeping with them that wept."[31] He was then "carried out of the camp into a tent where he lay speechless being overwhelmed for a considerable time with the mighty – Power of God."

Five days after the "glorious time" at the camp meeting, Bangs was able to describe, with a little more distance, "such an operation upon me as I never before felt." He wrote that late on Sunday night:

[I] felt a spark of Divine power come upon me and I immediately lifted up my voice in Exhortation but was soon so filled that I was held by some of my friends whilst I shouted forth the praises of my dear redeemer. I was carried out of the Camp and it seemed that my body was benumbed with the praises of God. I tried to speak but my lips and tongue was stiff. I was then laid in the tent where the blessing of the Lord seemed to circulate all through my body as well as soul. I lay there overwhelmed for some time until the Glory of God filled the tent ... O what love did I feel for souls. I wanted to take them in my arms. The dear children of God seemed as my heartstrings and I am sure I would have laid down my life for them if it would have done them any good. I have felt the divine flame ever since running through my soul which makes all within me rejoice.

Soon after being carried to the tent, Bangs discovered that it was "soon crowded," and when he finally chanted "a single utterance" through his "stiff lips," the entire group "fell to the ground."[32] This was the occasion for "the work of the Lord" to run "like fire in a dry stable until 10:00 next morning." With the lighting of the new version of the "Canada fire," Bangs discovered that his arms were "now immediately released." He first felt "a prickling sensation over the whole body, like that felt when a limb is said to be asleep; but this was followed by a soft, soothing feeling, as if," he stated, "I were anointed with oil, and such consciousness of the presence and peace of God pervaded me as I cannot describe."[33]

Bangs had never felt closer to his fellow Methodist Christians than he did on that long Sunday night and Monday morning. Nor had he ever felt as intimately close to his Saviour, Jesus Christ, who seemed to be an integral part of his very being. The Holy Spirit had infused Bangs with divine perfection, and the experience was mystical, intense, and unforgettably ecstatic. The Hay Bay Camp Meeting had added another level of spiritual intensity to the Wooster-inspired Upper-Canadian variant of Methodist sanctification; and other Methodists at Hay Bay were to share something of Bangs's "heaven on earth."

By noon on Monday, 30 September, most of the approximately 2,500 Upper Canadians who had come to the Hay Bay Camp Meeting had left for their homes, some of which lay more than fifty miles away. Bangs, Ryan, Case, and the other Methodist preachers who remained behind found it virtually impossible to leave. A shared common intense religious experience bound them together and seemed to glue them to what they were now convinced was indeed holy ground. As they gathered together for the last time, an unnamed "local Elder," who "had been an instrument in converting many souls" in Upper Canada, began "to feel the happy effects of ... the oil of God's grace still continuing to circulate through our hearts." As the elder experienced the power of the Holy Spirit, he was quickly surrounded by Ryan, Case, Bangs, and the others who

with their hands clasped around each others necks, tears streaming from many of their eyes, and hearts uplifted to God, broke out in such expressions of gratitude to God, and love one to another, while the presence of him who fulfills all in all filled our hearts with raptures of Divine Joy ... whilst our souls were thus expanded and filled with the pure stream of the Water of Life, we seemed to be absent from the body and present with the Lord, enlisting that pure and perennial bliss where the saints of the most high shall Eternally bask in the bright beams of the smiling countenance of God ... Surely heaven smiled at this hour and we doubt not but if the curtain had been drawn aside we should have beheld a multitude of the heavenly Host – praising God and saying Glory, honour, praise, and power be unto God and the Lamb forever whose loving spirit inspires such reciprocal love in the souls of men.[34]

In this concluding sentence of the description in his manuscript journal of the actual events of the Hay Bay Camp Meeting, Bangs perceptively underscored what the meeting had meant to many of the participants. What seemed so obvious to him was the Holy Spirit's real and actual presence, which "inspired" the "reciprocal love," which in turn created a powerful sense of Christian *communitas*. Never before had the Christian believers and seekers experienced in Upper Canada such an intense collective feeling of oneness in Christ and fellowship with one another. The individualism fostered by the frontier had been replaced by an almost exaggerated sense of community shaped by shared beliefs and shared religious experiences. They had actually felt the transforming power of the Holy Spirit, and this ecstatic moment of religious reality was something they shared with their fellows and something that was further energized by the unleashed power of "reciprocal love." It was a love without boundaries and limits – at least, in sacred space – a love that reached out in all directions, touching family members, neighbours, and even strangers for what seemed to be both a fragile moment and eternity.

When Bangs reluctantly left Hay Bay on 30 September, he remembered his feelings and those of his ministerial colleagues. They were pleased with the "sum total" results of the camp meeting: "30 Justified, 28 Backsliders reclaimed and 39 Sanctified 97 in all." But they were also obviously exhilarated by the total camp-meeting experience: "The hour came that we must part but even after we had been about 3 days and nights upon the ground and taken very little sleep and rest, yet there seemed to be an unwillingness ... to leave the spot. And even after we started we cast a longing, lingering look behind feeling a regret at evacuating the place where God had so recently blessed us and given us such a Signal Victory over our Enemies."[35] "The spot" was indeed a sacred place and would remain so for decades – for Bangs, Ryan, and hundreds of other Upper Canadians who had been there, including perhaps a woman very much like an anonymous one referred to in the writings of the Upper Canadian Methodist itinerant, Elijah Woolsey.[36]

According to Woolsey, the woman – let us call her Alida Allen Munroe – had been born in the extreme western part of Massachusetts in the midst of the Seven Years' War. Her parents were Congregationalists of the Old Light variety, considering New Light revivalism to be a particularly virulent form of pernicious, divisive religious enthusiasm. Alida attended church regularly, and as the only child in the family she was the apple of her parents' eyes. The family farm was fairly prosperous, but not escessively so. The Allens were solidly respectable, but they found themselves in the early 1770s increasingly alienated in their community as American Patriot resistance was suddenly transformed into revolution. The Allens were suspicious of Patriot motives, seeing no good reason why the old Anglo-American connection should be severed. The year of the Quebec Act, 1774, witnessed Alida's marriage to James Munroe, a close family friend who shared her father's increasingly pro-British and what would later be called Loyalist views. Although they were married by her minister, neither Alida nor James was a member of the church. James was not really outwardly irreligious, merely indifferent to all things religious; but he was widely regarded as a good provider, owning a large, prosperous farm and having a thriving cooper's trade.

Like other young women in her new community, Alida took very little interest in the polarization of political life in Massachusetts and the other insurgent colonies. She knew, of course, that her father and James were vociferously opposed to the Patriots and were committed to George III and all he represented. They believed in the need for order and stability in society – a need more than satisfied, in their view, by the British constitution. And they were increasingly fearful of the political and social disruptions unleashed by the growing Patriot preoccupation with liberty, freedom, and equality. Even before the Declaration of American Independence on 4 July 1776, both James and Alida's father had resolved to join the British side in what to them was an unnecessary civil war. Eventually, the two men made their way to Quebec, where in 1777 they became part of General Burgoyne's unsuccessful military expedition southwards to eradicate, once and for all, the Patriot threat to British "peace, order and good government."

Life was not easy for Alida once her husband joined the British side. She had two young children with her, and it seemed to her that as soon as James had made his decision, Patriot scavengers suddenly descended on the farm, taking away everything of value. Although Alida tried to cope, she found herself increasingly alienated in a bitterly hostile environment. As her sense of alienation intensified, she became increasingly critical of her husband's decision to abandon her and the children and battle for the obviously insane George III. Moreover, it bothered Alida that James had not written to her once since his departure.

Alida's neighbours – at least, those who still talked to her – tried to persuade her that James was dead and that she should cut her ties to him and to Loyalism by marrying a good Patriot man. How else was she going to look after her growing family? She began to have visits from a "young man," William White, who "having a desire to make her his wife, and finding that he could not have access to her without using deception, forged a letter in the name of her father, stating that her husband was dead."[37] On receiving this letter, Alida "dressed in mourning"; and after "a suitable time," William White proposed marriage and Alida reluctantly accepted. She felt extremely vulnerable in the midst of the American Revolution as a single mother with close Loyalist connections, and she hoped that marriage would provide security for herself and the two children as well as giving her some much-coveted companionship. But she knew, deep in her heart, that she would have to work hard to learn to love her new husband. Elijah Woolsey, who knew Alida well, described simply and graphically what happened to her at the end of the Revolutionary War:

After the end of the war the husband [James] came home; but before he arrived he heard that his wife was married to another man, and that she had heard that he was dead. He then concluded that she had been deceived, and that he would go and see her. She had never heard from him until he came in at the door. She recognized him as soon as she saw him. She was rocking the cradle at the time, in which lay an infant which she had by the man that had married her in her husband's absence.[38]

As might be expected, Alida "was very much frightened" when she saw James Munroe, but he urged the disoriented, confused, and guilty young woman "not to be frightened" and to direct him immediately "to the father of her child." Thus, James Munroe, husband of Alida Munroe, soon confronted William White, husband of Alida White. James introduced himself to William "by telling him his name." He then pointed to Alida and shouted, "That is *my* wife." An angry William White replied, "No, she is *my* wife." An even angrier James Munroe retorted, "She is my *wife*, and you have deceived her, and since she has been *deceived*, if she is willing to go with me, I shall never reflect on her." James then turned to Alida and said, "I have nothing but my blanket, and my knapsack," whereupon Alida blurted out, "I will go ... I will go with you, James back to Canada." A furious William White, on being unmasked as an "imposter" and "deceiver," then turned on Alida and, using the last weapon in his verbal arsenal declared, "You must go with only your clothes," and you will "not have the babe." Alida found it very difficult to utter her final few words to William White, but she bravely stated, "I will go with only the clothes on my back." She "left the babe in the cradle, and took her other two children with her" and sadly departed for British territory with James Munroe.[39]

The family actually walked all the way to Upper Canada, where James received for his loyalty "two hundred acres of land for himself, fifty for his wife, and two hundred for his children, and two years' provision with farming utensils." The Munroe grant was situated on the St Lawrence River somewhat to the east of Kingston. When they first arrived to take possession of "their bounty," the Munroes were confronted by a thick forest of trees. Like other Loyalist pioneers, James "cut down the trees, and rolled the logs together, and built a hut for his family, and afterwards a house etc." Eventually, Alida's daughter by her second husband ran away from Massachusetts and "came to [her mother] and introduced herself, and was received joyfully by all the family."[40]

Sometime in the 1790s, probably during the Wooster-inspired Canada-fire revival, Alida became a convert to Methodism, experiencing a life-transforming New Birth. She remembered declaring to her friends and neighbours: "I love God, and God loves me, I love Jesus and Jesus loves me: I love the Christians and the Christians love me: I love everybody and everybody loves me."[41] Although converted, Alida apparently found it impossible, "despite the Canada fire," to experience sanctification. She tried over and over again, but the Holy Spirit seemed carefully to avoid her, leaving her spiritually listless and devoid of her earlier witnessing zeal. Nevertheless, she continued to attend class meetings, and her home became a place where the Methodists itinerants usually visited and where they often spoke to thirty or more eager listeners.[42] Meanwhile, her husband gradually became more sympathetic to things religious, and by the time of the Hay Bay Camp Meeting her three children had "embraced religion and were ornaments to the cause."[43]

It is not known if the Munroe family actually attended this camp meeting. What is certain is that news of Hay Bay "excited great interest far and near."[44] Some people, perhaps even the Munroes, sailed or rowed to the Bay of Quinte, taking with them their entire families and even a few neighbours. They had heard about the "extraordinary display of the favour and power of God,"[45] especially at Cane Ridge, and like hundreds of other Methodists in eastern Upper Canada, they expected these same "extraordinary displays" to occur on British territory too. It is clear that many women hoped that the camp meeting would be the heaven-sent opportunity for them to experience sanctification. Many prayed that their husbands' fragile faith would be substantially reawakened and revived and would be transformed into real conversion. After pitching their tents a little distance from the stage and the semicircle of log benches, families like the Munroes made their way to the noon meeting on Saturday, 28 September 1805. As they took their places at the beginning of the meeting, the women and children sat on one side, the men and older boys on the other.[46]

Most of those present on that Saturday could look around and see the hundreds who were worshipping with them and the hundreds beyond the ring of tents who were spectators. They heard the huge, handsome, imposing preacher, Henry Ryan, yell out his text from the platform for all to hear: "My people are destroyed from lack of knowledge." Ryan's emotion-charged words seemed particularly aimed at his audience, especially when he suddenly bent over and looked directly at them and screamed, "You must get into God" and "You'll only get into God" when the "devil yes the devil be scared right out of you, and then right out of this field, right into Lake Ontario."[47] A woman on one of the front benches found herself in tears, as "the bursting power of God descended upon her." Not only was she sobbing uncontrollably, but she had fallen off the bench and was writhing about on the ground. It was as though someone had shot her. As she cried and yelled and kicked her legs and raised her arms to the heavens, she felt the steady hand of Nathan Bangs on her head, comforting her, encouraging her, and demanding with Christlike authority that all the remaining evil be removed and be replaced by the sanctifying power of the Holy Spirit.

Bangs was joined by others – by the women who surrounded her, and by some of the preachers – as they all tried to help in the healing of this woman, who had obviously been "wounded by the spirit of God." The young woman felt a fierce struggle taking place somewhere at the very centre of her being; and as the struggle raged, she continued to yell and sob, and to writhe on the ground. Then there was almost a magical peace; she stopped moving; her sobbing ended and her lips were miraculously sealed. She was certain that she felt God within her and that all her sin had been carved out by the power of the Holy Spirit. She felt boldly ecstatic and slowly pulled herself from the ground, hugged those gathered around her, including Bangs; and then she felt a deep inner compulsion to witness to her new state of holiness.

This woman had never exhorted before; she had never spoken to a group larger than her family. But she knew that the Holy Spirit had emboldened her, equipping her to do the Lord's special work, at a special place, at a special time. Her exhortation was one of many that, according to Bangs, "penetrated the very heavens and

reverberated through the neighbourhood."[48] The woman did not
return to her tent until sunrise on Sunday morning. Although physically exhausted, she was spiritually exhilarated and was unable to
sleep. She exhorted her drowsy and confused husband to emulate
her in climbing to the mountain peak of Methodist spirituality, but
despite her loud entreaties, which were punctuated by sobbing, her
husband could not respond in the way she was convinced he had to.
Feeling rebuffed, she went without her husband to attend the "love-
feast" and the communion. At both of these celebrations she felt
blissfully intimate with her Saviour. But Ryan's preaching on the text
"Many are called but few are chosen" once again shattered her composure, and she burst into tears and jumped from her log pew,
running wildly "from place to place," exhorting all who could hear
her to "flee the wrath to come."[49] She was probably one of the
"daughters of Jerusalem" described in Bangs's account of the camp
meeting. Clearly, she loved being involved in this cosmic drama that
was being played out on the shore of Lake Ontario. She witnessed
the furious struggle between the "wicked children of the devil" and
the "forces of righteousness" over the soul of the "pathetic demoniac,"
and her shouts and prayers supported those advocates of "the Spirit
of Adoption."

After nightfall, this unnamed woman fell to the ground exhausted,
shouting aloud "the praises of Immanuel." As she did so, she was
joined by other women, who embraced her, stroked her hair, cried
over her, and repeated over and over again, almost like an incanta-
tion, "the Holy Spirit is in you – God loves you – and we love you."
She thought she had never felt as close to any group of people –
including her husband and her children. She saw Jesus Christ in her
new friends, women so much like herself, and she therefore loved
them unconditionally and intensely. There was no sleep for her on
Sunday evening; there was only prolonged spiritual ecstasy – an
extraordinary and intense experience of collapsed time, which made
all other sensory experiences inconsequential. She did not want to
leave Hay Bay on Monday morning. She wanted to stay there for
ever, recapturing every rapturous spiritual moment; she wanted to
stay there because she had been free at last to be herself – to speak,
to exhort, to pray, and to be the equal of any man in a society
permeated by patriarchy. She had, she was convinced, been empowered by the mighty "power of God" to be a special instrument for
(as one of the preachers put it) "Christ our wisdom, righteousness,
sanctification and redemption."[50] She felt certain that she was now
an absolutely "new creature in Christ," and this certainty was shared

with the many other men and women who had been particularly blessed at the Hay Bay Camp Meeting.

Very little is known about people like this woman. Most Canadian religious history is written from the top down, from the vantage point of such people as Nathan Bangs rather than Alida Munroe or Barbara Smith. At Hay Bay, in September 1805, the leader and the follower met; the so-called articulate minority confronted the so-called inarticulate majority. Their experiences, their actions, at each point of the meeting, coincided and were one because this was what radical evangelicalism was. It was the essential resonance created by intense Christians who were seeking, in all their frailty, to be more like their Saviour, Jesus Christ.

10 The Rage for Dipping: Joseph Crandall, Elijah Estabrooks, and Believer's Baptism, 1795–1800

The "rage for dipping,"[1] or what has recently been called the Baptist Reformation,[2] which affected much of Nova Scotia and New Bruns-wick at the turn of the eighteenth century, was not simply a carefully orchestrated policy implemented by recently minted Baptist ministers who were determined to impose their unique kind of hegemonic order over a deeply divided popular and radical evangelical move-ment. Most of the so-called Maritime Baptist patriarchs in the 1790s – men such as Harris Harding, James and Edward Manning, Thomas Handley Chipman, Theodore Seth Harding, and Joseph Dimock – were in fact extremely reluctant Baptists. Their fear of the excesses unleashed by antinomianism, as well as their growing preoccupation with respectability, prestige, and order unquestionably moved some of the patriarchs from a radical New Light position to a more or less Massachusetts Calvinist evangelical Baptist position. But these men, it should be kept in mind, could have followed their former friend and close associate John Payzant into New Light Congregationalism in order to avoid antinomian anarchy. But they must have suspected that if they had done so, few of the growing number of radical evangelicals would have followed them. These former Allinites would have been shepherds with no sheep to look after. The patriarchs may have briefly considered Methodism, but here too they confronted the very real possibility that few of their followers would even have considered coming along with them. Thus, the Baptist patriarchs became more or less ardent Baptists largely because they were com-pelled to do so in order to survive as ministers, when faced with the remarkable popular movement that swept through the Yankee heart-land of Nova Scotia and the Chignecto-Shepody region of New Brunswick and the Saint John River Valley in the late eighteenth century and the early years of the nineteenth. This powerful social and religious movement created an intense and widespread demand for "believer's baptism."

How does one account for what Bishop Charles Inglis spitefully referred to in 1800 as an almost irrational obsession with "total immersion" in Yankee regions of Nova Scotia?[3] According to Professor David Bell, it was yet another manifestation of the radical evangelical concern with religious and spiritual innovation. "Baptism by immersion," according to Bell, "was just the latest phase of a whole generation of religious novelties that had begun with Alline himself."[4] Yet this explanation begs a further question: why this particular novelty? Why not "speaking in tongues" or "divine healing" or "intense sanctification"? There were some outbreaks of "glossolalia" in 1793 in New Brunswick and also in Nova Scotia (both a little earlier and a little later). Surely, in the context of the 1790s, speaking in tongues was as innovative a practice, if not more radically innovative, than believer's baptism by immersion? Both believer's baptism and glossolalia were, of course, marvellous examples of Christian primitivism – an emphasis on the return to the pristine purity of apostolic Christianity. Furthermore, Christian primitivism was a powerful force at work in late-eighteenth-century Maritime Canada as well as in central Canada. Believer's baptism, however, unlike other primitivist practices endorsed by the New Testament, was a ritual permeated not only by religious meaning but also by folk belief and by a sense of almost medieval magic. It was also a ritual which, like the camp meeting, was energized from the bottom up and could be so effectively controlled from the top down.

One must never underestimate what Mary Douglas has perceptively referred to as a universal belief in "the revivifying role of water in religious symbolism."[5] According to Mircea Eliade:

In water everything is "dissolved," every "form" is broken up, everything that has happened ceases to exist; nothing that was before remains after immersion in water, not an outline, not a "sign," not an event. Immersion is the equivalent, at the human level, of death at the cosmic level, of the cataclysm (the Flood) which periodically dissolves the world into the primeval ocean. Breaking up all the forms, doing away with the past, water possesses this power of purifying, of regenerating, of giving new birth ... Water purifies and regenerates because it nullifies the past, and restores – even only for a moment – the integrity of the dawn of things.[6]

Believer's baptism by immersion was, among other things, a purity ritual that helped both create and consolidate "a sense of community shaped by an intense public experience."[7] This new community was (in theory), because of the purifying power of believer's baptism, "a new society which would be free, unbounded and without coercion or contradiction."[8] Maritime Baptists could never forget Paul's letter to the Galatians (Galatians 3:28): "In being baptized into Christ, you have put on Christ: there can be neither Jew, nor Greek, neither bond nor free, neither male nor female, for you are all one in Christ Jesus." Moreover, believer's baptism was the means whereby thousands of Maritime evangelicals reversed the widespread Protestant "tendency to suppose that any ritual is empty form" and that "any external religion betrays true interior religion."[9] In believer's baptism, Maritime Baptists appropriated for themselves their own unique ritual, a ritual inspired by Jesus Christ and the New Testament. It permitted them to gain control over their total universe, where the cosmic overlapped with the mundane world, and it also provided them with a divinely sanctioned framing function that enabled them, in a profound psychological sense, to "shut in desired themes or shut out intruding ones."[10] We are always trying to create boundaries for ourselves to help define who we are and who we are not. Believer's baptism, in a sense, sanctified the rejection of the world and the acceptance of Christ's salvation triggered by conversion. It was the outward and visible sign of the acceptance of "Christ as Saviour and Lord."

As the eighteenth century blurred into the nineteenth, an increasing number of Maritime radical evangelicals – particularly, of course, those who were to become Baptists – began to regard the moment of baptism as being as important or even more important than the actual instant of conversion. There is some fragmentary evidence suggesting that for some early Baptists there was such a thing as baptismal regeneration. Thus, for some new Baptist Christians, believer's baptism helped "frame" the precise moment when they "became new creatures in Christ."[11] The ritual encapsulated the entire conversion and sanctification process in public, not in private. But it was a ritual that only an ordained Baptist minister could administer. A lay baptism was worse than worthless; it was perceived to be both evil and anti-Christian.

In the pre-1812 period, there is, in the hundreds of pages of records available, not one instance of a Maritime layperson baptizing another layperson. Only an ordained Baptist minister, it should be stressed, could immerse a new convert. Some isolated converts in the Maritimes waited for months, and some for years, to be baptized by an itinerant Baptist preacher; others, including women in their eighties, were baptized by immersion in large holes cut out of the Saint John River ice in the middle of winter – because a Baptist minister was at last available. Why would men and women risk pneumonia or worse in order to be baptized by a visiting minister, often a stranger, at such an inconvenient time and in such horrendous circumstances? What factor or factors actualized into Maritime reality, at a specific time, a growing popular preoccupation with the Baptist ritual of purification and cleansing?

There was, it seems, at the popular grassroots level, whether in the Yankee heartland of Nova Scotia or the Saint John River Valley of Loyalist New Brunswick, a powerful primitive belief in the regenerative efficacy of believer's baptism. The Baptist minister, who administered the ritual to someone who had first publicly declared her or his conversion, was believed to possess special spiritual powers. In baptizing a believer in the name of the "Father, Son and Holy Spirit," the minister was not only obeying the command of Christ to "make disciples of all the nations baptizing them in the name of the Father and of the Son and of the Holy Spirit"; he was actually transforming the temporal into the cosmic by spiritually purifying the individual for eternity. In late-eighteenth-century New Brunswick and Nova Scotia, there was a growing popular belief (some would call it a primitive prejudice) that without both conversion and believer's baptism, one could not "enter the Kingdom of Heaven." Christ's words as captured by John 3:5 could not be easily forgotten: "Except a person be born of water and the spirit, the person cannot enter into the Kingdom of God." It is noteworthy that in this key verse, upon which the "doctrine of Baptismal Regeneration is usually rested,"[12] being immersed in water is explicitly referred to before being born of the spirit. But the question of why this popular belief swept certain regions of New Brunswick and Nova Scotia in the late eighteenth century is not necessarily answered in a satisfactory way by merely stressing either the extraordinary convergence, in many minds, of the New Light conversion experience and baptism by immersion or the primacy given to baptism by water over being born of the spirit.

What seemed to exacerbate the "rage for dipping" was a growing and widespread belief that the end of the world was imminent and that Jesus Christ would soon return to earth and gather into his presence only those who were indeed "born of water and the Spirit." At the turn of the century, many people seemed to devote inordinate time and attention to "listening intently for the 'Midnight Cry.'"[13] One of these people was Elijah Estabrooks, a New Brunswick New

Light, who in 1800 was baptized by immersion. We know that soon after his baptism in the Saint John River, Estabrooks

asked the patience of the people, till he communicated his thoughts of the near approach of the millennium day, when Christ will reign a thousand years. Mr. Estabrooks had spoken but a few minutes before his mind seemed to awake in possession of the glorious day. A divine spark catched in the hearts of Mr. [Theodore] Harding, Mr. [Joseph] Crandall, and some others, and increased to a mighty flame. One sang glory, glory, glory to God in the highest, and others hallelujah, hallelujah, amen, so let it be; indeed, sir, the people were overshadowed with power divine.[14]

Other New Lights in the Cornwallis region, a few years earlier, and in the eastern extremity of New Brunswick, a few years later, also emphasized the imminent return of Christ, especially as they looked forward to the coming of the new century and as they viewed the myriad and complex repercussions of both the French and American revolutions.[15] There was a powerful compulsion to return to the practices of the New Testament church in order to usher in the "End Times."

Another way to try and come to grips with something of the appeal and something of the socio-psychological substance of the "rage for dipping" is by looking at the purification ritual as a crucially important element in evolving Maritime popular and radical evangelicalism at the turn of the eighteenth century. This approach is a largely biographical one, an attempt to see and understand believer's baptism from the immediate vantage point of a Baptist minister, Joseph Crandall (1771–1858), and a person he actually baptized, Elijah Estabrooks (1756–1825). The biographical approach obviously is much more specific and explicit than the more general and theoretical approach. But the two together, when sensitively combined, may provide some convincing clues to the actual origins of the so-called Maritime Baptist Reformation.

According to Crandall's most recent biographer, the New Brunswick Baptist patriarch was, without question, "the most influential and venerated Baptist leader" in the colony "during the first years of the nineteenth century."[16] Yet it would be a serious mistake to argue, as I.E. Bill did in 1880, that "probably to him more than to any other single individual, this Province [New Brunswick] stands indebted for the diffusion of correct sentiments regarding the matter of civil and religious liberty."[17] As a politician in the New Brunswick Assembly from 1818 to 1824, Crandall accomplished virtually nothing and was certainly neither "a radical" at odds with the political

Joseph Crandall, 1771–1858
Acadia University

and religious establishment nor "a regional power broker."[18] His contemporaries knew him for what he was, a very successful Baptist evangelist – nothing more and nothing less.

Joseph Crandall was born in 1771 in Tiverton, Rhode Island.[19] While still a child, he accompanied his emigrating parents to Nova Scotia "the year before the American Revolution, and settled in Chester."[20] In his highly stylized autobiography, penned near the end of his life, Crandall described his being "called to the death bed" of his mother. He was "much alarmed," he wrote, "to see my beloved mother so pale and deathlike. She said to me 'that she had sent for me to hear her last farewell.' She said 'she was going to leave us all and go to her Saviour where she would be happy.' After some time she looked earnestly at me and said 'Joseph the Lord has a great work for you to do when I am dead and gone.'"[21] Well after the event, Crandall was absolutely certain that his mother had indeed been "under the influence of the Holy Spirit," and it is clear that her words haunted him for the rest of his life. Nor did he ever forget what his father told him soon after the latter had heard Henry Alline preach for the first time: "That this preacher Henry Alline was a 'New Light' and that the 'New Light' were the people of God for they were Christians and that none could go to Heaven unless they were converted."[22]

Despite the New Light commitment of his parents, and despite hearing New Light evangelistic sermons preached in Chester in the mid-1780s by Thomas Handley Chipman and Harris Harding, Crandall found that his "heart was hard and unmoved." He observed: "I thought at the time that the Lord had left me to perish in my sins and justly too for I was one of the greatest sinners on earth."[23] Disoriented because of the death of his parents, Crandall was keen to make a new start in life, and while still in his teens he made his way to Liverpool, where he "was employed … in Cod fishing." Finding himself "more hardened in sin and … often in despair," he soon returned to Chester. From there he went to Falmouth and then to Newport and "was engaged for a time in freighting lumber from Shubenacadie to Windsor."[24] In July 1795, the twenty-four-year-old Crandall attended a New Light "Sabbath morning" service in a private home in Onslow, where Harris Harding preached a memorable sermon. The disciple of Henry Alline had been "high" in Crandall's "esteem" since the "time of the reformation at Chester." The service was also attended by Joseph Dimock, who was at the time pastor of the Chester New Light Congregational Church. This was the occasion when Crandall at last experienced what Jack Bumsted has recently referred to as his almost stereotypical New Light "adult conversion experience."[25] Crandall described it in an evocative Allinite manner:

When I entered the house the glorious majesty of the Divine Being appeared to open before the eyes of my understanding (I beheld no object with my bodily eyes) and I saw myself justly condemned to endless misery. I saw no way of escape until suddenly a glorious light shone from the excellent Majesty and I saw the way of Salvation was Gods work and not mine. I felt as I had never felt before although among strangers. I could not hold my peace. My hard heart was at last broken and I had such a view of a perishing world lying in ruin as I never could express.[26]

Then, to the "great surprise of all present," an excited, agitated, and seemingly inspired Crandall "began to speak and try to tell" what he "felt and saw." It was an unforgettable experience:

My mind was completely absorbed in the solemn and marvellous scene. It appeared to me that the whole human race lay in open ruin and were altogether at the disposal of that Holy Being whose bright glory had so overwhelmed my soul. I saw mercy so connected with the justice of God that they were both one that what God had done in the person of Christ was alone sufficient to save all that came to God for mercy through Jesus Christ. I felt that the whole world ought to know what I felt and saw for indeed it appeared of more importance to me than the whole world.[27]

Words of testimony and exhortation, shaped by his parents' New Light faith and his own former "despair," poured out of the new convert's mouth "for more than an hour," since he could not hold his peace. To Crandall, his salvation involved the infusion of the Holy Spirit, which he described as "a stream of living water flowing into my soul and then bursting forth like a stream from an overflowing fountain." While Crandall was exhorting, he experienced the Almighty's powerful and unmistakable call to preach the gospel; it was a distinct call within a context of a "vision" or "scene," in which, as he noted, "The work of sinners lay before me like a broad field to which I could see no end."[28]

Crandall's totally unexpected hour-long exhortation amazed Dimock and Harding and moved them to uncontrollable "weeping," and many others in the crowded room found themselves weeping with them. Crandall remained in the Newport-Onslow region in the summer. "The *World* had no charms for me now," he noted. He discovered, much to his delight, that he "had no comfort" unless he was praying or exhorting, which he did "whenever opportunity offered." There were many such opportunities for Crandall in the Onslow region and then in his home town of Chester, to which he returned in the autumn. But by late autumn, Crandall was no longer satisfied with merely "praying and exhorting" after Dimock had preached the sermon; he, too, wanted to preach, rather than playing ministerial second-fiddle to another man, even his much-beloved pastor. Opposition to Crandall's becoming a minister – actually being ordained – was, as he put it, "like thorns to my soul." Then, towards the end of 1795, Crandall had a dream, one that was very much in the Allinite tradition and that also seems to have been influenced by the "world of wonders" inhabited by Harris Harding. Crandall, the former fisherman, experienced this "strange dream" late on a Saturday night or early on a Sunday morning. He described it as follows:

I was standing by a broad stream of smooth water thousands of men and women were floating down the stream in a standing position with their heads and shoulders above the water, they seemed quite unconscious of their danger. I watched them until they reached the cataract below when they suddenly disappeared. All below the rocky cataract was dense darkness. I also saw in the dream a man with a long pole and a bow on the end of it: He came to me and told me to wade in and save all the people I could. I thought in the dream that I did so and all that I could throw the bow over I led to a delightful bank covered with green grass and beautiful flowers and there they united in singing the praises of God in a delightful manner.[29]

While Crandall was "musing on this strange dream" early on the Sunday morning, "the 28th chapter of Matthew came to my mind," he noted, "and when I came to the two last verses I was struck with a great surprise."[30] The two verses contain the last words of the resurrected Christ to his disciples:

19 Go therefore and make disciples of all the nations, baptizing them in the name of the Father and of the Son and the Holy Spirit;
20 Teaching them to observe all things that I have commanded you; and lo, I am with you always, even to the end of the age.

When taken in its entirety, this dream (only part of which Crandall was willing to relate in his autobiography) compelled the New Light convert to view believer's baptism by immersion not as Alline and his followers still viewed it – as "a non-essential" – but as a ritual that was divinely ordained and absolutely essential. "Had I been present when John baptised the Saviour and stood on the bank of the Jordan and witnessed the whole scene," Crandall declared, "I could not have been more convinced." The Sunday morning "divine illumination" had, in a remarkable and unanticipated manner, driven away all the existing doubts that Crandall still had about his conversion and his calling. In addition, it had suddenly transformed him into an ardent advocate of believer's baptism. On "that same sabbath day," probably in late October or early November, after pressuring his pastor, Crandall was, as he put it, "buried with my Lord in a watery grave by Elder Joseph Dimock." This public baptism by immersion in the frigid waters of Chester Basin became the defining experiential religious moment for Crandall, who from that precise moment "never since had one doubt" about his "conversion nor mode of baptism."[31]

From Crandall's own account, there were three major reasons why he became a Baptist. First, his memorable dream, which he considered to be an amalgam of "divine impression" and "command," persuaded him that in order to save all the people he could, he would have to "wade" in the water, in a deep ritualistic sense. Second, the dream compelled him to see the urgency of Christ's command to go "and make disciples of all nations, baptizing them ... " It was obviously not enough to help convert people to evangelical or even New Light Christianity; conversion had to be followed by baptism by immersion, because this was what Christ commanded. Third, Crandall powerfully connected the believer's-baptism imperative of the last two verses of Matthew with Christ's own baptism in the Jordan River by John the Baptist. If baptism by immersion in the Jordan by John the Baptist was good enough for the Saviour, it was good enough for Joseph Crandall. The dream had enabled Crandall to see the Scriptures in a radically different manner and through a newly ground lens provided by the Holy Spirit. By November 1795, Crandall had his message and his empowering ritual – a ritual that had touched, it seemed, in almost every conceivable way, the innermost recesses of his being.

In late November 1795, Crandall accompanied his spiritual mentor, Harris Harding, to Liverpool, where the two men helped preach a religious revival into existence. Crandall then spent most of the next four years itinerating throughout Yankee Nova Scotia and the eastern corner of New Brunswick. Despite his 1795 obsession with the efficacy of believer's baptism, there is absolutely no mention of any of his converts being baptized by immersion in 1796, 1797, 1798, or even 1799, the year in which, on 8 October in Sackville, New Brunswick, he was finally ordained as a minister of the gospel. The timing of Crandall's ordination[32] is of critical importance in explaining why his preaching did not produce baptisms. Of course, he could not baptize any of his converts until he was properly ordained; Crandall knew this and so did the hundreds of Nova Scotians and New Brunswickers who flocked to hear his New Light evangelistic message. Moreover, his mentor in the faith, Harris Harding, was not baptized by immersion until 1799 – four years after Crandall. And even after his baptism, Harding still regarded the question of baptism in a strictly Allinite light – as a matter of little real consequence. What remained absolutely central for Harding, throughout the latter part of the eighteenth century and early years of the nineteenth, was the New Light conversion experience. Furthermore, despite his own baptism by immersion as early as 1787, Joseph Dimock, Crandall's pastor, did not consider the ritual to be of special significance until at least 1811; and even after that date, Dimock continued to place more stress on the centrality of the New Light–New Birth than he did on believer's baptism.[33]

Without ministerial support from his closest colleagues and friends for the gospel of "conversion-baptism," the twenty-seven-year-old Crandall had found himself, by late 1798, becoming increasingly dysfunctional. The mood of intense and disconcerting spiritual immobilization had been intensified by his recent marriage and his move to the Salisbury area of eastern New Brunswick, where he farmed "quite in the wilderness" and where his "troubles of mind became almost overwhelming." Two years earlier, in 1796, Crandall had already been having doubts: "There was a possibility that I had deceived myself, and if myself, then others." Beset by these "depressing fears," he resolved "to preach no more."[34] But it is clear that by early October 1799 these fears had disappeared. Crandall's ordination, even as minister of "a mixed church" (in which the immersed and the merely converted were members) was the means whereby he could both spread his gospel of believer's baptism and also implement it.

It was less than two months before Crandall's ordination that Harris Harding was finally baptized by immersion. The baptism was performed in Yarmouth by James Manning, who described it in the following manner: "At the time of the ordinance of baptism was administered the people looked as solemn as the grave. Mr. Harding's coming to the water seemed like Christ coming to Jordan. After he came from the water he prayed with the people in the street. It seemed as though he had a double portion of the Spirit. Some of the dear christians broke forth in praises to God and the Lamb."[35] The Harding baptism poured fuel on the revival fires that had begun to blaze down the Annapolis Valley in 1798. By 1800, this religious and social movement had become what David Bell has accurately described as the first distinctly Baptist reformation in Maritime history,[36] and it had spread to the Yarmouth region and to neighbouring New Brunswick. In the spring of 1798, the "mass immersions began under Thomas Chipman" in the Annapolis-Granville region. Within thirteen months, Chipman had "dipped 173 persons,"[37] and scores of others were baptized by immersion in Kings and Yarmouth counties.

By 1800, the Baptist Reformation had begun to concern Bishop Charles Inglis. According to Inglis, the new Baptists "formerly ... were Pedobaptists, but by a recent illumination, they have adopted the Anabaptist scheme, by which their number has been much increased and their zeal inflamed."[38] Inglis stressed the popular, almost populist, impulse within the new Baptist movement. And he knew from his local Anglican sources in "Annapolis, Granville, Wilmot and Aylesford," that this was indeed the case. The New Light ministers were themselves being swallowed up by what Inglis spitefully referred to as the "rage for dipping."[39] Inglis reported to his SPG superiors that this rage for dipping "or total immersion prevails all over the western counties of the Province, and is frequently performed in a very indelicate manner before vast collections of people. Several hundreds have already been baptized, and this plunging they deem to be absolutely necessary to the conversion of their souls." As has already been pointed out, Inglis explicitly connected the popular Baptist movement to what he called a "democratic ... general plan of total revolution in religion and civil government." "All order and decorum are despised by them," he railed. "Fierce dissentions prevail among the most intimate; family government is dissolved; children are neglected and become disobedient."[40]

Despite his somewhat exaggerated claims, there were flashes of shrewd insight to be found in Inglis's report. There was indeed a "rage for dipping" in the Yankee heartland of Nova Scotia in 1798 and 1799 – a rage not created by the Baptist patriarchs from above but forced on most of them from below. The Baptist Reformation had, of course, more than just religious implications. As Inglis realized, there was to be found in the ritual of cleansing a powerful democratic and egalitarian impulse. The disconcerting question that hovered over the Baptist Reformation – for some Anglicans, at least – was whether the "rage for dipping" would be channelled or deflected from the largely religious realm to that of the secular sphere. Most of the Baptists involved in the movement, however, considered the question to be an irrelevant one, since for them the religious realm was everything.

As Crandall itinerated throughout New Brunswick in the years after his ordination, he carried with him his own version of "total immersion," a version that owed virtually nothing to the Baptist

Reformation in southwestern Yankee Nova Scotia. In early January 1800, Crandall felt a call to preach the "true gospel" along "the River Saint John."[41] At this time, there was only one tiny Baptist church – Crandall's own – in the entire colony of New Brunswick, and only a handful of people had been immersed. Thus, out of the total New Brunswick population of approximately 20,000 inhabitants in 1800, fewer than fifty were Baptists.[42] Seventy-one years later, out of a total population of 285,594, some 70,595 (or 25 per cent) were Baptist – almost one-half of the Protestant population.[43] During the first six decades of the nineteenth century the religious life of New Brunswick had obviously been significantly affected by the Baptist Reformation – which might also be referred to, with good reason, as the Baptist Revolution.

Assisting in the transformation of Yankee New Lights into Nova Scotia Baptists was one thing; being part of the same complex transformation process in Loyalist New Brunswick – where demographic heterogeneity and not homogeneity was the norm – was a radically different thing, or so it would seem.[44] The 1798–1800 Baptist Reformation in Yankee Nova Scotia brought like-minded Yankees together by enabling them to continue "to regard themselves as a people with a unique history, a distinct identity, and a special destiny."[45] In New Brunswick, the Yankee element was of little numerical consequence; most of the population was of Loyalist background, a rough cross section of American colonial society before the revolution. These Loyalists shared little in common except a sense of defeat and despair. But in David Bell's view, this apparent obstacle had, in fact, become a Baptist advantage at the turn of the century. "Economically and demographically the colony was stagnant," he argued. "Politically," he continued, New Brunswick "was bitterly factionalized. Far from becoming the boasted 'envy of the American states,' New Brunswick was reduced to the status of a remote backwater in the empire's struggle against the revolutionary French. One symptom of this loss of hierarchical consensus is the fact that some Loyalists felt free to demonstrate that they had no more regard for the elite's Church of England than the Church had shown for them."[46] Consequently, according to Bell's very persuasive analysis, "the Loyalist frontier needed the social organization religion could provide, and Baptist preachers arrived at a time when many no longer feared taking a stand with religious dissent."[47] Bell could have also mentioned that the first Baptist itinerant to arrive in New Brunswick in the first decade of the nineteenth century was greeted by large numbers, Loyalists and Yankees alike, who needed little if any convincing to be immersed. They too were caught up in the "rage for dipping" – part of a complex tendency natural among neighbouring societies to borrow, despite the absence of explicit and direct contact, "cultural elements from one another freely."[48]

Joseph Crandall, in January 1800, was the human agent largely responsible for actualizing what may be regarded as the pro-Baptist process of cultural osmosis then affecting certain regions of New Brunswick. In January 1800, Crandall was twenty-eight, and according to Jarvis Ring, who met him at this time, he was "a seallator [slender] Lacky [lanky] man not clothed much like a minister."[49] His "voice," it was said, was especially "commanding, and his intonations at times peculiarly touching."[50] He was always an eager itinerant and saw in his first expedition an opportunity to spread his New Light–Baptist message up and down the Saint John River Valley. But he still wondered where his "path of duty lay."[51] In his autobiography, Crandall stated, "It was now midwinter and how to get there I could not tell but it seemed by going there was the only door of hope open to my troubled mind."[52]

What did Crandall really mean by this statement? Why was itinerating in the midst of winter in the Saint John River Valley his "only door of hope"? Why was Joseph the Baptist going to convert and baptize New Brunswickers, people with whom he had so little in common, at the time of the year when all the available rivers and lakes were covered with thick ice? And why was he again suffering from a "troubled mind" only months after his ordination? Was it because he felt himself to be hypocritical in that he was a minister of a church that "was organized on gospel grounds with the exception that unimmersed Christians might commune"?[53] He was obviously caught on the horns of a real dilemma. In order to baptize by immersion, he needed to be an ordained minister; and in order to be ordained by Edward Manning, Joseph Dimock, and T.S. Harding (the three ministers who had ordained him in October 1799), Crandall had to accept "mixed communion," a practice buttressed by the Allinite conviction that the form of baptism was not an "essential." How could Crandall resolve this dilemma without splitting his church and without being immobilized himself? He could not, but in good New Light and Allinite fashion, he could leave his problems behind, however temporarily, by itinerating far from home; and this is precisely what he decided to do in early 1800, at a most inappropriate time it seemed, especially for a Baptist itinerant.

Crandall finally arrived at his destination of Waterborough, on the Saint John River, "uninvited and unknown towards the middle of March."[54] On his journey to Waterborough by snowshoe and later by "a sleigh on the ice," Crandall preached frequently but apparently met only one person, a "Mrs. Case ... who had been immersed."[55] At Waterborough, where there was a small Allinite congregation led by "a very Godly man ... Elijah Eastabrooks," Crandall spent time with the members but not with Estabrooks who, he noted, "was absent during my visit."[56] Crandall felt that his preaching had helped the "spirit of the Lord" affect "the minds of the people" but that only "one or two ... found mercy."[57] Somewhat disappointed, he decided to strike out towards the west – to Kingsclear, a few miles beyond the colonial capital of Fredericton – an area where "Edward Manning had had his most spectacular success in 1793."[58] There Crandall seemed to discover a totally unanticipated pro-Baptist sentiment. "The Lord wrought wonders in ... Kingsclear," he recorded. "On the Lord's day a pious woman asked me how she could proceed in order to be immersed. I pointed out the way, and announced that sister Cole would be immersed at ten o'clock the next day at a certain place. Long before the hour arrived people came in from all directions for many miles around."[59] It is noteworthy that the initiative for a winter baptism by immersion definitely came from "sister Cole." Obviously, she had already experienced the New Birth, most likely under the Allinite preaching of Edward Manning in 1793. She now demanded "immersion," and it is clear that this was not forced upon her by a manipulative Crandall. He simply "pointed out the way." Moreover, the news about her imminent baptism spread quickly throughout the region, triggering an amazingly positive popular response. The novelty of the ritual of believer's baptism unquestionably drew many people, who were both fascinated and attracted by it.

"Four or five hundred people surrounded the watery grave" at ten in the morning, and what they saw left an indelible impression on their collective memory:

The ice being open the candidate related a clear experience and was immersed. When we came up out of the water, two men came forward and related what the Lord had done for their souls. We could not leave the water until fourteen happy converts were immersed in the same manner as our Saviour. Truly this was the Lord's work ... it was wonderful to see the young converts going around among the people they came out of the cold water praising the Lord and exhorting others to come and embrace the Saviour. Surely this was the beginning of good days, the work of the Lord spread in every direction. As they returned from the meeting they said the bible was altogether a new book to them.[60]

In his preaching and his dipping, Crandall had provided the Kingsclear area residents with a new pro-Baptist grid to apply to their reading of the New Testament, a grid that transformed the Bible into an "altogether ... new book." Thus, the divinely inspired Word of God, read by an increasingly literate population through divinely inspired Baptist eyes, enabled paedo-Baptists (whether Anglicans, Congregationalists, or Presbyterians) to become Baptists in a complex process that sanctified their primitive urge to be purified, thus blotting out a bleak and disconcerting past and also restoring a faith in the future, in both a local and a cosmic sense.

The Kingsclear baptisms are noteworthy because they were administered in icy waters. In immersing fourteen men and women, Crandall would have had to spend at least twenty minutes up to his waist in the frigid Saint John River. Each candidate would have had to walk over the slippery ice and then slowly descend into the water to stand near the minister. Neither person, of course, had special waterproof boots or clothes for the occasion. Once they were in place and their feet firmly on the flat bottom of the river, Crandall used his left hand to grasp the candidate's two hands that were clasped in prayer, while his right cupped the candidate's neck. Just before the immersion, Crandall shouted to the hundreds crowded along the shore, "I baptize you [and then he stated the name of the individual] in the name of the Father, the Son, and the Holy Ghost." The candidate would then fall slowly into the water, and Crandall would be careful to ensure that the person was completely immersed and that she or he was quickly lifted back into an upright position. There were a number of instances of people not being totally immersed who demanded to be rebaptized properly. Both minister and candidate probably then left the water, Crandall to get warm and dry – if only for a moment – and the candidate to put on dry clothes. The Kingsclear winter baptisms must have been both an exhilarating and physically debilitating experience for both baptizer and baptized. Moreover, the extraordinary conditions in which they were done must have added an almost ethereal quality to the occasion – a quality readily exaggerated, in a myriad of ways, as those present told others about the amazing event, both soon afterwards and then over and over again as the years passed.

Revitalized by the baptisms, Crandall moved up to present-day Woodstock "preaching and immersing believers."[61] Then, in late May, he returned to Waterborough. Because of heavy flooding in the region, he "could not see how the Lord's work could be carried forward just then as the people could not attend the meetings." However, Crandall had underestimated the power of the Saint John River Valley system of oral communication. Just when he "began to think it was about time ... to return home," he saw arriving from east and west "boats ... loaded with anxious inquirers asking about the reformation up the river for they had heard about such numbers being immersed." This unexpected intelligence had compelled "many ... to read their bibles and were prepared to yield obedience to the Lords commands." An astonished Crandall was quickly surrounded by scores of men and women, and soon "the Lords Work commenced and a number rejoiced in the Lord." "It was wonderful" for the visiting preacher "to see the aged, the middle aged, and the youths relating in the language of the Holy Scripture what the Lord had done for their souls." The revival fires were fanned by the enthusiasm and support of "Brother Elijah Estabrooks." Not only did Estabrooks support the revival preaching of Crandall, but the old Allinite also unequivocally accepted the Baptist immersionist argument. Within a few days "there were about thirty immersed," including Estabrooks and Zebulon Estey, hitherto a vociferous opponent of believer's baptism. Estey, according to Crandall, was "an old New England Congregationalist rooted and grounded in the old puritan practice of Infant sprinkling."

On first meeting Crandall, Estey had declared, "I see you are going to break up our church." Crandall replied, "Sir, if your church is built on Christ the gates of hell cannot prevail against it." Estey shot back, "Do you not call us a church of Christ?" To this, the New Light Baptist itinerant replied, "I consider you are a company of pious christians but not walking in the order of the gospel as commanded by Christ." A furious Estey turned his back on Crandall and spat back at him, "My parents had given me up to the Lord in infancy and from that I would not depart." But before Estey could leave, Crandall confidently declared "Squire, I have one word to say to you. The Scribes and Pharisees rejected the council of the Lord against themselves not being immersed."[62]

This confrontation took place on Saturday during a ten-hour "conference meeting" at which it was announced that the special baptismal service would be held the following morning "being Lord's day ... at the water side at 9 o'clock." That Sunday, among the "great host of people assembled to see the effects of the new religion," Crandall was surprised to find that Estey, "the old gentleman who was determined 'never to depart from his infant sprinkling,' was the first to yield obedience to the commands of Christ."[63] Estey was followed into a somewhat warmer Saint John River by his close friend Elijah Estabrooks and eight others. Crandall declared, "Such a day of the Lord's power was I believe rarely witnessed on earth." He went on:

This meeting did not breakup until after the sun had gone down. And it was truly solemn and delightful as well to hear the praises of the Lord sung by great numbers of happy converts returning home in their Boats from the solemn scene. The work of that day I can never forget. The clear setting sun, the broad expanse of smooth water spreading over a large extent of land, the serenity of the atmosphere, the delightful notes of the feathered songsters and the solemn tone of the hymns from the many happy voices presented to me an emblem of the very presence of God. It seemed as though the very Heavens had come down to earth and I was on the brink of the external world.[64]

On the following Monday, Crandall "passed over the river and at 8 o'clock in the morning immersed a number [twenty-one, in fact] that came into liberty the day before."[65] Then, early in June, he began his return journey to his Salisbury home and his Baptist church. On the way, he "preached several times and immersed quite a number," always, he was certain, under "the watchful eye of God over me and mine."[66]

Crandall was often to return to the Saint John River Valley. He was a very effective Baptist itinerant until almost the end of his long ministerial career, which only terminated with his death in February 1858. But as one of his biographers, I.E. Bill, observed in 1881, Crandall was not a particularly successful pastor. "The fact is that steady pastoral guidance, in connection with an individual Church, was not his *forte*,"[67] noted Bill. "Notwithstanding" that he "was in his eighty-seventh year, he nevertheless died with his armour on." According to Bill, who knew Crandall well:

Only six weeks before he died, he preached the Gospel to the people, supported by two of his deacons, and took his leave of his affectionate and weeping Church; and during his last illness, though his sufferings were at times severe, yet he staggered not at the promise through unbelief, but was strong in faith, giving glory to God. Sensible to the very last, he met the King of terrors with perfect composure, and feeling that death was doing its work, he closed his eyes and died without a struggle.[68]

Elijah Estabrooks, at the time of his 1800 baptism by Joseph Crandall, was forty-four years old. He was born in Haverhill, Massachusetts, in May 1756, and his parents "belonged to the Church of England, and educated him conformably to the sentiment of that denomination."[69] In 1763 the Estabrooks family joined thousands of New Englanders as they moved northeastwards to settle in Nova Scotia. After three years in the Horton region, they moved in "about 1768 to St. John (N.B.)" and then nine years later, in 1777, "they settled in Waterbury, on the River St. John."[70] In the early summer of 1778, at the age of twenty-two, Elijah Estabrooks experienced a

New Light conversion brought about by a powerful evangelistic sermon preached by a Yankee itinerant, Elisha Freeman.[71] Throughout his life, Estabrooks remembered Freeman's text from John 8:36: "If the Son therefore shall make you free, ye shall be free indeed." A "deep and permanent impression" was made "on his mind," but it was not until August that he actually experienced "regeneration," what he referred to as obtaining "a hope in Christ, – *a good hope through grace*."[72] A year later, Estabrooks first heard Henry Alline preach, and soon afterwards he became a member of the local New Light Congregational Church. According to a contemporary, at this time, Estabrooks "was much esteemed for his exemplary piety, and it soon became manifest, that he possessed gifts for public usefulness. After a few years he commenced preaching and laboured to general acceptance."[73]

It is known that "about the year 1790," Estabrooks was very active in the Allinite New Light services being held in the Waterborough area. At these house services, there would be prayer, some exhorting or witnessing, and "Alline's hymns were commonly sung."[74] It is also known that in the summer of 1791 the black Loyalist Baptist, David George, became the first "Baptist to preach and immerse on the River St. John."[75] George may or may not have made contact with Estabrooks; it is certain, however, that his black disciple Sampson Colbert did so later in the year, but these Baptists failed to persuade the Allinites to accept their New Light black Baptist gospel. Instead, Estabrooks and several of his friends seem to have become enamoured with radical evangelical Methodism. At some of these New Light–Methodist meetings in Waterborough in 1792, a British Calvinist Methodist missionary, John James, observed, "About 25 or thirty have been bawling as loud as they could at the same instant of Time consisting of Male and Female, old and young, and many of them Persons of infamous Character."[76] These men and women were transformed into preachers "by the mere impulse of a heated imagination."[77] According to the Scots traveller Patrick Campbell who, by a "remarkable coincidence,"[78] was visiting Waterborough at the same time, James's description was indeed accurate:

As we were conversing along, I heard a great noise in a house at some distance, on which I stopped to listen, and told the gentleman that there were some people fighting in that house; at which he smiled and answered, "That he knew the place well; that it was a house of worship, where a number of religious fanatics assembled at all hours of the night and day, there no body preached, every one prayed for himself, and the louder they roared, the more sincere and devout they were supposed to be; so that the one vied with the other who should bawl out loudest." When we had come nearer, I was struck with amazement at the hideous noise they made ... I asked him if he supposed they would permit me to go in to see them; he said I might, provided I behaved properly, and did not laugh, or offer to ridicule them in any shape; that they would not prevent me, or give me the least trouble; thus encouraged, I went in, and found they consisted of about three score persons, of both sexes, all on their knees, and in tears, every one praying for himself ... and bawling out, O Lord! O Lord! which were the only expressions I understood of what they said. After standing a few minutes in the house, my hair almost standing on end at the horror of the scene these miserable people exhibited, I returned, and just as I was passing the window of their apartment, someone called out, that the devil was among them; upon which they all gave a yell, louder and more horrible than any Indian war hoop I had ever heard; and if the devil himself was to show his physiognomy in all the frightful grimaces ascribed to him in the middle of them, every door bolted, so that none possibly could escape his clutches, their screaming could not have been louder or more horrible.[79]

Although Campbell had little sympathy for what he called New Brunswick New Light "fanaticism,"[80] he certainly did notice in the worship service the importance of lay preachers and exhorters, gender equality, and enthusiasm. In all likelihood, Estabrooks, now thirty-six years old, was one of the men on his knees, praying and yelling, almost delirious in his Allinite ecstasy. However, Estabrooks drew the line at having sexual relations with women during worship services, as some reportedly did. These antinomian excesses, called by some "liturgical sex," split these Waterborough Allinites into two major camps late in 1792 and 1793. The antinomian camp was led by John Lunt, who was described by a contemporary as "an abandoned profligate character, a sort of necromancer and fortune teller."[81] The other camp, which was spitefully referred to by the Luntites as the "pharisaical," was apparently led by Estabrooks and Estey.[82] A rape charge against Lunt, heard in the Queen's County circuit court on 29 June 1793,[83] seemed to strengthen Estabrook's resolve to create theological distance and space between his position and that of his former close friends. In 1794 or 1795, it is known that Estabrooks was seriously considering being ordained a Methodist minister; but during his "public examination" he stubbornly refused to accept certain key features of Wesleyan Arminianism because of his deep commitment to the Allinite emphasis on the "perseverance of the Saints."[84]

After his flirtation with the Methodists, Estabrooks returned to his struggling New Light congregation which, according to David

Bell, had "become consciously more formalistic."[85] For the latter half of the last decade of the eighteenth century, although still active as a New Light preacher (though not ordained), Estabrooks began to raise serious and disconcerting questions about "the correctness of some of his sentiments."[86] While "endeavouring to maintain the views which he then entertained," he found that "his mind was seriously exercised with doubts." According to a friend who knew him very well at the time, Estabrooks had slowly come to the realization late in the 1790s that many of his Allinite views "had been adopted without a due examination of the Scriptures."[87] He "proceeded, therefore, to a prayerful and attentive investigation. This terminated in a full conviction, that salvation is wholly of grace, proceeding from the *eternal purpose* of JEHOVAH. On pursuing a similar inquiry relative to the ordinances of the Gospel, he came to the conclusion, that the immersion of a professed believer in Christ is the only scriptural baptism."[88]

Estabrooks's religious and spiritual trajectory from Allinism to Baptist Calvinism may not have been as straightforward as his biographer seemed to suggest in 1829.[89] What is certain, however, is that by "about the commencement of the year 1800," Estabrooks had definitely replaced Allinite "impressionism" with "a due examination of the Scriptures" and had replaced New Light anarchy with an almost exaggerated emphasis on decorum and order.[90] Moreover, like hundreds of New Brunswickers in the Saint John River Valley and thousands of Yankees in Nova Scotia, Estabrooks had seen in believer's baptism not only a possible answer to the various complex problems unleashed by manifestations of New Dispensationalism, but also a powerful ritual that had actually been endorsed and experienced by his Saviour. Perhaps his double espousal of Calvinism and believer's baptism was more common than many have assumed, though the available contemporary evidence suggests that this was not the case, especially at the popular level. The evidence suggests that Calvinism was espoused first by some members of the Baptist ministerial élite, influenced by events and personalities in Massachusetts and by their almost palpable desire to become respectable and to avoid, as one of their members put it, being "looked upon as nobody."[91] Estabrooks, early in 1800, had abandoned the Allinite indifference to the mode of baptism and now considered believer's baptism to be an essential of the evangelical Christian faith. His espousal of Calvinism and closed communion would come later, despite what some of his Baptist contemporaries might have thought in the 1820s. These men were eager to rewrite the Baptist past –

and in many respects, until quite recently, they were amazingly successful in this mission.

By late May 1800, Estabrooks, "having embraced" his pro-immersion "sentiments ... did not hesitate to make a public avowal of them."[92] On that early Sunday morning he saw his close friend, Zebulon Estey, baptized by Joseph Crandall. After Estey's baptism, Estabrooks entered the "watery grave." He walked out on the firm sandy bottom to where Crandall was standing up to his hips in the Saint John River. In all likelihood, Estabrooks was dressed simply in homespun trousers and a light shirt; he was also barefoot. When he reached Crandall, he looked back and saw scores of his friends crowded along the flat riverbank. There were many others to be seen farther up the bank, men, women, and children who did not consider themselves to be believers. There was symbolic space, therefore, between those who believed and those who did not – something that both groups almost instinctively created for themselves. Those crowded along the river felt that they, like the Hay Bay Camp Meeting Methodists, were on sacred ground, and they regarded the water contiguous to them as sacred space as well – their New Brunswick Jordan. In this sacred space, the events of the New Testament could indeed be replicated. As had been the case when John the Baptist baptized Jesus or when the apostle Philip baptized the "Ethiopian eunuch," the Holy Spirit was expected to be present in its full transforming power.

Estabrooks proudly faced the shore. Then, while Crandall, with his left hand, gently grabbed Estabrooks's hands, clutched together in prayer, and placed his right behind Estabrooks's neck, the Baptist minister shouted for all to hear, "I baptize you, Elijah Estabrooks, in the name of the Father, the Son, and the Holy Spirit." Then Estabrooks bent his knees slightly and Crandall both pushed and guided him under the water. Estabrooks closed his eyes and mouth, and held his breath. He felt himself transported through centuries of time to the Jordan; and in Crandall's touch, he felt the touch of his Saviour. Immersed in the Saint John River, Estabrooks experienced again his New Light regeneration of 1778 and the boundless grace of Christ's ultimate sacrifice. For a brief and glorious moment he felt almost one with the divine. Then, suddenly, he found himself being helped to his feet by Crandall. And as he wiped his face, straightened his trousers, and regained his balance, he may have seen Crandall look at the people on the shore and slowly bend over and scoop up some water in the palm of his right hand. Then, while Crandall let the water dribble back into the Saint John, he might have shouted out the question, quoting from Acts 8:36: "See, here is water; what hinders *you* from being baptized?" It is noteworthy that for Estabrooks, as had been the case with Crandall, the public baptism by immersion became the defining moment of his religious life. In addition, this mode and style of immersion was to become the norm for Baptists in nineteenth-century New Brunswick. There would be some additions such as antiphonal singing and testimonies, and even some sermonizing from "the watery grave"; yet at the core of the ritual of believer's baptism was to be found the "revivifying role of water in religious symbolism" and the almost magical powers of purification and regeneration dispensed by the ordained minister – but always within a narrowly conceived New Testament framework.

Estabrooks's baptism led to his ordination as a Baptist minister on 15 September 1800.[93] It was hoped that he would be the human means of spreading the Baptist Reformation up and down the Saint John River Valley; and so he was, despite some setbacks along the way. When this Baptist "Elijah" of New Brunswick was on the verge of death in September 1825, it seemed that "the spirituality and comfort which he had enjoyed while labouring successfully in the cause of his dear Redeemer, appeared to continue unabated, and even to increase, as he approached the close of his mortal existence."[94]

The Crandall-Estabrook story provides something of the particular "New Brunswick character" that is necessary in order to evaluate the essential nature of the more generalized "Baptist circumstance." Social anthropological theory, the description of virulent critics and that of unreconstructed supporters, when applied to the actual accounts of two of the principal actors involved in the Baptist Reformation, adds both depth and substance to a descriptive analysis of a crucially important social and religious movement – the "rage for dipping." This Baptist ritual significantly influenced Maritime evangelical culture at the turn of the eighteenth century and beyond. Moreover, the widely perceived transforming power of this ritual was so obvious to contemporaries that it seldom drew much serious attention from them. Nor has it drawn much attention from some twentieth-century scholars who remain critically suspicious of the obvious – especially in the realm of religion.

11 New Lights, Presbyterians, James MacGregor, and Nova Scotia's First Long Communion, July 1788

From his own unique New Light evangelical vantage point, Henry Alline, during the American Revolution, found it virtually impossible to have anything positive to say about the two Scots Presbyterian ministers with whom he had two extremely bitter confrontations, one in 1777, the other in 1782. Nor was Alline overly impressed with the Christian qualities of the Scots Presbyterian laypeople to whom he preached. The New Light critique of Presbyterianism was matched in its animus by the often vituperative Scots Presbyterian denunciation of the extreme New Light disciples of Alline. The "fanaticism" of the Allinites, it was asserted, had at its core a peculiar Yankee "mixture of Calvinism, Antinomianism and enthusiasm."[1]

There was an important evangelical component, however, to Scots Presbyterianism in pre-1812 Nova Scotia, New Brunswick, and central Canada. But the Scots brand of evangelicalism was, in certain important aspects, very different from the indigenous North American New Light variety, especially during the pre-1800 period. Yet despite these fundamental differences – differences grounded on a Scots Presbyterian preoccupation with the religion of the head and the heart rather than only the heart, and with Calvinism and the Westminster Confession rather than the "priesthood of all believers" – the two brands of evangelicalism had something significant in common. They both advocated, first, belief in the Bible as the inspired word of God; second, the crucial importance of accepting Christ's unique redeeming work of salvation on the cross, and, third, the importance of spreading the Christian gospel. Something of the complex relationship of radical evangelicalism and the moderate evangelicalism of Scots Presbyterianism, especially in the Maritimes, may be discerned by examining Alline's experiences and the early career of that very gifted man, the Reverend James MacGregor, who in 1786 came to Nova Scotia as an anti-Burgher Secessionist Presbyterian missionary. MacGregor died in his much-beloved Pictou on 3 March 1830.[2]

In early June 1777, about a year after Alline had begun to preach, he found himself in Cornwallis confronting two angry Scots Presbyterian ministers, the Reverend Daniel Cock and the Reverend David Smith. Cock, a native of Clydesdale, Scotland, was an ordained minister of the Burgher "Associate Synod" of the Secessionist Church. The Secessionist Church had broken away from the Established Church of Scotland in 1733, only to be split in 1747 into two warring factions – the Burgher and anti-Burgher – over the question of whether the Secessionist leaders should be willing to swear an oath of allegiance to the crown. The Burghers were willing to do so, while the anti-Burghers were not, since they considered the oath to be a giant first step back to an established church and élite control of their denomination. After teaching at the Associate Synod College, Cock had been appointed in 1770 by the Associate Synod to serve as a minister to the Scotch-Irish Presbyterian inhabitants of Truro, Nova Scotia. He was joined by Smith, who had been ordained in 1767 and who made his way to nearby Londonderry in 1770. Both were well-educated men, Scots to the core, and committed to the Burgher Secessionist version of Presbyterianism. Cock was to die in Truro in 1805; Smith, in Londonderry in 1795.[3]

According to Alline, the reason Cock and Smith came to Cornwallis in June 1777 was "to inquire into my principles and preaching."[4] Curious about the two Presbyterian visitors, he went to hear them preach in the local Presbyterian church. "I ... had reason to hope," commented the condescending Alline, "that one of them was a minister of Christ, although something sunk into a form without power."[5] During "the week following," Cock and Smith, accompanied by "a number" of local inhabitants whom Alline knew to be "enemies to the power of religion," resolved to examine Alline in order to compel him to vindicate his "principles of religion." When the two Presbyterian ministers inquired after Alline's right to preach, he simply replied, "I trusted my authority was from heaven; but I did not know whether it was needful to discover it to them, finding them much against the power." Reacting against Alline's arrogance, Cock and Smith demanded his credentials, whereupon Alline calmly showed them what he had from his Cornwallis New Light Church – which "credentials" the Presbyterians "condemned," noted Alline in his

Journal, "because it was not from a society of ministers, which caused a dispute to begin, they affirming that I had no right to preach without a license from a society of ministers, and I affirmed that I had." The Scots visitors then emphasized that as far as they were concerned, it was "next to impossible for a man to be called to preach, who had no college learning." Furthermore, they asserted that their ordinations, unlike Alline's, had been "handed down by a successive chain *from the Apostles*"; they therefore represented apostolic tradition and order while Alline "was breaking through all order."

The young Nova Scotia itinerant was not in any way intimidated by the "book-learning logic" of Cock and Smith. "I told them," Alline proudly noted in his *Journal*, "that there was no people in the world more s[t]rict to the orders and traditions of men than the church of Rome; and where was all their religion, or what had they but a dry form? and therefore, although I strictly held to all the orders of God's house, yet I looked on the power of God's Spirit far more important than the traditions, the bare traditions of men." In this reply, Alline cut to the heart of his New Light position and contrasted it to the Cock-Smith brand of Presbyterianism. Alline considered the "power of God's Spirit" to be far more important than "the bare traditions of men."

On realizing that Alline had put them on the defensive and would not be "easily moved," Cock and Smith suddenly shifted the discussion and "began to be more moderate." They made him "an offer of their libraries," noted Alline, "and what assistance they could give me, if I would leave off preaching until I was better qualified." Alline "thanked them for their kindness" and then twisted his knife into their offer. "I told them," he proudly declared, "that the Lord knew before he called me, how unqualified I was *as to human learning*, and as he had called me, I trusted he would qualify me for whatever he had for me to do. I told them besides, that the work of God was then prospering in my hands, and therefore I did not dare to desert it." Stung by Alline's seeming hubris, Cock and Smith informed the newly ordained itinerant that they looked on him "as a stiff young man" and then they went away. Alline's response was to remain a further five days in Cornwallis, where he preached "and visited those under conviction." "The Lord was with me," he observed, "and blessed my labours." The Almighty had rewarded and blessed Alline with "the power of God's Spirit." Cock and Smith would have to be satisfied with their libraries, their college learning, and the dry bones of their Presbyterian traditions.[6]

Not until early August 1782 did Alline again meet Cock and Smith – this time on the latter's home turf in the Cobequid townships of Truro, Onslow, and Londonderry. As Alline travelled through this

Scotch-Irish heartland, he met with open hostility at first. Cock and Smith, whom Alline now referred to as the "two dark ministers," had spitefully "informed the people, that there was a strange imposter from the countries up the bay, who ... was coming among them; who was neither college learned, nor authorized by the presbytery. He was a new light, he was a separatist, and one that broke up their churches." As a result of these public warnings, recorded Alline, the "poor dark people (most of them) conceived such an opinion of me, that they would gaze at me, as I passed their doors, with as much strangeness, as if I was one [of] the antediluvians; and when I came down to the public house I was even refused a bed or a room for any money."[7]

Eventually, Alline found lodging in a private home. As he was being led to his room by an obviously reluctant owner, the curious neighbours "looked on me as if I had some distemper, that was catching." The curiosity of the Truro people soon got the better of them, however, and "some of them hearing me sing" asked if they could "come and hear me sing." Alline, who had a marvellous sense of humour, began to poke fun at his growing audience. He replied, "Yes, if they thought it was safe for them," especially since they had been so concerned earlier "that there was a danger of being caught with that spirit, that I went about with." It was the New Light "distemper," and of course Alline knew that it was most certainly contagious. Soon he was invited to preach at a private home, despite the objections of Cock, the local minister, who sent Alline two letters demanding an immediate meeting. During the meeting, which lasted "about three hours," Cock and Alline debated "the call and qualifications of a minister; the door into the ministry; the power of ordination; and original sin." Eventually, a disgruntled Cock "got up and broke off from the discourse," having realized to his horror that many of his parishioners regarded the Yankee New Light evangelist as the clear winner of the theological debate.[8]

After preaching "three or four days in Truro," an elated Alline made his way to Onslow and then to Londonderry, where he faced the Reverend David Smith "in a great rage." After a brief period of verbal shadow boxing, the two ministers began a furious theological debate – for all in the region to hear. Smith began by denouncing Alline's "principles" – his theology: his heterodox view of "original sin," his denunciation of "predestination," and his peculiar view of "God's incarnation." According to the Falmouth tanner-farmer, who unlike Smith had never seen the inside of a synod college, the educated Presbyterian from Scotland was no match for the uneducated Yankee New Light, who made theological mincemeat of the

Westminster Confession. Alline emphasized the inconsistency of Smith's argument concerning original sin. He savagely mocked Smith for declaring "that God was making souls now in these days, and made a soul for every body, when the body was once conceived in the womb, and after he makes the soul and sends them into the bodies, he imputes Adam's guilt to them." In response to Smith's orthodox Presbyterian view of predestination, Alline replied that this was "impossible; for God could neither be the author of sin nor decree a thing against his own nature."[9]

Alline appeared to be most pleased with his critique of Smith's view on the incarnation. He described their heated discussion in the following manner:

I asked him [Smith] what God made Christ of: he said, that his body was made of the elements (which I did not oppose) but that his soul was made out of nothing. Out of nothing, I replied, why then he may return to nothing. Besides, if that be the case, then he is but a creature, which once was nothing, and is this the Christ you worship, and expect to worship forever? I then told him the Saviour I worshipped was the eternal Son of God, and that God had declared that the word was God, and that the Word was made flesh, and that that very infant that was born, was declared to be the everlasting Father, the Prince of Peace, and therefore he was not a created man, but God manifest in the flesh. And then I told him that I believed his people never knew before now, that their minister believed that Christ was made out of nothing; and that I was glad, he has discovered himself.

On hearing this last statement, Smith "rose up in a passion and left the house." Everyone else remained behind – not to experience conversion but to begin "to get their eyes opened to see where the darkness was."[10]

Henry Alline never again visited the Cobequid townships, and his New Light gospel did not have a significant permanent impact on this Scotch-Irish section of Nova Scotia. His two major confrontations with Smith and Cock certainly reveal the theological differences that separated his Christianity from that preached and practised by the two Presbyterian ministers. Cock and Smith were, in almost every respect, orthodox Secessionist Presbyterians – apart from the fact that they apparently placed relatively little importance on the New Birth. They were concerned with Old Light order and discipline, and they shared an Old Light suspicion of enthusiasm in all its North American manifestations. Their preoccupation with British and Presbyterian order and their often vociferous critique of New Light enthusiasm owed a great deal to their response to the American

Revolution. As far as Alline was concerned, in 1777, at the beginning of the Revolution, Cock and Smith could have been considered to be "ministers of Christ," despite a few obvious flaws. In other words, they preached the New Light gospel, or at least its Presbyterian variant. But five years later, in 1782, Alline regarded the two men as "minions of the Antichrist," without any redeeming features. Their drift to Loyalism obviously affected their already fragile Scots Presbyterian evangelicalism; to prove their loyalty to the crown, they had to prove that their Calvinism, unlike that of thousands of their fellow religionists in the republic to the south, was not transforming them into evangelical Patriots. Furthermore, it is clear that during Nova Scotia's First Great Awakening, Cock and Smith became increasingly concerned about the possible inroads the New Lights could make among the Scotch Irish. And in order to counter the New Light offensive, they attacked the invaders, and in the process they exaggerated the theological and cultural differences that may have separated the two groups. In making the New Lights appear to be dangerous religious radicals, Cock and Smith had to strip away some of their own residual evangelicalism. In an ironic twist of historical development, these Secessionist Presbyterians, by 1792, had become as "moderate" and "as anti-evangelical" as most "moderate" Presbyterian kirkmen in Old Scotland.

Alline's negative view of Cock and Smith (though not necessarily his reasons for it) was shared by the Reverend James MacGregor, a newly arrived anti-Burgher missionary, after his first meeting, in 1786, with the two Burgher ministers. Without question, MacGregor was the most influential Presbyterian in Nova Scotia during the three decades following the end of the American Revolution. His Calvinist evangelicalism was affected – some would say significantly muted or moderated – by his almost sectarian anti-Burgher convictions. When MacGregor arrived in Halifax on his way to Pictou, on 11 July 1786, he was, according to his most recent biographer, "a large man, six foot tall ... with a gift of conversation." His Secessionist "fiery adherence to principle" often encouraged him, at least in his early years in Nova Scotia, to be rigidly judgmental and doctrinally arrogant. "His ardent Christian zeal" during his first decade in the colony seemed to be readily, some would say too readily, channelled away from North American–oriented evangelical compassion towards bitter internecine Scots Presbyterian theological warfare.[11]

MacGregor was born in December 1759 in Portmore (St Fillans) in the rural parish of Comrie, Perthshire. His father was a farmer and weaver, and a committed anti-Burgher Secessionist. Fluently bilingual in Gaelic and English, James attended grammar schools at

Kinkell and Dunblane, and then studied at the University of Edinburgh, where he matriculated in 1779. He also attended the anti-Burgher theological college, the General Associate Hall, from 1781 to 1784. He was a teacher as well as a probationer minister before his ordination in Glasgow on 31 May 1786 – three days before his embarkation for Pictou, where his synod had unanimously appointed him "as their first missionary to the Maritimes."[12]

According to MacGregor, his father "was a man of so gentle a spirit, and so interested in spiritual matters, as almost to regard his worldly interests with carelessness." His mother, "with the spirit of a Martha ... was a woman of decided piety, and also one of a turn of mind which fitted her to be a help-meet for him."[13] At his infant baptism, as was the custom in many Highland homes, MacGregor was "solemnly dedicated" by his father "to the work of the Lord, should it be his gracious will, in the ministry of his Son."[14]

Little is known about MacGregor's early years, apart from the fact "that he bore the character of a lively and active, yet gentle boy, of very inquisitive disposition, and occasionally giving evidence of a quick temper."[15] "Throughout his early life," it has been persuasively argued, "his conduct was characterized at least by morality and outward respect for religion."[16] According to his first biographer, the Reverend George Patterson, who knew a great deal about him, MacGregor never actually experienced a sudden New Birth. Rather, "from his enquiring turn of mind" and "from the manner in which religion filled the mind of his father, and pervaded his whole household arrangements," MacGregor "must have had his attention directed to the subject" of becoming "decidedly pious ... at a very early age; and from any information we have received, we are inclined to believe that he was one of those who are sanctified from their mother's womb, – that the seeds of religious truth took root in his childish mind with the first impressions of a pious home, and the first instructions of his parents' lips."[17] Thus, for MacGregor, being suddenly "born again," in a cathartic, emotional, and transforming conversion experience, was something quite foreign and almost distasteful. He had become "pious" gradually, as he was able to love his Lord with "all of his mind and all of his heart." If anything, the mind (the head) was far more important to him than the heart (the feelings) in establishing a relationship with Christ as "Saviour and Lord."[18]

MacGregor never expected to go to Nova Scotia as a missionary; he was certain, early in 1785, that he would be called to a church somewhere in the Highlands, where his Gaelic could be put to good use. Bug according to his "narrative," in the "fall of 1784, the settlers of Pictou sent a petition to Scotland for a minister, who could preach Gaelic and English." At the time there were only eighty Scots families in the region, fifty of which had arrived before the American Revolution and thirty since the end of the hostilities. "A majority of the whole," observed MacGregor, "were Highlanders and Presbyterians, but there was a number of Roman Catholics and other denominations."[19] (When Alline had visited the region in late July 1782, he had found only "four Christians in the place, who were greatly revived, and rejoiced that the gospel was sent among them." The others in the community "crowded night and day" to hear the charismatic itinerant, but their curiosity was not transformed into conviction and conversion, and Alline failed to coax even a minor revival into existence.)[20]

When the Pictou petition was "laid ... before the General Associate Synod [anti-Burgher] in May, 1786," it was decided that since MacGregor was the only available bilingual recruit, he should immediately be ordained and "should take the first opportunity of sailing for Nova Scotia."[21] MacGregor was, understandably, "thunderstruck by this decision of Synod" since he "by no means expected it." He described with considerable sensitivity some of his feelings at the time:

It put me into such a confusion, that I did not know what to say or think. I had considered it a clear case, not to myself only, but to the majority of the Synod, that I was called to preach to the Highlanders of Scotland, and of course that I could not be sent abroad. I had never met with an event to deprive me wholly of a night's sleep till then. That night I slept none, but tossed upon my bed, till it was time to rise next morning. Through the day several friends helped much to reconcile me to the Synod's appointment. Upon reflection I observed that there was at present no opening of great consequence for my preaching the gospel to the Highlanders at home, – that souls were equally precious wherever they were, and that I might be as successful abroad as at home. I resolved to go, but still overwhelming difficulties were before me. The mission was vastly important, and I was alone and weakness itself. I had to go among strangers, probably prejudiced against the religious denomination to which I belonged. Though the Synod told me, and I felt it comfort too, that I was not sent to make Seceders, but Christians; yet as there was no minister before me, except two or three Burgher ministers, nor any likely to come after me with whom I could hold communion, I felt as an exile from the church. Besides Nova Scotia was accounted so barren, cold and dreary, that there was no living in it with comfort.[22]

Eventually, MacGregor came to realize that the Almighty had indeed called him to Pictou, and this deep sense of calling was to permeate his entire Nova Scotia ministerial career. It has been recently pointed out that, "influenced by his own youthful intellectual prowess and the moulding of his mentors, MacGregor brought to Nova Scotia the cultural baggage of his Scottish education."[23] Within a few days of his Halifax arrival, he was invited to join "the Presbytery of Truro, then forming among the Burgher ministers already settled in the province."[24] "The immorality of Halifax" shocked MacGregor "not a little," and he "hastened out of it hoping better things of the country."[25] Cock and Smith expected MacGregor to join with them to sustain and strengthen the cause of Presbyterianism in the colony, but MacGregor had other ideas. After visiting Pictou briefly, he returned to Truro, where he informed his fellow Presbyterian ministers that he was unwilling to abandon his anti-Burgher principles in order to establish a united Nova Scotia Presbyterian Church. His intense general and imported antipathy to the Burghers was significantly intensified by certain specific local concerns. MacGregor was revolted by the Truro presbytery's American-influenced acceptance and "use of Watts's Psalms," and by their peculiar "mode of electing elders." In addition, he felt that "the Presbytery had not adopted the Westminster Confession of Faith in terms sufficiently explicit," but rather had agreed to a version of "the Creed of Pope Pius the IV." Of particular concern to MacGregor, who was a staunch abolitionist, was the fact that Cock "held a coloured girl in slavery." On this point, MacGregor apparently "went so far as to say, that he hoped he would rather burn at the stake than keep communion with one who did so."[26] MacGregor's antislavery rhetoric was soon matched by his abolitionist actions. According to Susan Buggey, he

put his convictions to practical use by applying £20 of the £27 he received for his first year's services toward purchasing the freedom of a slave girl from her Nova Scotian master, and he subsequently aided in the release of others. MacGregor extended this commitment when he confronted Cock, who was a slave owner, with the immorality of a Christian's enslaving God's children. The publication in Halifax in 1788 of MacGregor's rebuke to Cock, and the Reverend David Smith's reply on Cock's behalf, formalized Mac-Gregor's split with the Presbytery of Truro.[27]

It should be kept in mind that as a zealous anti-Burgher, Mac-Gregor stubbornly refused "to hold communion" with those who disagreed with him even "on the minutest points," since he believed that in doing so he would compromise his own faith and testimony. For "holding fellowship with error" meant "partake[ing] in its guilt."[28] "Forbearance in matters of religious opinion" could be countenanced, but having communion with proponents of "error or wrong doing" was sin.[29]

MacGregor discovered that "Pictou had no church, road bridge, mill, [though it had hand mills] and scarcely any convenience." He quickly learned "to walk on snow-shoes in winter, and to paddle a canoe in summer, and to cross brooks and swamps upon trees overturned or broken by the wind, and to camp in the woods all night, for there is no travelling the woods at night, where there is no road."[30] Since there was no church building for services, on his arrival MacGregor preached "in the open air, till ... compelled by the cold" to go indoors.[31] He was, from the beginning, a somewhat reluctant itinerant. "This circulating plan of preaching," he once noted, "was no little inconvenience to me. For six weeks in eight I was from home, almost totally deprived of my books and of all accommodation for study, often changing my lodging, and exposed to frequent and excessive cold."[32] MacGregor's parish was huge, stretching inland for about twenty miles and along the Gulf of St Lawrence for approximately fifty miles.[33] His theological training in Scotland had certainly not prepared him adequately for his wilderness parish in "Nova Scarcity."

During his "circulating," MacGregor resolved "not to confine my visitations to Presbyterians, but to include all, of every denomination, who could make me welcome; for I viewed them as sheep without a shepherd."[34] Soon after arriving in Pictou, he cogently summed up his missionary strategy: "The purport of my visitations was, to awaken them to a sight of their sinful and dangerous state, to direct them to Christ, to exhort them to be diligent to grow in religious knowledge, and to set up and maintain the worship of God in the family and closet morning and evening."[35] Some responded enthusiastically to his ministrations, and a few were actually, as MacGregor explained, brought "to Christ."[36] Many others rebuffed the itinerant, especially the half-pay Scots officers, veterans of the Revolutionary War, who "threatened to shoot me," observed MacGregor, "and burn the house in which I lodged."[37] This virulent and persistent opposition fed his homesickness, particularly in the summer of 1787. The acute homesickness did not leave him until he had a "remarkable" dream on the same day he heard from Scotland about his mother's sudden death. Like many New Lights, MacGregor saw in some of his dreams the almost miraculous guidance of the Almighty.[38]

By the late summer of 1787, MacGregor found himself under considerable community pressure "about dispensing the sacrament of the Supper," especially since two · church buildings had at last been built. He delayed "partly because" he "believed that not many of the people were prepared" but "chiefly because" he "thought it too heavy a burden first to converse with the candidates one by one, and then go through all the customary services in both languages."[39] He was obviously afraid that the long communion would become a "*Very, Very Long Communion.*" Despite some setbacks, However, MacGregor could report:

As to the success of my ministrations this summer, I had more reason to be content than to complain. People in general attended public ordinances diligently and attentively. There was much outward reformation; and I doubt not, some believers were added to the Lord. On considering, as maturely as I could, the circumstances of the people, I thought it my duty to sound the alarm of the law in their ears. Accordingly, I preached a course of sermons on the Ten Commandments, with the view of showing them the holiness of God, their duty, and their fearful condition under the curse for breaking it; the impossibility of justification before God by their own works, and, of course, the necessity of fleeing to Christ, the hope set before them; and finally, the faith, love, gratitude, and obedience and suffering under the curse. I afterwards found that these sermons were not in vain.[40]

During the fall and winter of 1787–88, as he itinerated throughout his huge parish, MacGregor was preparing his parishioners for Nova Scotia's first long communion. His Highland congregation desperately wanted the long communion, considering it to be the essence of their Presbyterian religion. Communion was to "be dispensed on the 27th of July, a little above the head of the tide on the Middle River, the most central place that could be found." Here was Presbyterian "sacred space" – a "beautiful green on the left bank of the river, sheltered by a lofty wood and winding bank."[41] On first viewing this sight, MacGregor had "an awful and delightful recollection of the religious exercises" of his youth, when he had participated in some of the memorable long communions held in Perthshire.[42]

MacGregor "published five weeks beforehand" the actual day "for dispensing the sacrament" and its location. He knew that he needed at least five weeks "for examining intending communicants; and they were all particularly examined."[43] These spiritual examinations were lengthy, exhausting, and, for MacGregor, absolutely essential; he used the occasion to test the orthodoxy of Christian commitment of members of his congregation. MacGregor cogently described "the first sacred Supper dispensed in Pictou," observing, "Though some, no doubt, communicated unworthily, yet I trust that a great majority were worthy."[44] He gave the following account of the proceedings:

It was agreed that the preceding Thursday should be observed as a day of public humiliation and prayer for preparation; and that the English should be first this year, and so on alternately. On the humiliation-day I earnestly exhorted the congregation to examine themselves impartially and thoroughly, to renounce hypocrisy and self-righteousness, to lay hold on the hope set before them in the gospel, and implore the gracious and merciful presence of God on the ensuing occasion, as I was a young and inexperienced minister, and the most of them were to be young and inexperienced communicants; and the first dispensation of the sacrament might have lasting effects of good or evil. I preached first in English, then in Gaelic, on the Thursday, the Saturday, and on the Monday. On Sabbath I preached the action-sermon, fenced the tables, consecrated the elements, and served the first two tables in English, at which all the English communicants sat. The singing in English continued till all the Highlanders, who were waiting, filled the table. I then served two tables, gave directions, and preached the evening sermon in Gaelic. The work of the Day was pretty equally divided between the two languages.[45]

There was a total of 130 communicants, "of whom one hundred and two were heads of families, ten widowers and widows, living with their children, eight unmarried men, and ten strangers from Merigomish."[46]

Early in the last week of July 1788, scores of expectant Presbyterians had already begun to arrive for "the dispensation of the Supper." Those who came from a distance were housed in barns and in the homes of those who lived near "the Intervale, on the Middle River," where a tent had been set up "for the minister" and where "the multitudes sat or reclined upon the green grass of the Intervale, or under the leafy shade of the trees on the bank, facing the minister."[47]

The long communion was, of course, "dispensed in the manner common at that time in Scotland" and consequently popular expectations demanded that MacGregor carefully follow the Highland schedule of events. Thursday was the first day of "holy convocation" and it was widely referred to as "the day of humiliation or fasting."[48] MacGregor preached two sermons on the Thursday, one in English and one in Gaelic, and both were "directed to the object of bringing sin to remembrance, and exhorting" men and women to "confession and repentance." The psalms that were sung emphasized the same general theme, "while the prayers were principally devoted to the acknowledgement of sins, and supplications for mercy on account of them." The rest of the day "was spent with the solemnity of a Sabbath, being devoted to such secret and family religious exercises, as were suitable to such a day." Like many others at Pictou, MacGregor observed the entire day "literally as a fast, abstaining entirely from food before preaching, and afterward partaking only of such slight refreshment, as was necessary to support nature."[49]

On Friday, the day described by Highlanders as "the day of the men," MacGregor did not preach; this was a day for "private religious meetings" conducted by the few elders who were available and by the more "experienced Christians." There were lay-led prayer meetings; there were many opportunities for praise, mutual exhortation, and the so-called "question," which involved "marks of grace"[50] – or the way one should actually live the Christian life.

On Saturday, MacGregor probably preached first on Joshua 3:5, "Sanctify yourselves; for to-morrow the Lord will do wonders among you," and then on Psalms 10:17, "He will prepare your heart." The outline of his Joshua 3:5 sermon is available, the first part of it being entitled "Of the wonders which God will do":

1 He will let you see the evil of sin. Christ the beloved Son of God was brought by it to death. This was done by your thoughts, words, and actions. If you can understand the whole sufferings of Christ, you may understand all the evil and all the desert of sin.
2 He will show the severity of God's justice. He would not be satisfied with thirty-three years' obedience. He required all the sufferings of his soul till his body was broken. "Awake, O Sword etc." God loved him and was gracious to him, but that would not do. What will become of self-flattering sinners?
3 The love of God: of the Father in giving his Son whom he infinitely loved to be broken for us, and the Son in suffering for us, and the Holy Ghost in coming into such hellish hearts to prepare us for eating the broken body of Christ.
4 The virtue of Christ's blood, to take away the guilt of sin, to give peace to the conscience, in spite of sin and hell, to purify the heart, to strengthen it for God's service, to fill it with the joy and peace of believing, to prevent our fears and exceed our hopes, to feed our souls.

The second part of his sermon was entitled "Of our Sanctification," and its outline was as follows:

1 This says that we should understand something of God's holiness. He is so holy that he cannot keep communion with sinners – that the angels cover their faces, and that no unclean thing is meet to come before him.

2 That we are sensible of our unholiness, our original and actual transgressions, and that by these we are altogether as an unclean thing, a lump of hell.

3 That we are to depend on the Spirit for sanctification. We cannot sanctify ourselves. The Spirit is promised to sanctify us, and there is influence in Christ's blood to sanctify us, and we must apply to this in the diligent use of means.

4 We are to retire from the world, and to examine our hearts, that we may part with whatever displeases a holy God, and that we may get a suitable frame of spirit to attend upon him. We are to cast out pride, the world, unbelief, malice, and vain thoughts. We are to be in a humble, spiritual, fixed, lovely, lively frame.

In the concluding section, MacGregor simply stressed that God "delights himself in them that are sanctified." Throughout the sermon, MacGregor's Calvinism was both explicitly and implicitly expressed – but never in such a way as to marginalize human initiative completely.[51] It is clear that MacGregor's approach to sanctification was radically different from that of a Nathan Bangs or even a Freeborn Garrettson. For the Presbyterian minister, sanctification was something to be accepted rationally, not something to be ecstatically experienced to the inner recesses of one's entire being.

In all likelihood, after the second Saturday sermon, the communion tokens were handed out by MacGregor, flanked by his elders, "as the intending communicants, one by one," slowly walked by the rough-hewn communion tables.[52] These tokens were not passed out indiscriminately, nor were they accepted without much soul-searching. The token provided the ticket to the communion service, where each worshipper either declared his or her oneness with Christ or else, in the wine and the bread, drank and ate his or her own damnation and sinned grievously against the Holy Spirit.

MacGregor and the hundreds of Scots who were in Pictou on Sunday, 27 July, would never forget that Sabbath. "The Great Day of the Feast" had finally come.[53] The 65th Psalm was announced, "lined" by MacGregor, and sung by the congregation "seated, many of them with eyes closed, their bodies slightly swaying to the music."[54] Many with tears in their eyes sang in a slow dirgelike fashion, both in Gaelic and English:

Praise is awaiting You, O God in Zion; and to You the vow shall be performed.
O You who hear prayer, to You all flesh will come.
Iniquities prevail against me; as for our transgressions, You will provide
  atonement for them ...

After singing the last verse, "The pastures are clothed with flocks;
the valleys also are covered with grain; they shout for joy, they also
sing," MacGregor prayed the "long prayer" in preparation for his
"action sermon." According to the Reverend George Patterson, the
action sermon was "usually devoted to the great central truths of
Redemption, specially exhibited in the ordinance of the Supper."[55]
The text for MacGregor's sermon was the Song of Solomon 2:16:
"My beloved is mine and I am his." In the first part, he stressed:

All his gracious promises are mine to quicken, sanctify, and save me. Faith
puts all the promises of grace in my possession, and then all the grace in
the promise in my property. Quickening grace ... reviving grace ... sanctifying grace ... saving grace ... grace to overcome sin, Satan, and the world.

In his conclusion, MacGregor declared, "Faith puts all the promises
of grace in my possession" and "All my sins are his ... my original
sin and all my actual sins are his by imputation ... My unworthy
communicating is his." He then made three points about the communion to come:

• What is the proper work of a communion Sabbath, to be saying, "My
  beloved is mine and I am his." God is for him in his soul. Give you
  yourselves to him in your soul.
• What will make us worthy communicants. Christ is the fountain of grace.
  Go to him for all that you need.
• How foolish they who despise Christ. "All that hate me love death? They
  lose the best jewels that exist for nothing."[56]

The sermon was followed by a prayer and the singing of another
psalm, possibly Psalm 18, which begins, "I will love You; O Lord,
my strength. The Lord is my rock and my fortress and my deliverer;
my God, my strength, in whom I will trust; my shield and the horn
of my salvation, my stronghold."[57] Next came "the fencing of the
table." This ritual consisted of "a plain statement of the character of
those who have or have not a right to observe the ordinance."[58]
MacGregor concluded by reading from the Beatitudes found in Matthew 5 and from Galatians 5:19–24:

19 Now the works of the flesh are evident, which are adultery, fornication, uncleanness, lewdness.

20 Idolatry, sorcery, hatred, contentious, jealousies, outbursts of wrath, selfish ambitions, dissensions, heresies.

21 Envy, murders, drunkenness, revelries, and the like; of which I tell you beforehand, just as I also told you in time past, that those who practice such things will not inherit the kingdom of God.

22 But the fruit of the Spirit is love, joy, peace, longsuffering, kindness, goodness, faithfulness.

23 Gentleness, self-control. Against such there is no law.

24 And those who are Christ's have crucified the flesh with its passions and desires.[59]

After a brief pause, MacGregor lined out a portion of the 103rd Psalm, which begins "Bless the Lord, O my Soul; and all that is within me, bless His holy name!" While the psalm was being sung, "the elders brought forward the elements and placed them upon the communion table," where the English-speaking "communicants slowly and reverently took their places" on the rough-hewn planks, which were the seats provided for them. There were "two long benches on which they sat facing one another, with a narrow table covered with a pure white cloth between them." When all the seats were filled, MacGregor "took his place at the head of the table, and having read as authority for observing the ordinance ... Paul's in 1 Cor XI 23–26, he offered up a prayer, especially giving thanks for the blessings of salvation, and for the ordinance in which it is commemorated." Then there followed what was called the "serving of the tables." "A Short address was delivered to those at the table" by MacGregor who, at the same time, "broke the bread and handed a portion of it and afterwards the wine to those nearest to him, repeating as he did ... the words of institution." The elements "were then passed along" from one communicant to the next "to the foot of the table, the attending elders supplying deficiencies," while MacGregor "continued his exhortation." When MacGregor had finished his address, he dismissed the first group of communicants with the words, "Go then from the table of the Lord singing his praises and may the God of peace go with you." At this, the congregation began to sing again from Psalm 103:

And as the singing proceeded, those who had been at the table rose, and began, many with moistened eyes, slowly and reverently, as if treading on holy ground, to retire, while another band with the same measured tread advanced and took their places. Another table service followed and another singing, and so on till all those who spoke the one language were served.

Now it was the turn of the Gaelic-speaking Presbyterians, who, after surrendering their tokens to the elders, made their way to the communion table. The exhausted MacGregor, digging deep into his spiritual, mental, and physical reservoir, carefully replicated in Gaelic what he had already done in English. After the Gaelic-speaking Presbyterians slowly made their way back to their seats, yet another psalm was sung. Then MacGregor "delivered the concluding exhortation – usually called 'the directions,'" which "consisted commonly of advices to those who had communicated, as to their future conduct, and an earnest appeal to those" who were mere spectators "to embrace the Saviour and profess his name." After an interlude for refreshment, MacGregor preached his evening sermon in Gaelic, and the service concluded well after sunset with "prayer and praise."[60]

On the Monday, commonly called Thanksgiving Day, there were two more sermons, one in English and the other in Gaelic.[61] After the afternoon service, the participants reluctantly made their way home by boat, foot, or horse, many of them travelling long distances. The Pictou long communion had encapsulated for many of them the essence of their Christianity; they had experienced directly, in a profound and personal way, the salvation provided by Jesus Christ, the forgiveness of the Almighty, and the presence of the Holy Spirit. The long communion was the means whereby they celebrated their acceptance of Christ, witnessed to their faith, and were both revitalized and assured of their salvation. For these Scots Presbyterians, there was considerable emotional and spiritual content to the Pictou long communion – a content shaped significantly by traditionalism. Since the long communion was an annual ritual, it helped renew and strengthen a person's faith to a considerable extent in much the same way as revivals, camp meetings, and believer's baptism did.

MacGregor's contribution to the remarkable success of Nova Scotia's first long communion was of crucial significance. Without him, there would not have been a long communion – in fact, there could not have been one, especially in 1788. His fluency in Gaelic and English obviously gave the Pictou ceremony a special quality, as did his unique preaching strengths and his almost limitless store of energy. According to those who often heard him preach at long communions:

He seemed to rise with the occasion, and in the vigour and unction of his address to increase to the end. Indeed ... his efforts on these occasions were the most astonishing of his life. It was on these occasions, particularly, that the remarkable power of his voice was exhibited. But few men could address large audiences in the open air as easily as he could. His voice was not indeed loud nor anything of what is called stentorian, but it was beautifully clear and melodious as a woman's. There was not the least harshness about it, but its tones were rather plaintive and tender, yet such was its compass that he was easily heard over the largest assembly; and so clear was his utterance, that he was heard as distinctly at the outer edge of the crowd, as at the very centre.[62]

Those who knew MacGregor well contended that within a half-mile radius "not only was his voice heard, but the words were distinguished." Furthermore, it was said that his voice, almost miraculously, "increased in fullness till the last day of services."

MacGregor had fully understood how important it was to find a suitable location for the long communion, a place where the "multitude assembled under the broad canopy of heaven to engage in the highest and holiest rites of our religion."[63] The "sacred spot" where the first long communion was celebrated was described as follows: "The quiet grassy glade, on which the tables were spread, with the wooded bank in front, looking down upon the river, and around the sloping hills covered with forest, then in all the verdure of summer, and only here and there broken by the small clearing of the settler, formed a scene from which the eye of even the mere lover of nature might drink in delight."[64] Thus, Nova Scotian nature provided the environment in which the communion ritual from Scotland was transplanted in the Maritimes. What eventually evolved was Highland Scots Presbyterian to the core but there was also a certain Nova Scotian evangelical element – distinct yet strangely muted.

There is yet another way to look at the Pictou long communion of 1787, namely, by using some of the insights to be found in Leigh Eric Schmidt's groundbreaking work, *Holy Fairs: Scottish Communions and American Revivals in the Early Modern Period* (1989). According to Schmidt, the long communion as "a set of intricate rituals and as an embodiment of a complex symbolic universe," is "a fertile field for the retrospective ethnographer":[65]

Though Protestants generally and evangelicals particularly are often seen as having so aggrandized the preached Word that sacramental actions paled in comparison, faith in the unsurpassed power of the eucharist was forever central to the revivalism of the evangelical Presbyterians.

He goes on:

Embodied in measured gestures and tangible elements, the gospel was caught up in the mystical actions of the Lord's Supper and set forth for all to see. "Looking upon these elements hath done more good than many sermons," John Livingstone testified; "the substance of the whole Bible is in these sacramental elements; the whole covenant, a whole Christ in a state of humiliation and exaltation." Or, as one preacher proclaimed at a Saturday preparation service on the eve of eucharistic celebration: "The Lord ... hath been calling to you by the still calm voice of the word, the trumpet will sound louder to-morrow, he hath been speaking to you this day by his word, but to-morrow he will speak by his bloody wounds."[66]

Thus, as "words gave way to eucharistic actions,"[67] the Scots Presbyterians actually saw the gospel; not only that, but some actually tasted the "blood and the body" of the sacrificed Saviour. For them, the entire Christian gospel was indeed embodied in the long communion. In this, their own unique ritual process, preparation was followed by penitence and then purification.[68] Schmidt holds that the white communion cloth (and this is only one of the examples he uses) represented far more than Christian purity. Those who came to the Lord's table saw far beyond the white linen cover: "Weeping over Christ's death and absence, symbolized in the linen, the saint might then meet with Christ as Mary did. Thus could sacral symbols of purity, such as these spotless coverings, evoke other meanings. Rituals and symbols of purity and preparation ultimately opened outward into fuller emblems of the faith."[69] And when the women and men "partook of the bread and the wine," they found themselves not only experiencing with their neighbours a heightened sense of mutuality and *communitas* but also the mystical presence of the divine.[70] The intense sense of *communitas* was strengthened by the shared experience of piercing the "fence" around the "table of the Lord." Moreover, seated around the table, some had a foretaste of heaven and the millennium to come; others saw ever so clearly the need for holiness in their lives while still in "this vale of tears."

It should be noted that much of the imagery used during the long communion (like that at the camp meetings, believer's baptism, and religious revivals) although understood perhaps "in wholly spiritual ways, bordered at times on the erotic."[71] Even at Pictou in 1787, emphasis was placed upon being united with Christ; Christ was the "beloved" who was "mine," and "all that he hath" was "mine."[72] It is not surprising therefore that Schmidt should conclude that being immersed "in such sensual metaphors and symbols, the saints used such biblical – and sexual – images to express a divine love that was for them little related to, and far greater than, earthy love."[73] The long communions thus "presented a compelling combination of solemnity and festivity."[74] At Pictou in 1788, the solemnity was more obvious than the festivity. But as the eighteenth century moved into the nineteenth, the Maritime Presbyterian long communion, like that in Scotland, inextricably combined, almost as equals, the sacred and the social.

In the long communion there was a peculiar mix of pre-Reformation Catholicism, eighteenth-century Scots evangelicalism, and an almost naive Highland-peasant obsession with magic and the occult. In the frontier wilderness of Nova Scotia during the period linking the coming of the Loyalists and the outbreak of the War of 1812, it helped to provide the Scots immigrants with an experiential bridge between the past and the present and between the Old World and the New. Moreover, it helped to carve off the jagged edges of the uprooting experience by adding shape and substance to a new sense of Scots identity and a new sense of group solidarity.[75] The long communion became the quintessential Scots Presbyterian religious ritual, pregnant with spiritual meaning, in the same way that the camp meeting was the quintessential Methodist evangelical ritual and believer's baptism was the Baptists'.

The Pictou long communion may have attracted a few hundred worshippers in 1788. Within two or three decades, thousands were attending – from a radius of sixty or seventy miles. These decades witnessed the arrival in Nova Scotia of thousands of Scots Presbyterian and Roman Catholic immigrants. By 1815, the population of Pictou County was estimated to have been 8,737, over half of whom were Presbyterians.[76] Out of a total Nova Scotia population of 60,000 in 1808, approximately one-third, or 20,000, were from Scotland, and of this number some 10,000 were, in all likelihood, Presbyterians. It is known that in December 1807, MacGregor estimated that Pictou County contained "600 or 700 families" of Highlanders, "of which the majority are Protestants." Not all of these Protestants were people whom MacGregor viewed as "believers." If 400 families were Protestant, perhaps half this number actually partook of communion. And of those who took communion, MacGregor was certain that "four-fifths of them" were indeed "worthy."[77] Obviously, there was a significant moderate evangelical group of Presbyterians in Pictou County; in 1808 they may have constituted almost one-quarter of the total population of the county. Pictou County was, all observers agreed, the Presbyterian evangelical heartland of the Maritimes.

During the period between the American Revolution and the War of 1812, there was not one resident Presbyterian minister in New Brunswick (the first arrived in 1817).[78] On Prince Edward Island, during this period, only the "Rev. Mr. Urquart, of the Church of Scotland, had laboured for two years in Prince Edward Island; being the only Presbyterian, during this period, to do so."[79] Obviously, therefore, Pictou County was the evangelical exception to the Presbyterian rule in the Maritimes.

When MacGregor arrived in Nova Scotia in 1786, he was one of only five Presbyterian ministers in the region. When he died in 1830, he was one of twenty-one.[80] The Halifax *Nova Scotian* commented on his death: "If he met a believer, he joined him as a traveller journeying on the same road, to the same country, and was happy that they had been brought together. If he found an unfortunate brother who needed consolation, he ... administered to him the comfort of the Gospel."[81] MacGregor was capable of "almost superhuman exertions,"[82] and as he grew older his closed-minded anti-Burgher Presbyterianism was replaced by an almost winsome Maritime evangelicalism. Two verses from one of the twenty-five spiritual songs he wrote, which were published originally in Gaelic in 1819 under the title *Dain a chomhnadh crabhuidh* captured something of his orderly Presbyterian evangelicalism:

To one who is anxious, because with him, he feels God is displeased
And whose sins appalling, in dense array, close in around him
Not knowing but that he's doomed to hell's agonizing torments,
E'er yet next morn arrives, with death, the grim monster, in his eye,
To one who the knowledge of truth from the Holy Spirit has learned
That the pleasure which this world imparts is empty, false and vain;
For during the present, it's no more than a fleeting shadow,
Whose brief existence death, most surely, shall then for ever end.

To tell of life and safety is news which great delight inspired,
From Jesus who his life resigned moved by love for all mankind,
His blood is the remedy in which exists the power to heal,
When with sympathizing tenderness it is at once applied
To a wounded heart and a stranger to happiness and joy,
But troubled, sorrowful, and without a guide in search of peace,
By the noble Spirit of powers invincible and divine.
When he descends upon it with mild and quickening influence.[83]

The "quickening influence" of the Holy Spirit may have been felt by a number of Presbyterians, especially in Nova Scotia, during the period 1784–1812. But there were, the evidence suggests, precious few evangelical Anglicans. Of the approximately thirty-five Anglican ministers who were stationed in Nova Scotia between 1783 and

1816,[84] only one was a professed evangelical; most of the others were embarrassing misfits who did little in a positive sense to build up the spiritual lives of the estimated 20 per cent of the population that was Anglican.[85] The Reverend William Twining of Cornwallis, who was an avowed evangelical, alienated most of his congregation and the Society of the Propagation of the Gospel because of his sympathy for the religious style of the despised New Lights and Methodists.[86] There was also an evangelical Anglican minister located on Prince Edward Island during this period, the Reverend Theophulus Desbrisay (1754–1823), who was described by MacGregor in 1791 as "a devoted Christian, and decidedly evangelical and Calvinist in his views."[87] A graduate of Trinity College, Dublin, Desbrisay had little influence on the religious life of Prince Edward Island or on his largely moribund denomination, which had virtually no impact on the religious life of the island.

As far as MacGregor was concerned, the Maritime Anglicans and Roman Catholics required "conversion" to become true Christians. On the other hand, the Baptists, New Lights, and Methodists needed only the steady glow of Presbyterian Calvinism in order to be "enlightened," since they clearly endorsed the central evangelical doctrine of "the necessity of regeneration" and were basically "good" men and women.[88] By the middle of the nineteenth century, whether in central Canada or the Maritimes, evangelical Presbyterians felt themselves to be closer, despite perceived ethnic and doctrinal differences, to the Baptists, Methodists, and other evangelicals than to non-evangelical Presbyterians. All these evangelical groups were an integral part of the evolving "evangelical alliance" within what was indeed the "evangelical century."[89] But it would not be the "radical evangelical century."

Conclusion

Some of the worst fears that the key Canadian Anglican Loyalist leaders had about the evils of American republicanism and religious enthusiasm seemed to be confirmed by the outbreak of the War of 1812. This negative view of Americans and the American republic considerably helped to strengthen a pro-British bias in what is now Canada, a bias that was further consolidated by the influx of hundreds of thousands of British immigrants after the war. Anti-Americanism triggered by the War of 1812, especially in central Canada, and the demographic transformation of British North America in the postwar period, together with the transformation of the sect mentality into the church mode of thought, meant, among other things, that radical evangelicalism was no longer on the leading edge of Protestantism. Instead, it was gradually pushed to the periphery by a leadership preoccupied with British order, British respectability, and a growing suspicion of democratic and populist evangelical enthusiasm.

Despite this gradual marginalization of radical evangelicalism, the nineteenth century in Canada has, with some justification, been called "the evangelical century."[1] As Goldwin French perceptively observed in 1968, it was an evangelicalism shaped by a creed[2] – a loosely constructed yet pervasive body of Christian beliefs and assumptions – rather than by a common collective traumatic religious conversion experience. It was also an evangelicalism that owed more to the evangelicalism of the James MacGregors than it did to that of a Henry Alline or Freeborn Garrettson.

As French has observed, in the period preceding the War of 1812 in particular, but also during the two decades following the war, even though there "was an evangelical element in the Anglican and Presbyterian churches," there were still "real differences between them and the genuine evangelical churches – the Methodists and the Baptists."[3] By the latter part of the nineteenth century, however, these so-called genuine evangelical churches, whether in Atlantic Canada, central Canada, or the West, had become more like the evangelical Anglicans and Presbyterians. This new evangelical alliance put more stress on the religion of the head and less on the religion of the heart, and easily "succumbed ... to the materialist delights" of late-Victorian Canada.[4]

Increasingly, as Canadian society changed in the so-called progressive milieu of the late nineteenth century, the old religious language about the New Birth and revivalism no longer articulated the changing experience and practice of many leading Canadian Protestants. In an attempt to find new wineskins for the old evangelical wine, the traditional conversionist piety was altered – some would say fundamentally – by key members of the denominational élites, and was replaced by a new piety that no longer placed much emphasis on the New Birth of the individual but saw its special mission in the "spread of scriptural holiness by reforming the nation."[5] This Social Gospel emphasis, however, was not enthusiastically accepted by many rank-and-file Canadian evangelicals, who preferred to embrace the old piety and the old verities. The accommodating Protestantism of the élites was very different from an accommodating popular evangelicalism that continued to be shaped largely by "enthusiasm" and, to a lesser degree, by the continuing influence of radical evangelicalism.

For many Canadian Protestant church leaders, the abandonment of "conversionism" was the first step leading to the disembowelling of traditional Christian orthodoxy. Having lost faith in themselves and having abandoned the faith of their fathers and mothers, many sought salvation in the gospel of "inhibited scientific inquiry."[6] Others turned to what has been called the "insidious antithesis to essential Christianity"[7] – the gospel of narcissistic therapeutic self-realization underpinning North American consumerism.[8] Many rank-and-file Canadian Protestants, however, refused in the twentieth century to follow their mad dash away from the coordinates of Christian orthodoxy. The forces of secularization in the twentieth century have, without question, significantly affected virtually every aspect of Canadian Protestantism. Yet despite the revolutionary changes unleashed by secularization, and despite what many recent scholars have maintained has been the victory of the religious liberals in blazing a path "not to the Kingdom of God on earth, as many had hoped, but, ironically, to the secular city,"[9] the legacy of radical evangelicalism has not been eradicated from the religious landscape.

It is becoming increasingly clear that the forces of nineteenth-century Canadian evangelical continuity were not completely and unceremoniously neutralized by the forces of secular progress and modernity. In early 1993, the Angus Reid Group did a series of surveys on Canadian religion (the largest scientific religious survey ever conducted in Canada).[10] The results, based upon four monthly surveys involving some 6,000 respondents, with a margin of error of plus or minus 1.3 per cent nineteen times out of twenty, seemed to support those advocates of evangelical continuity and questioned the conclusions put forward by those who have argued that "supernatural Christianity" is virtually dead in Canada.

In answering the question "I feel that through the life, death and resurrection of Jesus, God provided a way for the forgiveness of my sins," 39 per cent "strongly agreed" and 22 per cent "moderately agreed." Moreover, 14 per cent of the adult Canadians surveyed "strongly agreed" that the "Bible is God's word, and is to be taken literally word for word," while 16 per cent "moderately agreed"; 47 per cent "strongly agreed" and 20 per cent "moderately agreed" that "Jesus was crucified, died and was buried but was resurrected to eternal life"; 20 per cent stated that they read their Bible daily or weekly, and 29 per cent stated that they pray daily.

It is also important to underscore some of the regional differences, which appear to buttress some of the major conclusions put forward in this volume. The region of Canada that was both most significantly affected by radical evangelicalism and least affected by the forces of modernity was Atlantic Canada. In the 1990s, as tables 1 to 3 suggest, Atlantic Canada continues to be the heartland of Canadian evangelicalism.

It is of some consequence that 17 per cent of adults in the Atlantic region have "had a profound religious conversion experience – a particularly powerful religious insight or awakening" – compared with the 14 per cent of all Canadians; 33 per cent of Atlantic adults have committed their lives "to Christ" and "consider [themselves] to be ... Converted Christians," in contrast to 28 per cent of Canadians; 18 per cent of Atlantic adults say they have been "Born Again or had a turning point in life when I committed myself to Christ," while only 15 per cent of Canadians do; 21 per cent of the former say they agree strongly or agree that they are "charismatic Christians," compared with 14 per cent of Canadians. Moreover, 37 per cent of

Table 1
Percentage of Canadian Adults Who Pray Daily

Atlantic provinces	36
Quebec	30
Ontario	29
Manitoba/Saskatchewan	32
Alberta	26
British Columbia	20
National	29

Source: Angus Reid survey, 1993

Table 2
Percentage of Canadian Adults Who Attend Religious
Services at Least "Once a week or so"

Atlantic provinces	37
Quebec	20
Ontario	24
Manitoba/Saskatchewan	29
Alberta	21
British Columbia	15
National	23

Source: Angus Reid survey, 1993

Table 3
Percentage of Canadian Adults Who Read the Bible or
Other Religious Writings at Least Weekly

Atlantic provinces	28
Quebec	13
Ontario	22
Manitoba/Saskatchewan	25
Alberta	20
British Columbia	16
National	20

Source: Angus Reid survey, 1993

Atlantic residents maintain that it is important to evangelize non-Christians, compared with 26 per cent of Canadians.

The 1990s may not be Canada's "Christian decade," but there is a greater residue of evangelicalism in general, and radical evangelicalism in particular, in the land than even the most ardent evangelicals had thought. From the vantage point of the élite, in the late twentieth century, Canadian Christianity was considered as dead and irrelevant as the Christian God. From the grassroots populist level, a radically different picture is emerging, with 13 per cent of the population evangelistic evangelicals, 11 per cent dormant evangelicals and 14 per cent ardent churchgoers (evangelistic evangelicals without the evangelism). Furthermore, it is important to note that one-third of Canadian evangelicals are now Roman Catholics – the "Catho-evangelicals." The religious enemy in much of the nineteenth and twentieth centuries has, in a remarkable reversal of roles, become in the last two decades of the twentieth century, an enthusiastic religious ally.

In the 1990s, in Canada, there is, I have recently discovered, a huge gap between those who both believe and practise their Christianity and those who have little faith in contemporary Christianity and its institutions. In the nineteenth and early twentieth centuries, the Christian church could be used by the Canadian élite to impose its values on society in general – and to impose a form of social control. This alliance, however, collapsed in the interwar years. The élite, having little real contact with the Canadian grass roots, believed that Christianity was a spent ideological force and that God was indeed dead. Their world was a secular world devoid of any sense of ultimate meaning other than that shaped by the shibboleths of consumerism, progress, and so-called scientific truth. In gutting Canadian Christianity, they alienated many Canadians whose religiosity remained orthodox; moreover, they failed to realize that Christianity had not, in fact, died in Canada.

There is still, after two centuries, a distinct populist, evangelical strain in Canadian Protestantism – still one at odds with the élite's view of reality. Thus, when religiosity in Canada is studied from the bottom up, using the data recently assembled by the Angus Reid Group, a radically different picture begins to emerge from that projected for decades from the top down. Some of this data, I am sure, will ripple back to the nineteenth century and compel scholars to ask new questions about the so-called new and old orthodoxies and also about the transforming power of radical evangelicalism, not only in the distant past but also in the increasingly disorienting present.

Notes

ABBREVIATIONS

AAS   American Antiquarian Society
AUA   Acadia University Archives
DCB   *Dictionary of Canadian Biography*
PANS   Public Archives of Nova Scotia
SPG   Society for the Propagation of the Gospel
UCA   United Church Archives

INTRODUCTION

1 Nehemiah Curnock, ed., *The Journal of John Wesley*, 8 vols. (London: Charles H. Kelly, 1909), 1:475–6.
2 *Arminian Magazine* (London, 1791), 68–70.
3 H. Alline, *The Life and Journal* (Boston: Gilbert and Dean, 1806), 35.
4 C.C. Goen, ed., *The Works of Jonathan Edwards*, vol. 4, *The Great Awakening* (New Haven: Yale University Press, 1972), 193.
5 "An Account of the Life of Mr. David George," reprinted in G. Gordon, *From Slavery to Freedom: The Life of David George, Pioneer Baptist Minister* (Hantsport: Lancelot Press, 1992), 171–2.
6 Lyman A. Kellstedt, "The Meaning and Measurement of Evangelicalism: Problems and Prospects," in *Religion and Political Behavior in the United States*, ed. T.G. Jelen (New York: Praeger, 1989), 5. According to Kellstedt, these four key doctrines establish what may be regarded as the "set of minimalist" criteria for evangelical membership. David Beb-

bington also stresses this point in his influential *Evangelicalism in Modern Britain* (London: Allen and Unwin, 1989).

7 See George Marsden, "The Evangelical Denomination," in *Evangelicalism and Modern America*, ed. G. Marsden (Grand Rapids: W.B. Eerdmans, 1984), x.

8 Nathan Hatch, *The Democratization of American Christianity* (New Haven: Yale University Press, 1989).

9 See my paper, "'A Total Revolution in Religious and Civil Government': The Maritimes, New England, and the Evening Evangelical Ethos, 1776–1812," presented at Wheaton College, April 1992.

10 M. Noll, "The American Revolution, the Interaction of Conceptual 'Languages,' and the Rise of Protestant Evangelicalism in the United States" (unpublished paper, presented at a conference at Prouts Neck, Maine, October 1991).

11 H. Alline, *The Anti-Traditionalist* (Halifax: Anthony Henry, 1783), 65.

12 My *New Light Letters and Spiritual Songs, 1778–1793* (Hantsport: Lancelot Press, 1983) is an attempt, among other things, to prove this thesis from the bottom up.

INTRODUCTION TO PART ONE

1 Nathan Hatch, *The Democratization of American Christianity* (New Haven: Yale University Press, 1989), 224.

2 *Ibid.*, 49.

3 Harry S. Stout, *The New England Soul: Preaching and Religious Culture in Colonial New England* (New York: Oxford University Press, 1986).

4 My definition of radical evangelicalism includes what Curtis Johnson has recently referred to as the "emotional faith" of the "Antiformalists" and the "liberating faith" of "African Americans." This radical evangelicalism was fundamentally different from "formal," or "orderly," evangelicalism; see Curtis D. Johnson, *Redeeming America: Evangelicals and the Road to Civil War* (Chicago: Ivan Dee, 1993), 7–9.

CHAPTER ONE

1 D.G. Bell, ed., *Newlight Baptist Journals of James Manning and James Innis* (Hantsport: Lancelot Press, 1984), xiii.

2 T. Vincent, "Henry Alline: Problems of Approach and Reading the *Hymns* as Poetry," in *They Planted Well: New England Planters in Maritime Canada*, ed. M. Conrad (Fredericton: Acadiensis Press, 1988), 203.

3 This theme is developed in greater detail in G.A. Rawlyk, *Ravished by the Spirit: Religious Revivals, Baptists and Henry Alline* (Montreal: McGill-

Queen's University Press, 1984) and *Champions of the Truth: Fundamentalism, Modernism, and the Maritime Baptists* (Montreal: McGill-Queens University Press, 1990).

4 See, in particular, James Beverley and Barry Moody, eds., *The Journal of Henry Alline* (Hantsport: Lancelot Press, 1982), 23–5.

5 J. Davis, *Life and Times of the Late Rev. Harris Harding, Yarmouth, N.S.* (Charlottetown: Printed for the Compiler, 1866), 178.

6 William James, *Varieties of Religious Experience* (New York: Longmans, Green, 1902), 159, 217.

7 M.E. Marty, *Modern American Religion: The Irony of It All: 1893–1919* (Chicago: University of Chicago Press, 1986), 1:42.

8 Beverley and Moody, *Journal of Henry Alline*, 53–4.

9 Ibid., 36–7.

10 Ibid., 39–40.

11 Ibid., 40.

12 Ibid., 41.

13 Ibid., 46–8.

14 Ibid., 48.

15 Ibid., 49.

16 Ibid., 49–50.

17 Ibid., 50–1.

18 Ibid., 50.

19 Ibid., 52–3.

20 Ibid., 61.

21 Ibid.

22 Ibid. The translation is from the King James version, which Alline used and huge sections of which he had memorized. He seems to have possessed a photographic memory.

23 Ibid.

24 Ibid., 61–2.

25 Ibid., 62.

26 Ibid., 63.

27 H. Alline, *The Anti-Traditionalist* (Halifax: Anthony Henry, 1783), 40.

28 See ibid., 62–3, and H. Alline, *Two Mites: Some of the Most Important and Much Disputed Points of Divinity* (Halifax: Anthony Henry, 1781), 20–1.

29 Alline, *Anti-Traditionalist*, 65.

30 Ibid.

31 Alline, *Two Mites*, 121–35.

32 Ibid., 124.

33 Ibid., 124–5.

34 Ibid., 126.

35 Ibid.

36 Ibid.
37 Quoted in a fragment of an unidentified letter in the Manning Papers, Acadia University Archives.
38 Alline, *Two Mites*, 128.
39 Ibid., 128–9.
40 Ibid., 132.
41 Ibid., 132–3.
42 Ibid., 150–1.
43 Alline, *Anti-Traditionalist*, 40.
44 Alline, *Two Mites*, 95.
45 M. Armstrong, *The Great Awakening in Nova Scotia 1776–1809* (Hartford: American Society of Church History, 1948), 101.
46 Beverley and Moody, *Journal of Henry Alline*, 216.
47 This point is stressed in S.A. Marini, *Radical Sects of Revolutionary New England* (Cambridge: Harvard University Press, 1982).
48 See Rawlyk, *Ravished by the Spirit*, 81–5, 89–101.
49 Henry Alline, *A Gospel Call to Sinners* (Newburyport: Blunt and March, 1795), 29.
50 H. Abelove, *The Evangelist of Desire: John Wesley and the Methodists* (Stanford: Stanford University Press, 1990), 82.
51 Quoted in Armstrong, *The Great Awakening in Nova Scotia*, 86.
52 "Matthew Byles III Journal," Public Archives of Nova Scotia (PANS), MG 1, vol. 163.
53 "Records of the Church of Jebogue in Yarmouth," 138, PANS.
54 Ibid., 140.

CHAPTER TWO

1 See my article "William Black, Henry Alline, and Nova Scotia's First Great Awakening," in *The Contribution of Methodism to Atlantic Canada*, ed. C.H.H. Scobie and J.W. Grant (Montreal: McGill-Queen's University Press, 1992), 79–91.
2 Quoted in G. French, *Parsons and Politics* (Toronto: Ryerson Press, 1962), 65.
3 Quoted in ibid., 38.
4 Quoted in ibid., 65.
5 See my "Freeborn Garrettson and Nova Scotia," *Methodist History* 30, no. 3 (April 1992): 157–8.
6 G.S. French, "William Black," *Dictionary of Canadian Biography* (hereafter cited as *DCB*) (Toronto: University of Toronto Press, 1987), 6:67.
7 *Arminian Magazine* (London, 1791), 14.
8 Ibid., 14–15.

9 Ibid, 15.
10 Ibid., 15–16.
11 Ibid., 68–70.
12 Ibid., 70–2.
13 French, "William Black," 62.
14 D.C. Harvey and C.B. Fergusson, eds., *The Diary of Simeon Perkins, 1780–1789* (Toronto: Champlain Society, 1958), 168–74.
15 Ibid., 177.
16 Ibid., 188.
17 Ibid.
18 Ibid., 189–90.
19 B.C. Cuthbertson, ed., *The Journal of John Payzant* (Hantsport: Lancelot Press, 1981), 28.
20 James Beverley and Barry Moody, eds., *The Journal of Henry Alline* (Hantsport: Lancelot Press, 1982), 180.
21 Ibid., 178.
22 Ibid., 179.
23 Ibid.
24 Ibid., 181.
25 Ibid., 197.
26 Ibid., 199.
27 M. Richey, *A Memoir of the Late Rev. William Black, Wesleyan Minister, Halifax, N.S.* (Halifax: William Cunnabell, 1839), 44–5.
28 Ibid., 50.
29 *Arminian Magazine* (London, 1791), 123.
30 Ibid., 178.
31 Richey, *Memoir of the Late Rev. William Black*, 66–7.
32 Ibid., 67.
33 Ibid., 69.
34 Ibid., 74.
35 Ibid.
36 Ibid., 76.
37 Ibid., 234.
38 *Arminian Magazine* (London, 1791), 78.
39 See Richey, *Memoir of the Late Rev. William Black*, 80–1.
40 Quoted in ibid., 98–9.
41 Ibid., 107.
42 Ibid., 107–8.
43 Ibid., 104.
44 See G.A. Rawlyk, *Wrapped Up in God: A Study of Several Canadian Revivals and Revivalists* (Burlington: Welch, 1988), 55–7.
45 French, "William Black," 67.

46 Quoted in ibid., 66.

CHAPTER THREE

1 "Macaulay Journal, Tuesday, April 25, 1797," quoted in Grant Gordon, *From Slavery to Freedom: The Life of David George, Pioneer Baptist Minister* (Hantsport: Lancelot Press, 1992), 144.

2 Gordon, *From Slavery to Freedom*, 163.

3 Ibid.

4 This theme is developed in greater detail in ibid., 25–7. Gordon's detailed treatment should be read in conjunction with Albert J. Raboteau, *Slave Religion: The "Invisible Institution" in the Antebellum South* (New York: Oxford University Press, 1980), 136–41.

5 See A.F. Walls, "The Nova Scotia Settlers and their Religion," *Sierra Leone Bulletin of Religion* 1, no. 1 (1959): 19–31; and, more recently, his suggestive paper, "Evangelical Revivalism, the Missionary Movement and Africa" (delivered at the Trans-Atlantic Evangelicalism Conference, Wheaton College, Wheaton, Illinois, April 1992).

6 "An Account of the Life of Mr. DAVID GEORGE," reprinted in Gordon, *From Slavery to Freedom*, 168.

7 Ibid.

8 Ibid., 169.

9 Ibid.

10 Ibid., 170.

11 Ibid., 171.

12 Ibid., 169.

13 Ibid., 171–2.

14 *Rippon's Register* 1:332, quoted in Gordon, *From Slavery to Freedom*, 24.

15 Clarence M. Wagner, *Profiles of Black Georgia Baptists* (Gaineville Georgia, 1980), 4, quoted in Gordon, *From Slavery to Freedom*, 24.

16 "DAVID GEORGE," in Gordon, *From Slavery to Freedom*, 172.

17 Ibid.

18 Mechal Sobel, *Trabelin' On: The Slave Journey to an Afro-Baptist Faith* (Westport: Greenwood Press, 1979), 160. See also Raboteau, *Slave Religion*, 128–37.

19 "DAVID GEORGE," in Gordon, *From Slavery To Freedom*, 172.

20 Ibid.

21 Ibid., 173.

22 Gordon, *From Slavery to Freedom*, 25.

23 Ibid.

24 "DAVID GEORGE," in Gordon, *From Slavery to Freedom*, 172.

25 Ibid., 173.

26 Ibid.

27 Ibid.
28 See G.A. Rawlyk, *Ravished by the Spirit: Religious Revivals, Baptists and Henry Alline* (Montreal: McGill-Queen's University Press, 1984), 80–9.
29 This entire section dealing with the Macaulay-George debate is based on the "Macaulay Journal" fragments to be found in Gordon, *From Slavery to Freedom*, 142–9.
30 See A.F. Walls, "The Nova Scotia Settlers and their Religion," *Sierra Leone Bulletin of Religion* 1, no. 1 (1959): 19–31; Christopher Fyfe, "The Baptist Churches in Sierra Leone," ibid., 5, no. 2 (1963): 55–60; "The Countess of Huntington's Connexion in Nineteenth Century Sierra Leone," ibid., 4, no. 2 (1962): 53–61; and "The West African Methodists in the Nineteenth Century," ibid., 3, no. 1 (1961): 22–8. Christopher Fyfe, *A History of Sierra Leone* (London: Oxford University Press, 1962), is also of great value.
31 See Walls, "Evangelical Revivalism." Walls developed this theme at greater length in the discussion following the paper.
32 "DAVID GEORGE," in Gordon, *From Slavery to Freedom*, 177.
33 Ibid.
34 Ibid., 178.
35 D.C. Harvey and C.B. Fergusson, eds., *The Diary of Simeon Perkins, 1780–1789* (Toronto: Champlain Society, 1958), 297.
36 "DAVID GEORGE," in Gordon, *From Slavery to Freedom*, 180.
37 Harris Harding to Joseph Dimock, 1 Sept. 1791, in G.A. Rawlyk, ed., *New Light Letters and Spiritual Songs, 1778–1793* (Hantsport: Lancelot Press, 1983), 155.
38 Harding to Lavina D'Wolf, 20 August 1791, in Rawlyk, *New Light Letters and Songs*, 131.
39 Quoted in J.M. Cramp, "Baptists of Nova Scotia (1760–1860)," 71, in Acadia University Archives (hereafter cited as AUA).
40 "DAVID GEORGE," in Gordon, *From Slavery to Freedom*, 181.
41 E.G. Wilson, *The Loyal Blacks* (New York: G.P. Putnam, 1976), 241.
42 James W. St G. Walker, "David George," *DCB* 5:341.
43 Black Nova Scotia Methodists also shared this intense New Light spirituality. See the primary material about two Nova Scotia Black Methodist leaders, John Marrant and Boston King, in G.E. Clarke, ed., *Fire on the Water: An Anthology of Black Nova Scotia Writing* (Lawrencetown Beach: Pottersfield Press, 1991), 1:40–56.

CHAPTER FOUR

1 See George A. Rawlyk, "Freeborn Garrettson," *DCB* 6:275–6, and "Freeborn Garrettson and Nova Scotia," *Methodist History*, 30, no. 3 (April 1992): 142–58.

2 W.C. Barclay, *Early American Methodism, 1769–1844* (New York: Board of Missions and Church Extension of the Methodist Church, 1949), 1:171.

3 J.M. Buckley, *A History of Methodism in the United States* (New York: Christian Literature Company, 1897), 1:369.

4 Quoted in T.W. Smith, *History of the Methodist Church within the Territories Embraced in the Late Conference of Eastern British America, including Nova Scotia, New Brunswick, Prince Edward Island and Bermuda* (Halifax, 1877), 193–4.

5 Quoted in N. Bangs, *The Life of the Rev. Freeborn Garrettson* (New York, 1832), 154.

6 Buckley, *A History of Methodism in the United States,* 1:171.

7 See R.D. Simpson, ed., *American Methodist Pioneer: The Life and Journals of The Rev. Freeborn Garrettson 1752–1827* (Rutland, Vt: Academy Books, 1984).

8 Ibid., 2.

9 Ibid., 40.

10 Ibid., 42.

11 Ibid., 43.

12 Ibid.

13 Ibid.

14 Ibid., 44.

15 Ibid.

16 Ibid.

17 Ibid.

18 Ibid., 44–5.

19 Ibid., 47.

20 Ibid., 48.

21 Ibid., 47.

22 Ibid., 47–8.

23 Ibid., 48.

24 Ibid., 49–50.

25 Ibid., 54–77.

26 Ibid., 79, 98–101.

27 Quoted in Bangs, *Garrettson,* 177.

28 Ibid., 172.

29 *Methodist Magazine* (1827), 272.

30 See G.A. Rawlyk, ed., *New Light Letters and Spiritual Songs, 1778–1793* (Hantsport: Lancelot Press, 1983), 31–3.

31 W.W. Williams, *The Garden of American Methodism: The Delmarva Peninsula 1769–1820* (Wilmington, Del.: Scholarly Resources, 1984), 32.

32 Ibid.

33 Quoted in ibid.

34 "Freeborn Garrettson Journal," transcript, United Church Archives, Toronto (hereafter cited as UCA).
35 Ibid.
36 Ibid.
37 Ibid.
38 Simpson, *American Methodist Pioneer*, 127.
39 Ibid.
40 "Freeborn Garrettson Journal," UCA.
41 Ibid.
42 Ibid.
43 Garrettson to John Wesley, 10 March 1787, in Simpson, *American Methodist Pioneer*, 248.
44 Ibid., 129–30.
45 Quoted in Barclay, *Early American Methodism*, 1:171.
46 Quoted in G. French, *Parsons and Politics* (Toronto: Ryerson Press, 1962), 34.
47 See Rawlyk, "Freeborn Garrettson and Nova Scotia," 148–58.

CHAPTER FIVE

1 J. Davis, *Life and Times of the Late Rev. Harris Harding, Yarmouth, N.S.* (Charlottetown: Printed for the Compiler, 1866), 178.
2 J.M. Cramp, "History of the Maritime Baptists," 35, AUA.
3 H. Harding, "Account of the Rise and Progress of the First Baptist Church in Yarmouth, Nova Scotia," in Davis, *Harris Harding*, 206.
4 See the chapter on Harding and the Second Great Awakening in G.A. Rawlyk, *Wrapped Up in God* (Burlington: Welch, 1988), 76–95.
5 I.E. Bill, *Fifty Years with the Baptist Ministers and Churches of the Maritime Provinces of Canada* (Saint John: Barnes, 1880), 201–2.
6 C.B. Fergusson, ed., *The Diary of Simeon Perkins, 1790–1796* (Toronto: University of Toronto Press, 1966), 177.
7 C.B. Fergusson, ed., *The Diary of Simeon Perkins, 1797–1803* (Toronto: University of Toronto Press, 1968), 18.
8 Fergusson, *Diary of Simeon Perkins, 1790–1796*, 428.
9 Davis, *Harris Harding*, 146–8.
10 T.S. Harding, "Recollections of Harris Harding," 10 March 1854, in ibid., 168.
11 See G.A. Rawlyk, "From New Light to Baptist: Harris Harding and the Second Great Awakening in Nova Scotia," in *Repent and Believe: The Baptist Experience in Maritime Canada*, ed. B. Moody (Hantsport: Lancelot Press, 1980), 11.
12 Davis, *Harris Harding*, 5.
13 Quoted in ibid., 5.

14 Quoted in ibid., 7–8.
15 Quoted in ibid., 10.
16 B. Cuthbertson, ed., *The Journal of John Payzant* (Hantsport: Lancelot Press, 1981), 37–8.
17 Ibid., 38.
18 Davis, *Harris Harding*, 143.
19 Alexander Crawford to Edward Manning, 2 October 1813, Manning Letters, AUA.
20 Fergusson, *Diary of Simeon Perkins, 1790–1796*, 174.
21 Davis, *Harris Harding*, 33.
22 See H. Harding to T. Harris, 14 May 1789, in G.A. Rawlyk, ed., *New Light Letters and Spiritual Songs, 1778–1793* (Hantsport: Lancelot Press, 1983), 94.
23 Harding to Dorcas Prentice and Keturah Whipple, 24 May 1791, ibid., 123.
24 Harding to Nancy Brown, 9 July 1791, ibid., 126.
25 Harding to John Payzant, 23 August 1791, ibid., 133.
26 This letter is to be found in the Manning Papers, AUA.
27 Harding to D. Prentice, 27 August 1791, in the Manning Papers, AUA.
28 Harding to D. Prentice, 17 September 1791, in Rawlyk, *New Light Letters and Songs*, 66.
29 Harding to E. Manning, 1 September 1792, ibid., 170.
30 Harding to W. Alline, 6 April 1792, quoted in Cramp, "A History of the Maritime Baptists," 33, AUA.
31 Harding to Dorcas Prentice, 27 August 1791, in Rawlyk, *New Light Letters and Songs*, 147.
32 Cramp, "History of the Maritime Baptists," 35, AUA.
33 "Freeborn Garrettson Journal," UCA.
34 Cuthbertson, *Journal of John Payzant*, 43.
35 Ibid., 44.
36 Ibid.
37 Ibid.
38 Ibid., 45–7.
39 Ibid., 47.
40 Ibid., 49.
41 Ibid., 52.
42 Ibid., 55.
43 Quoted in Cramp, "History of the Maritime Baptists," 24.
44 Ibid.
45 Harding to T.H. Chipman, 12 December 1792, in Rawlyk, *New Light Letters and Songs*, 171.
46 Fergusson, *Diary of Simeon Perkins, 1797–1803*, 45.

47 Harding to J. Dimock, 27 January 1792, in Rawlyk, *New Light Letters and Songs*, 161.

48 Harding to T. Bennett, 6 April 1792, ibid., 163.

49 Cramp, "History of the Maritime Baptists," 36.

50 Quoted in ibid., 36.

51 Fergusson, *Diary of Simeon Perkins, 1790–1796*, 386.

52 Ibid., 387.

53 S. Wright to T. Bennett, 26 September 1793, in Rawlyk, *New Light Letters and Songs*, 178.

54 Cuthbertson, *Journal of John Payzant*, 74.

55 Davis, *Harris Harding*, 73.

56 See Cramp, "History of the Maritime Baptists," 73.

57 Ibid.

58 See the report from Inglis in *Classified Digest of the Records of the Society for the Propagation of the Gospel in Foreign Parts, 1701–1892* (London: SPG, 1893), 118.

59 Quoted in E.M. Saunders, *History of the Baptists of the Maritime Provinces* (Halifax: J. Burgoyne, 1902), 115.

60 Ibid.

61 See Cuthbertson, *Journal of John Payzant*, 79.

62 See James Beverley and Barry Moody, eds., *The Journal of Henry Alline* (Hantsport: Lancelot Press, 1982), 20.

63 Cramp, "History of the Maritime Baptists," 75.

64 Davis, *Harris Harding*, 78.

65 J. Fingard, *The Anglican Design in Loyalist Nova Scotia, 1783–1816* (London: SPC, 1972), 60.

66 Quoted in Davis, *Harris Harding*, 79.

67 Quoted in ibid., 23.

68 P. Miller, *Errand into the Wilderness* (Cambridge: Belknap Press of Harvard University Press, 1964), 167.

69 Davis, *Harris Harding*, 220.

70 Ibid.

71 Ibid., 101.

72 Ibid., 102–3.

73 Quoted in Cramp, "History of the Maritime Baptists," 94.

74 Ibid., 100.

75 Ibid.

76 See G.A. Rawlyk, "Nova Scotia Baptists and Ethnicity: A Preliminary Probe," *Revista Di Studi Canadesi* 4 (1991): 12.

77 Davis, *Harris Harding*, 136.

78 Ibid., 136–7.

79 See Beverley and Moody, *Journal of Henry Alline*, 222.

CHAPTER SIX

1 See G.A. Rawlyk, ed., *New Light Letters and Spiritual Songs, 1778–1793* (Hantsport: Lancelot Press, 1983).

2 This description of Manning's conversion is based upon his 1789 account, "Edward Manning's Conversion," in ibid., 287–9. See also his "Reminiscence," in the Manning Papers, AUA.

3 See J.M. Cramp, "A History of the Maritime Baptists," 52–4, in AUA.

4 See Professor Barry Moody's important paper on Manning's long career, "From Itinerant to Settled Pastor: The Case of Edward Manning" (delivered at the meeting of the Canadian Society of Church History, Halifax, June 1981).

5 Rawlyk, *New Light Letters and Songs*, 241.

6 See the biographical sketch of Charlotte Prescott-Boyle in the *Baptist Missionary Magazine*, January 1835, 1–8.

7 B.C. Cuthbertson, ed., *The Journal of John Payzant* (Hantsport: Lancelot Press, 1981), 19.

8 Rawlyk, *New Light Letters and Songs*, 332.

9 Ibid.

10 Ibid., 333.

11 G. Boyle to T. Bennett, 19 September 1790, in ibid., 113–14.

12 B. Fergusson, ed., *Diary of Simeon Perkins, 1804–1812* (Toronto: University of Toronto Press, Champlain Society, 1964), 245.

13 Helen Grant to Harris Harding, March 1790, in Rawlyk, *New Light Letters and Songs*, 96.

14 Nancy DeWolf to her mother, 5 January 1791, Lawrence Papers, American Antiquarian Society (hereafter cited as AAS).

15 Ibid.

16 See the three letters covering this period in the Lawrence Papers, AAS.

17 Quoted in Rawlyk, *New Light Letters and Songs*, 352–3.

18 Ibid., 353–4.

19 Ibid., 355.

20 Ibid., 273.

21 Ibid., 273–4.

22 Elizabeth Prescott to Joseph Dimock, April 1790, ibid., 99.

23 Hannah Webber to Joseph Dimock, 1790, ibid., 97–8.

24 Charlotte Lusby to Thomas Bennett, 4 August 1790, ibid., 103.

25 Charlotte Lusby to Thomas Bennett, 3 November 1790, ibid., 115.

26 Rawlyk, *New Light Letters and Songs*, 106–7.

27 Ibid., 108–9.

28 Ibid., 112.

29 H. Harding to Dorcas Prentice, 27 August 1791, ibid., 147.

30 Sylvia Wright to Thomas Bennett, 26 September 1793, ibid., 176.

31 Rawlyk, *New Light Letters and Songs*, 240.

32 Ibid.

33 Ibid., 238.

34 Ibid., 239.

35 See ibid., 336.

36 Ibid., 244.

37 E.C. Wright, "Without Intervention of Prophet, Priest or King," in *Repent and Believe in the Baptist Experience in Maritime Canada*, ed. Moody (Hantsport: Lancelot Press, 1980), 66–74.

38 Nathan Hatch, *The Democratization of American Christianity* (New Haven: Yale University Press, 1989).

39 See John Walsh, "Methodism at the End of the Eighteenth Century," in *A History of the Methodist Church in Great Britain*, vol. 1, ed. R. Davies and G. Rupp (London: Epworth Press, 1965), 275–315.

40 H. Abelove, *The Evangelist of Desire: John Welsey and the Methodists* (Stanford: Stanford University Press, 1990), 89.

41 V. Turner, *The Ritual Process* (Ithaca: Cornell University Press, 1979), 139–40.

42 Hatch, *Democratization of American Christianity*, 209.

CHAPTER SEVEN

1 See J.C. Deming and M.S. Hamilton, "Methodist Revivalism in France, Canada, and the United States" (paper presented at the Evangelicalism in Trans-Atlantic Perspective Conference, Wheaton College, April 1992), 27.

2 Quoted in A. Wilson, *The Clergy Reserves of Upper Canada: A Canadian Mortmain* (Toronto: University of Toronto Press, 1968), 17. See also C. Fahey, *In His Name: The Anglican Experience in Upper Canada* (Ottawa: Carleton University Press, 1991), 9.

3 Simcoe to Dundas, 6 November 1792, quoted in Fahey, *In His Name*, 9.

4 *Journals and Proceedings of the House of Assembly of the Province of Ontario, 1792*, Sixth Report of the Bureau of Archives of the Province of Ontario, ed. E. Cruikshank (Toronto, 1901), 17 September 1792, 1–2.

5 *Journals and Proceedings, House of Assembly*, 18 September 1792.

6 See Janice Potter, *The Liberty We Seek* (Cambridge: Harvard University Press, 1983), and Jane Errington, *The Lion, the Eagle and Upper Canada: A Developing Colonial Ideology* (Montreal: McGill-Queen's University Press, 1987).

7 See Errington, *The Lion*, especially ch. 3.

8 Quoted in Fahey, *In His Name*, 9.

9 See John Stuart to Bishop Mountain, 1 November 1795, in *Kingston before the War of 1812*, ed. R. Preston (Toronto: University of Toronto Press, Champlain Society, 1959), 308–9.

10 Stuart to Mountain, 11 May 1801, ibid., 319.

11 Mountain to SPG, 24 October 1804, quoted in ibid., 326.

12 See H.E. Turner, "John Langhorn," in *DCB* 5:474–6.

13 A. Stevens, *Life and Times of Nathan Bangs D.D.* (New York: Carlton and Porter, 1863), 42.

14 Stuart to Inglis, 25 June 1793, quoted in Fahey, *In His Name*, 40.

15 Fahey, *In His Name*, 40.

16 Pollard to SPG, 20 March 1810, quoted in ibid., 15.

17 J. Mountain, *A Charge Delivered to the Clergy of the Diocese of Quebec in August, 1803* (Quebec: John Neilson, 1803), 13, 26–27.

18 Stuart to Inglis, 25 June 1793, quoted in Fahey, *In His Name*, 40.

19 Stevens, *Bangs*, 119–20.

20 Ibid., 120.

21 N. Bangs, *A History of the Methodist Episcopal Church* (New York: Mason Lane, 1840), 2:85.

22 G.S. French, "Nathan Bangs," *DCB* 11:27.

23 Bangs, *A History*, 2:84.

24 Ibid., 72.

25 Ibid.

26 A.S. Sutherland, *Methodism in Canada: Its Work and Its Story* (Toronto: Methodist Mission Rooms, 1904), 40.

27 John Carroll, *Case and His Contemporaries* (Toronto: S. Rose, 1881), 1:36.

28 John Carroll, *Past and Present* (Toronto: Alfred Dredge, 1860), 171.

29 G.P. Playter, *A History of Methodism in Canada* (Toronto: Green, 1862), 156.

30 Carroll, *Past and Present*, 171.

31 Bangs, *A History*, 72.

32 Ibid., 73.

33 Ibid.

34 Ibid.

35 Ibid., 73–4.

36 Ibid., 74–5.

37 Ibid., 75–6.

38 Ibid., 83–4.

39 J. Dowling, ed., *The Dealings of God, Man, and the Devil: As Exemplified in the Life, Experience, and Travels of Lorenzo Dow* (New York: Nafis and Cornish, 1850), i.

40 Ibid., 67.

41 Ibid.

42 Ibid., 72.
43 Ibid., 67.
44 Bangs, *A History*, 2:85.
45 Ibid.
46 Stevens, *Bangs*, 120.
47 See chapter 1 of John H. Wigger's, Ph.D. dissertation, still in progress, Notre Dame University.
48 Bangs, *A History*, 1:121.
49 Stevens, *Bangs*, 15–29.
50 A.H. Tuttle, *Nathan Bangs* (New York: Eaton and Main, 1909), 33.
51 Stevens, *Bangs*, 34.
52 Ibid.
53 Ibid., 39.
54 Ibid., 120.
55 Ibid., 41.
56 Ibid., 44.
57 Ibid., 45.
58 Ibid., 47.
59 Ibid., 48–9.
60 Ibid., 50–3.
61 Ibid., 58.
62 Ibid., 58–9.
63 Ibid., 50–9.
64 Ibid., 54.
65 Ibid., 59.
66 Ibid., 61–5.
67 Ibid., 87.
68 Ibid., 86.
69 Tuttle, *Nathan Bangs*, 54.
70 Stevens, *Bangs*, 87.
71 Ibid., 87–8.
72 Ibid., 89.
73 Ibid., 92–3.
74 Ibid., 95.
75 Ibid., 101–2.
76 Ibid., 102–6.
77 Ibid., 120.
78 Ibid., 123.
79 Ibid., 126.
80 Ibid., 131.
81 Ibid., 136–7.
82 Ibid., 137.
83 Ibid., 135–41.

84 Ibid., 148.

85 Ibid.

86 See chapter 9 for my descriptive analysis of the Hay Bay Camp Meeting as a crucially important Methodist religious ritual.

87 Steven, *Bangs*, 153.

88 Ibid., 155.

89 Ibid., 156.

90 Ibid., 158–65.

91 French, "Nathan Bangs," 26.

92 This is based on N. Hatch and M. Hamilton, "Can Evangelicalism Survive Its Success?" *Christianity Today*, 5 October 1992, 21.

93 See Wigger's Ph.D. dissertation, ch. 1.

94 M. Betts, "From Butcher's Block to Cathedral: The Methodists in Kingston 1788–1852," (M.A. thesis, Queen's University, 1989), 27.

95 See S. Ivison and F. Rosser, *The Baptists in Upper and Lower Canada before 1820* (Toronto: University of Toronto Press, 1956).

96 See G.A. Rawlyk, "From New Light to Baptist," in *Repent and Believe: The Baptist Experience in Maritime Canada*, ed. B. Moody (Hantsport: Lancelot Press, 1980), 24–5.

97 These are merely enlightened (or some would prefer to say unenlightened) guesses, since the population data is so fragmentary for the 1812 period. From my ongoing work on the Baptists in Nova Scotia in the early nineteenth century, it is becoming increasingly clear to me that to argue that for every Baptist Church member there were eight adherents is indeed a very conservative contention.

CHAPTER EIGHT

1 See my description of the Babcock Tragedy in G.A. Rawlyk, *Ravished by the Spirit: Religious Revivals, Baptists and Henry Alline* (Montreal: McGill-Queen's University Press, 1984), 100–101. See also D.G. Bell, ed., *New Light Baptist Journals of James Manning and James Innis* (Hantsport: Lancelot Press, 1984), 331–54.

2 See G.A. Rawlyk, ed., *New Light Letters and Spiritual Songs, 1778–1793* (Hantsport: Lancelot Press, 1983), 38–75.

3 "Inglis Journal, 24 Aug. 1791," Public Archives of Nova Scotia, Halifax (hereafter cited as PANS).

4 K.W.F. Stavely, review of a variety of books about seventeenth-century New England, in *The William and Mary Quarterly* 49 (January 1992): 142.

5 M.W. Armstrong, *The Great Awakening in Nova Scotia 1776–1809* (Hartford: American Society of Church History, 1948), 101.

6 Henry Alline, *Two Mites: Some of the Most Important and Much Disputed Points of Divinity* (Halifax: Anthony Henry, 1781), 93.

7 Henry Alline, *The Anti-Traditionalist* (Halifax: Anthony Henry, 1783), 42.

8 See Henry Alline, *Life and Journal* (Boston: Gilbert and Dean, 1806), 174.

9 "Account of Mr. Black," *Arminian Magazine* (London, 1791), 178.

10 Ibid.

11 Ibid., 234.

12 Ibid., 298.

13 "Freeborn Garrettson Journal," UCA.

14 Ibid.

15 Quoted in N. Bangs, *The Life of the Rev. Freeborn Garrettson* (New York: Emory and Waugh, 1832), 167.

16 See J. Bailey to Samuel Peters, 29 April 1785, in *The Frontier Missionary: A Memoir of the Life of the Rev. Jacob Bailey*, ed. W.S. Bartlet (Boston: Ide & Dutton, 1853), 222–3.

17 Quoted in Armstrong, *The Great Awakening in Nova Scotia*, 124.

18 J. Marsden, *A Narrative of a Mission* (Plymouth-Dock: J. Johns, 1816), 49.

19 See Rawlyk, *New Light Letters and Songs.*

20 See Gordon Wood, "Evangelical America and Early Mormonism," *New York History* 61 (October 1980): 366.

21 See ibid., 360–73.

22 Nathan Hatch, *The Democratization of American Christianity* (New Haven: Yale University Press, 1989), 209.

23 M. Noll, "The American Revolution and Protestant Evangelicalism," *Journal of Interdisciplinary History* 23 (1993): 615–38.

24 Alline, *Journal*, 84.

25 Alline, *Two Mites*, 20.

26 N. Christie, "In These Times of Democratic Rage and Delusion: Popular Religion and the Challenge to the Established Order, 1760–1815," in G.A. Rawlyk, *The Canadian Protestant Experience 1760–1990* (Burlington: Welch, 1990), 21.

27 Ibid., 34.

28 Ibid., 37.

29 Quoted in I.E. Bill, *Fifty Years with the Baptist Ministers and Churches of the Maritime Provinces of Canada* (Saint John, N.B.: Barnes & Co., 1880), 191.

30 Quoted in Armstrong, *The Great Awakening in Nova Scotia*, 130.

31 Quoted in Bill, *Fifty Years*, 190.

32 See P. Campbell, *Travels in the Interior Inhabited Parts of North America in the Years 1791 and 1792*, ed. H.H. Langton and W.F. Ganong (Toronto: Champlain Society, 1937), 255–6.

33 See Armstrong, *The Great Awakening in Nova Scotia*, 129.

34 See the disjointed Manning correspondence from the 1790s, in Acadia University Archives (hereafter cited as AUA).

35 G.E. Levy, ed., *The Diary and Related Writings of the Reverend Joseph Dimock (1768–1846)* (Hantsport: Lancelot Press, 1979), 43.

36 Ibid., 52.

37 Ibid., 67.

38 Ibid., 19.

39 Quoted in G. French, *Parsons and Politics* (Toronto: Ryerson Press, 1962), 34.

40 This theme is developed at greater length in G.A. Rawlyk, *Wrapped Up in God* (Burlington: Welch, 1988), 63–75.

41 See their correspondence in the *Massachusetts Baptist Missionary Magazine* for the year 1808 in particular. See also the Case Papers, located at Colby College, Waterville, Maine.

42 T. Vincent, "Henry Alline: Problems of Approach and Reading the *Hymns* as Poetry," in *They Planted Well: New England Planters in Maritime Canada*, ed. M. Conrad (Fredericton: Acadiensis Press, 1988), 203.

43 See H.E. Scott, ed., *The Journal of the Reverend Jonathan Scott* (Boston: New England Historic Genealogical Society, 1980).

44 E. Mancke, "Two Patterns of New England Transformation: Machias, Maine and Liverpool, Nova Scotia, 1760–1820" (unpublished Ph.D. thesis, Johns Hopkins University, 1989), iii.

45 Ibid., 7.

46 Ibid.

47 Ibid., 284.

48 Ibid., 288–9.

49 Ibid., 330–1.

50 J. Adams to H. Stiles, 13 February 1818, in *The Works of John Adams*, ed. C.F. Adams (Boston: Little Brown, 1856), 10:282–3.

51 See Gordon Stewart and G.A. Rawlyk, *A People Highly Favoured of God: The Nova Scotia Yankees and the American Revolution* (Toronto: Macmillan, 1972).

52 Ibid., 61–2.

53 See M.W. Armstrong, "Neutrality and Religion in Revolutionary Nova Scotia," *New England Quarterly*, 9 (March 1946): 50–62.

54 See Grant Gordon, *The Life of David George (1743–1810)* (Hantsport: Lancelot Press, 1992).

55 See, for example, A. Taylor, *Liberty Men and Great Proprietors: The Revolutionary Settlement on the Maine Frontier, 1760–1820* (Chapel Hill: University of North Carolina Press, 1990).

56 S. Marini, *Radical Sects in Revolutionary New England* (Cambridge: Harvard University Press, 1982).

57 Taylor, *Liberty Men*, 181–207.

58 "Manning Journal, 24 August 1821," AUA.

59 This paragraph is based upon G. Wood, *The Radicalism of the American Revolution* (New York: Knopf, 1992), 96.

60 Ibid., 133.

61 Ibid., 232.

62 Quoted in ibid., 232–3.

CHAPTER NINE

1 N. Bangs, *History of the Methodist Episcopal Church* (New York: Mason and Lane, 1840), 2:172.

2 See G.A. Rawlyk, *Ravished by the Spirit: Religious Revivals, Baptists and Henry Alline* (Montreal: McGill-Queen's University Press, 1984), 102, 117.

3 Quoted in G.S. French, "William Case," *DCB* 8:132.

4 J. Carroll, *Case and His Contemporaries* (Toronto: Rose, 1867), 1:112.

5 French, "William Case," *DCB* 8:134.

6 From J. Carroll, *Past and Present, Or a Description of Persons and Events Connected With Canadian Methodism for the Last Forty Years by a Spectator of the Score* (Toronto: Alfred Dredge, 1860), quoted in M. Betts, "From Butcher's Block to Cathedral: The Methodists in Kingston 1788 to 1852" (M.A. thesis, Queen's University, 1989), 36.

7 G.S. French, "Henry Ryan," *DCB* 6:670.

8 G. Playter, *The History of Methodism in Canada with an Account of the Rise and Progress of the Work of God among the Canadian Indian Tribes and Occasional Notices of Civil Affairs of the Province* (Toronto: Green, 1862), 84.

9 French, "Henry Ryan," 670.

10 Ibid.

11 Carroll, *Case and His Contemporaries*, 1:24.

12 Quoted in French, "Henry Ryan," 670.

13 Quoted in ibid.; see also Playter, *History of Methodism*, 370.

14 French, "Henry Ryan," 670.

15 Ibid.

16 A. Stevens, *Life and Times of Nathan Bangs* (New York: Carleton and Porter, 1863), 148.

17 Carroll, *Case and His Contemporaries*, 1:113.

18 See C. McDannell, "Lourdes Water and American Catholicism, 1870–1896" (paper delivered at Notre Dame University, 10 November 1992), 4.

19 Carroll, *Case and His Contemporaries*, 1:114.

20 J.E. Sanderson, *The First Century of Methodism in Canada* (Toronto: William Briggs, 1908), 1:43.

21 Paul Conkin, *Cane Ridge: America's Pentecost* (Madison: University of Wisconsin Press, 1990). This is the most recent account.

22 Stevens, *Bangs*, 149–50.

23 A xeroxed copy is available at the United Church Archives, Victoria University, Toronto. The original is to be found at Drew University. All the references in this section are to the Bangs manuscript journal unless there is a specific footnote to the contrary.

24 Stevens, *Bangs*, 151.

25 Ibid., 152.

26 "Bangs Manuscript Journal," 27 September to 5 October 1805, UCA.

27 Stevens, *Bangs*, 152.

28 Ibid., 153.

29 Ibid., 154.

30 Ibid.

31 Ibid., 155.

32 Ibid.

33 Ibid., 156.

34 "Bangs Manuscript Journal."

35 This final quotation is also from the manuscript journal. One should note how this account evolved over the years. Compare the manuscript account with the edited version in Stevens, *Bangs*, 151–6, and Carroll, *Case and His Contemporaries*, 1:114–18. It is interesting to note how certain key sections were removed from the journal by Stevens and Carroll. In addition, Bangs added to his manuscript version some material that Stevens gladly included in his biography.

36 The section on Alida Munroe owes a great deal to G. Goles, *The Supernumerary; or Lights and Shadows of Itinerancy Compiled from Papers of Rev Elijah Woolsey* (New York: Lane and Tippett, 1845). Woolsey was a contemporary of Bangs and was also, for a brief time, a Methodist itinerant in Upper Canada. Further background material was provided by Janice Potter-MacKinnon, *While the Women Only Wept: Loyalist Refugee Women in Eastern Ontario* (Montreal: McGill-Queen's University Press, 1993). There was a Loyalist woman whom I have called Alida Munroe; she was the unnamed woman discussed by Woolsey. She may also have been described by Bangs in the unfolding Hay Bay drama.

37 For the background material, see Coles, *The Supernumerary*, 41.

38 Ibid., 41–2.

39 Ibid., 42–3.

40 Ibid., 43–4.

41 Ibid., 40–1.

42 Ibid., 37–40.

43 Ibid., 43.

44 Carroll, *Case and His Contemporaries*, 1:114.

45 Stevens, *Bangs*, 151.
46 For the most recent study of Upper Canadian camp meetings, see Guiseppe E. Dardano, "The Frontier Camp Meeting and Popular Culture in 19th Century North America" (M.A. thesis, Queen's University, 1991).
47 See Betts, "From Butcher's Block to Cathedral," 37; and for a very interesting British Baptist view of the Upper Canadian camp meeting and the Ryanlike interjections, see F.A. Cox and J. Hoby, *The Baptists in America: A Narrative of the Deputation from the Baptist Union in England to the United States and Canada* (London: Stevens and Pardon, 1836), 219–21.
48 "Bangs Manuscript Journal," UCA.
49 Ibid.
50 Carroll, *Case and His Contemporaries*, 1:114.

CHAPTER TEN

1 Quoted in E.M. Saunders, *History of the Baptists of the Maritime Provinces* (Halifax: J. Burgoyne, 1902), 115.
2 D. Bell, ed., *Newlight Baptist Journals of James Manning and James Innis* (Hantsport: Lancelot Press, 1984), 23.
3 Quoted in Saunders, *History of the Baptists*, 115.
4 Bell, *Newlight Baptist Journals*, 21.
5 Mary Douglas, *Purity and Danger: An Analysis of the Concepts of Pollution and Taboo* (London, 1979), 161.
6 M. Eliade, *Patterns in Comparative Religion* (London: Sheed and Ward, 1958), 194.
7 Douglas, *Purity and Danger*, 2.
8 Ibid., 158.
9 Ibid., 61.
10 Ibid., 63.
11 See ibid., 64.
12 *Christian Messenger*, 12 February 1841.
13 Bell, *Newlight Baptist Journals*, 184.
14 Z. Estey to James Manning, 10 March 1802, in Fredericton Baptist Churchbook, 271, AUA.
15 See Bell, *Newlight Baptist Journals*, 184–5, 257–8.
16 J.M. Bumsted, "Joseph Crandall," DCB 8:179. There are some major typographical errors in this biography, for example, the date of Crandall's birth is given as 1761 instead of 1771, and his age at death as 97 instead of the correct 87.
17 I.E. Bill, *Fifty Years with the Baptist Ministers and Churches of the Maritime Provinces of Canada* (Saint John: Barnes, 1880), 213.

18 D. Britton, "Joseph Crandall: Preacher and Politician," in *An Abiding Conviction: Maritime Baptists and their World*, ed. R.S. Wilson (Hantsport: Lancelot Press, 1988), 110.

19 Ibid., 111.

20 Bill, *Fifty Years*, 204.

21 J.M. Bumsted, ed., "The Autobiography of Joseph Crandall," *Acadiensis* 3, no. 1 (Autumn 1973): 81 (hereafter cited as "Crandall Autobiography").

22 Ibid., 81.

23 Ibid., 82.

24 Ibid.

25 Bumsted, "Joseph Crandall," 179.

26 "Crandall Autobiography," 82–3.

27 Ibid., 83.

28 Ibid.

29 Ibid., 83–4.

30 Ibid., 84.

31 Ibid.

32 Bumsted, "Joseph Crandall," 179.

33 See G.E. Levy, ed., *The Diary of Joseph Dimock* (Hantsport: Lancelot Press, 1979), passim.

34 "Crandall Autobiography," 86.

35 J.M. Cramp, "A History of the Maritime Baptists," AUA.

36 Bell, *Newlight Baptist Journals*, 23.

37 Ibid., 21.

38 Quoted in Saunders, *History of the Baptists*, 114–15.

39 Ibid., 115.

40 Ibid.

41 "Crandall Autobiography," 87.

42 Bell, *Newlight Baptist Journals*, 249–50.

43 See G.A. Rawlyk, *Ravished by the Spirit: Religious Revivals, Baptists and Henry Alline* (Montreal: McGill-Queen's University Press, 1984), 171.

44 See E.C. Wright, *The Loyalists of New Brunswick* (Fredericton: E.C. Wright, 1955), passim.

45 See G.A. Rawlyk, *Nova Scotia's Massachusetts* (Montreal: McGill-Queen's University Press, 1973), xvi.

46 Bell, *Newlight Baptist Journals*, 85.

47 Ibid.

48 G.P. Murdoch, "Ethnographic Atlas: A Summary," *Ethnology* 1, (April 1967): 112.

49 Jarvis Ring Papers, AUA.

50 Bill, *Fifty Years*, 214.

51 "Crandall Autobiography," 87.

52 Ibid.
53 Ibid., 86.
54 Bell, *Newlight Baptist Journals*, 85.
55 "Crandall Autobiography," 87.
56 Ibid., 88.
57 Ibid.
58 Bell, *Newlight Baptist Journals*, 85.
59 "Crandall Autobiography," 88.
60 Ibid.
61 All quotations in this paragraph are from "Crandall Autobiography," 88.
62 Ibid., 88–9.
63 Ibid., 89.
64 Ibid.
65 Ibid.
66 Ibid., 90.
67 Bill, *Fifty Years*, 214.
68 Ibid., 215.
69 "Memoir of the Rev. Elijah Estabrooks," *Baptist Missionary Magazine of Nova Scotia and New Brunswick* 1, no. 1 (April 1829): 289 (hereafter cited as "Estabrooks Memoir").
70 Ibid.
71 Bell, *Newlight Baptist Journals*, 35.
72 "Estabrooks Memoir," 289–90.
73 Ibid., 290.
74 Bell, *Newlight Baptist Journals*, 72.
75 Ibid.
76 John James to unidentified correspondent, 18 October 1792, transcript in the possession of G.A. Rawlyk. The original letter is in the Archives of Westminster College, Cambridge, U.K.
77 Ibid.
78 Bell, *Newlight Baptist Journals*, 77.
79 P. Campbell, *Travels in the Interior Inhabited Parts of North America: in the Years 1791 and 1792*, ed. H.H. Langton and W.F. Ganong, 1793 (Toronto: University of Toronto Press, Champlain Society, 1937), 255–6.
80 Ibid., 256.
81 Quoted in Bell, *Newlight Baptist Journals*, 80.
82 Quoted in ibid., 80.
83 This trial is superbly dealt with in ibid., 81–3.
84 Jarvis Ring Papers, AUA.
85 Bell, *Newlight Baptist Journals*, 84.
86 "Estabrooks Memoir," 290.
87 Ibid.

88 Ibid.
89 For a further discussion of this problem with respect to some of the other Baptist patriarchs, see Rawlyk, *Ravished by the Spirit*, 73–105.
90 Ibid., 88–93.
91 Quoted in Cramp, "History of the Maritime Baptists."
92 "Estabrooks Memoir," 290.
93 Ibid.
94 Ibid., 294.

CHAPTER ELEVEN

1 G. Patterson, *Memoir of the Reverend James MacGregor D.D.* (Philadelphia: J.M. Wilson, 1859), 72.
2 S. Buggey, "James Drummond MacGregor," *DCB* 6:457. For further background material on MacGregor, see N. Smith, "James MacGregor and the Church in the Maritimes," in *Enkindled by the Word: Essays on Presbyterianism in Canada* (Toronto: Presbyterian Publications, 1966), 9–18.
3 See I.F. MacKinnon, *Settlement and Churches in Nova Scotia 1749–1776* (Montreal: Walker Press, 1930), 80.
4 James Beverley and Barry Moody, eds., *The Journal of Henry Alline* (Hantsport: Lancelot Press, 1982), 83.
5 Ibid.
6 Ibid., 83–5.
7 Ibid., 201–2.
8 Ibid., 202–3.
9 Ibid., 204–5.
10 Ibid., 205. For a further discussion of this confrontation, see G. Stewart and G. Rawlyk, *A People Highly Favoured of God* (Toronto: Macmillan, 1972), 131–2.
11 Buggey, "MacGregor," 461.
12 Ibid., 457.
13 Patterson, *Memoir of MacGregor*, 17.
14 Ibid., 22.
15 Ibid., 23.
16 Ibid., 24.
17 Ibid.
18 Ibid., 32–5, 46.
19 G. Patterson, ed., *A Few Remains of the Reverend James MacGregor D.D.* (Edinburgh: Oliphant, 1859), 250.
20 Beverley and Moody, *Journal of Henry Alline*, 200.
21 Patterson, *Memoir of MacGregor*, 47.
22 Ibid., 47–8.

23 Buggey, "MacGregor," 457.

24 Ibid. For further material on MacGregor and Pictou County, see G. Patterson, *History of the County of Pictou, N.S.* (Montreal: Dawson Bros., 1877), especially 136–397.

25 Patterson, *Memoir of MacGregor*, 60.

26 Ibid., 112.

27 Buggey, "MacGregor," 458.

28 Patterson, *Memoir of MacGregor*, 113.

29 Ibid.

30 Patterson, *A Few Remains*, 250.

31 Patterson, *Memoir of MacGregor*, 119.

32 Ibid., 122.

33 See D. Campbell and R.A. MacLean, *Beyond the Atlantic Roar: A Study of the Nova Scotia Scots*, (Toronto: McClelland & Stewart, 1974), 35–6.

34 Patterson, *Memoir of MacGregor*, 122.

35 Ibid., 122–3.

36 Ibid., 123.

37 Ibid., 124.

38 Ibid., 131.

39 Ibid., 135.

40 Ibid., 137–8.

41 Ibid., 158–9.

42 Ibid., 159.

43 Ibid.

44 Ibid., 160.

45 Ibid., 159–60.

46 Ibid., 160.

47 Ibid., 195.

48 Ibid.

49 Ibid.

50 Ibid.

51 Ibid., 160–1.

52 G.A. MacLennan, *The Story of the Old Time Communion Service Worship; Also the Metallic Communion Token of the Presbyterian Church in Canada* (Montreal, 1924), 2.

53 Ibid., 4.

54 Ibid.

55 Patterson, *Memoir of MacGregor*, 196.

56 Ibid., 162–3.

57 MacLennan, *Old Time Communion*, 4.

58 Patterson, *Memoir of MacGregor*, 196.

59 Ibid.

60 Ibid., 197–8.

61 Ibid., 198.

62 Ibid.

63 Ibid., 199.

64 Ibid.

65 Leigh E. Schmidt, *Holy Fairs: Scottish Communions and American Revivals in the Early Modern Period* (Princeton: Princeton University Press, 1989), 6.

66 Ibid., 69.

67 Ibid.

68 Ibid., 76.

69 Ibid., 83.

70 Ibid., 97.

71 Ibid., 162.

72 Patterson, *Memoir of MacGregor*, 162.

73 Schmidt, *Holy Fairs*, 163.

74 Ibid., 218.

75 L. Stanley, *The Well-Watered Garden: The Presbyterian Church in Cape Breton, 1798–1860* (Sydney: University of Cape Breton Press, 1983), xi.

76 Campbell and McLean, *Beyond the Atlantic Roar*, 21.

77 Patterson, *Memoir of MacGregor*, 160.

78 W. Gregg, *History of the Presbyterian Church in the Dominion of Canada* (Toronto: Presbyterian Printing and Publishing Co., 1885), 265.

79 Ibid., 273.

80 Ibid., 262.

81 *Nova Scotian*, 10 March 1830.

82 Buggey, "MacGregor," 461.

83 Patterson, *A Few Remains*, 272.

84 J. Fingard, *The Anglican Design in Loyalist Nova Scotia 1783–1816*, (London: SPCK, 1972), 53.

85 Ibid., 165, 223.

86 Ibid., 69.

87 Patterson, *Memoir of MacGregor*, 211.

88 Ibid., 71.

89 M. Gavreau, *The Evangelical Century: College and Creed in English Canada from the Great Revival to the Great Depression* (Montreal: McGill-Queen's University Press, 1991).

CONCLUSION

1 M. Gauvreau, *The Evangelical Century: College and Creed in English Canada from the Great Revival to the Great Depression* (Montreal: McGill-Queen's University Press, 1991).

2 See G. French, "The Evangelical Creed in Canada," in *The Shield of Achilles*, ed. W.L. Morton (Toronto: McClelland & Stewart, 1968), 16–35.

3 G. French, "The Impact of Christianity on Canadian Culture and Society before 1867," *Theological Bulletin* (McMaster Divinity College), no. 3 (Jan. 1968): 29.

4 French, "The Evangelical Creed," 16.

5 P. Airhart, *Serving the Present Age: Revivalism, Progressionism and the Methodist Tradition in Canada* (Montreal: McGill-Queen's University Press, 1992), 144.

6 C. Johnston, *McMaster University: The Toronto Years* (Toronto: University of Toronto Press, 1976), 1:72.

7 See G.A. Rawlyk, *Wrapped Up in God* (Burlington: Welch, 1988), 136.

8 See G.A. Rawlyk, "A.L. McCrimmon, H.P. Whidden, T.T. Shields, Christian Education, and McMaster University," in *Canadian Baptists and Christian Higher Education*, ed. Rawlyk (Montreal: McGill-Queen's University Press, 1988), 31–62.

9 R. Cook, *The Regenerators: Social Criticism in Late Victorian English Canada* (Toronto: University of Toronto Press, 1985), back cover. See also David Marshall, *Secularizing the Faith: Canadian Protestant Clergy and the Crisis of Belief, 1850–1940* (Toronto: University of Toronto Press, 1992).

10 The survey results are in the possession of G.A. Rawlyk, Queen's University. See also *Maclean's*, 5 April 1993, for a cover story devoted to the Angus Reid surveys. The preliminary analysis of the data was done by Mr Andrew Grenville, vice-president of the Angus Reid Group. Andrew has been a remarkably helpful and astute research associate who has imposed a sophisticated framework on the data that was collected in early 1993. I am very much indebted to him and to Angus Reid, who has been so financially generous in supporting this research project, as have, of course, the Pew Charitable Trusts.

Index

DATE DUE